TOWARD A CONTEMPORARY WISDOM CHRISTOLOGY

A Study of Karl Rahner
and Norman Pittenger

Leo D. Lefebure

UNIVERSITY
PRESS OF
AMERICA

Lanham • New York • London

Copyright © 1988 by

University Press of America,® Inc.

4720 Boston Way
Lanham, MD 20706

3 Henrietta Street
London WC2E 8LU England

British Cataloging in Publication Information Available

Library of Congress Cataloging-in-Publication Data

Lefebure, Leo D., 1952–
Toward a contemporary Wisdom Christology : a study of Karl Rahner
and Norman Pittenger / Leo D. Lefebure.
p. cm.
"Developed as a doctoral dissertation presented to the Divinity
School of the Universityof Chicago"—Acknowledgments.
Bibliography: p. Includes index.
1. Jesus Christ—Person and offices—History of doctrines—20th
century. 2. Wisdom—Religious aspects—Christianty—History of
doctines—20th century. 3. Rahner, Karl, 1904- —Contributions
in Christology. 4. Pittenger, W. Norman (William Norman), 1905- —
contributions in Christology. 5. Wisdom—Biblical teaching. I. Title.
BT205.L44   1988   232'.2'0922—dc 19   88–22798 CIP
ISBN 0–8191–7151–4 (alk. paper)
ISBN 0–8191–7152–2 (pbk. : alk. paper)

To Richard and Evelyn Lefebure,

who first taught me to search for wisdom.

ACKNOWLEDGEMENTS

In writing this book I owe much to a great many people. This essay developed as a doctoral dissertation presented to the Divinity School of the University of Chicago. I express my deep gratitude to my advisor, David Tracy, for his unfailing interest, encouragement, and guidance in directing this project. I also thank the other members of my dissertation committee, Anne Carr and Langdon Gilkey, for their most helpful comments, suggestions, and criticisms on the shaping and development of this work. The weaknesses and limitations of this essay are fully my own.

My debts extend far back into earlier studies, for the lessons and insights of earlier teachers were a constant resource in formulating and exploring this topic. I owe a special debt of thanks to the person who introduced me to the biblical wisdom tradition and who guided my first explorations of Wisdom Christology, John J. Collins of the University of Notre Dame, and to Timothy O'Connell of Loyola University of Chicago, who introduced me to the vision of Karl Rahner, and to Charles R. Meyer of the University of Saint Mary of the Lake, who guided my first reading of Alfred North Whitehead.

I would like to thank the people and staff of Our Lady Help of Christians Church in Chicago, with whom I worked and prayed and played during the writing of this work. Their understanding, cooperation and support made possible the undertaking and completion of this project.

I would also like to thank Patrick Lyons, Peggy Lyons, and James P. McIlhone for introducing me to the world of computers and thereby making possible the preparation of this manuscript.

Grateful acknowledgement is made for permission to quote copyrighted material from the following publications:

Excerpts from THE JERUSALEM BIBLE, copyright (c) 1966 by Darton, Longman & Todd, Ltd. and Doubleday, a division of Bantam, Doubleday, Dell Publishing Group, Inc. Reprinted by permission.

From FOUNDATIONS OF CHRISTIAN FAITH by Karl Rahner. Copyright (c) 1978 by The Crossroad Publishing Company. Reprinted by permission of the publisher.

Reprinted with permission of Macmillan Publishing Company from PROCESS AND REALITY, by Alfred North Whitehead. Corrected Edition. Copyright (c) 1978 by The Free Press.

TOWARD A CONTEMPORARY WISDOM CHRISTOLOGY:
A STUDY OF KARL RAHNER AND NORMAN PITTENGER

TABLE OF CONTENTS

AI   Alfred North Whitehead. Adventures of Ideas. New York:
        Free Press, 1967.

BZAW   Beihefte zur Zeitschrift für die alttestamentliche
        Wissenschaft.

CBQ   Catholic Biblical Quarterly.

CR   Norman Pittenger. Christology Reconsidered. London: SCM
        Press, 1970.

FR   Alfred North Whitehead. The Function of Reason. Boston:
        Beacon Press, 1962.

GW   Karl Rahner. Geist in Welt: Zur Metaphysik der endlichen
        Erkenntnis bei Thomas von Aquin. Ed. Johannes
        Baptist Metz. 2nd ed. Munich: Kösel-Verlag, 1957.

HR   History of Religions.

HTR   Harvard Theological Review.

HW   Karl Rahner. Hörer des Wortes: Zur Grundlegung einer
        Religionsphilosophie. Ed. J.B. Metz. 2nd ed.
        Munich: Kösel-Verlag, 1963.

Int   Interpretation.

JAAR   Journal of the American Academy of Religion.

JBL   Journal of Biblical Literature.

JR   The Journal of Religion.

MT   Alfred North Whitehead. Modes of Thought. New York: Free
        Press, 1968.

NTS   New Testament Studies.

PR   Alfred North Whitehead. Process and Reality: An Essay in
        Cosmology. Eds. David Ray Griffin and Donald W.
        Sherbourne. Corrected ed. New York: Free Press,
        1978.

RM   Alfred North Whitehead. Religion in the Making. New
        York: New American Library, 1974.

1QH	Qumran. _Hodayoth_ (Hymns of Thanksgiving).
1QS	Qumran. _Rule of the Community_.
SMW	Alfred North Whitehead. _Science and the Modern World_. New York: Free Press, 1967.
SW	Karl Rahner. _Spirit in the World_. Trans. William Dych. New York: Herder & Herder, 1968.
Sym	Alfred North Whitehead. _Symbolism: Its Meaning and Effect_. New York: Capricorn Books, 1959.
TI	Karl Rahner. _Theological Investigations_. 20 vols. Various translators. Vols. 1-6. Baltimore: Helicon, 1961-69. Vols. 7-10. New York: Herder & Herder, 1970-73. Vols. 11-14. New York: Seabury, 1974-76. Vols. 15-20. New York: Crossroad, 1979-83.
TS	_Theological Studies_.
WI	W. Norman Pittenger. _The Word Incarnate: A Study of the Doctrine of the Person of Christ_. Digswell Place: James Nisbet & Co., 1959.
ZNW	_Zeitschrift für die neutestamentliche Wissenschaft_.
ZTK	_Zeitschrift für die Theologie und Kirche_.

INTRODUCTION

The wisdom tradition of ancient Israel has exerted a major influence upon the interpretation of Jesus of Nazareth both in the New Testament and the later Christian tradition. New Testament texts such as 1 Corinthians 8:6, the prologue of John, and Colossians 1:15-20 attributed to Jesus Christ the cosmological role that had been characteristic of Lady Wisdom in the Hebrew Bible and Septuagint. These texts claim a cosmic dimension for the revelation of God experienced in Jesus Christ. By describing Christ as the one in whom all things hold together, the Logos through whom all things were made, these passages claim that the power of God revealed in Jesus Christ has been at work throughout all creation from the beginning. This perspective establishes a close relation between the universal presence of God in all human experience and the specific historical revelation of God in Jesus Christ.

The relationship between the universal activity of God in creation and the historical event of Jesus Christ has been at the center of the long tradition of Logos Christology. Two contemporary representatives of this tradition are Karl Rahner and Norman Pittenger.

Recent biblical scholarship has stressed that the biblical antecedents of the tradition of Logos Christology are to be found in the writings of the wisdom tradition. By the wisdom tradition I mean the books of Proverbs, Job, Qoheleth, Ben Sira, and the Wisdom of Solomon. In this discussion I will generally use the term "Wisdom Christology" rather than "Logos Christology." By Wisdom Christology I mean the interpretation of Jesus as the incarnation of Lady Wisdom.

What the Hebrew Bible and Deuterocanonical Books meant by Wisdom is very closely related to what the Greek tradition meant by Logos. Both Wisdom and Logos are attempts to describe the ordering principle of the universe. By using the terminology of "Wisdom Christology" I am not suggesting a major conceptual distinction from Logos Christology. I am interested in the roots of this trajectory in the wisdom tradition of Israel and in the fact that Lady Wisdom is a feminine figure.

In recent years the biblical wisdom tradition has been the focus of intense study. Biblical scholars have stressed the importance of the wisdom tradition for the emergence of Logos Christology.[1] As representatives of the tradition of Logos

---

[1]Raymond E. Brown, _The Gospel according to John_, Anchor Bible, vols. 29-29A (Garden City, N.Y.: Doubleday & Co., 1966,

Christology, Rahner and Pittenger participate in the history of effects of the biblical wisdom tradition, and their theologies find biblical analogies and precedents in the perspectives of the ancient sages. However, they themselves do not refer to the wisdom tradition in a major way, and there has been no major comparison of the Christologies of Rahner or Pittenger with the biblical wisdom tradition.

My purpose in this investigation is to examine the relationship between the biblical trajectory of Wisdom Christology and the Christologies of Rahner and Pittenger and to explore the contribution that the wisdom tradition can make to the contemporary interpretation of Jesus Christ. It is my contention that the understanding of Jesus Christ as the incarnation of Lady Wisdom can offer a basis for expressing his significance for Christians today. At each stage of the investigation I will explore the relationship between the specific historical event of Jesus Christ and the universal presence of God in all human experience.

The highly conceptual language of philosophical theology used by Rahner and Pittenger is obviously on a very different level from the more concrete poetic and metaphorical images and hymns of the biblical wisdom trajectory. There are, however, important concerns that are shared by Rahner, Pittenger, and the ancient sages, and there are relations between the abstract conceptual frameworks of the contemporary theologians and the more concrete language of the ancient sages.

John Mark Thompson has argued that proverbs have an incipient philosophical function, for they are expressions of a search for order in nature and human relationships.[2] Roland E. Murphy has explicitly suggested an analogy between the approach of the wisdom tradition and the theological anthropology of Karl Rahner.[3] John J. Collins has interpreted the wisdom tradition in light of the categories of systematic theology of David Tracy.[4] Charles E. Carlston has suggested that serious consideration of the wisdom sayings in the teaching of Jesus in the Synoptic tradition

---

1970), I, cxxii-cxxv; C.H. Dodd, The Interpretation of the Fourth Gospel (Cambridge: Cambridge University Press, 1965), 272-85.

[2]John Mark Thompson, The Form and Function of Proverbs in Ancient Israel (The Hague: Mouton, 1974), 69).

[3]Roland E. Murphy, "The Interpretation of Old Testament Wisdom Literature," Int 23(1969):292 and n. 11.

[4]John J. Collins, "The Biblical Precedent for Natural Theology," JAAR 45 Supplement(1977):35-67.

might even bring biblical scholars into contact once more with our own theologians, re-establishing a dialogue which the imperialism of a misplaced exegetical science has too frequently broken off.[5]

Paul Ricoeur has also lamented the split between the conceptual language of philosophical theology and the more concrete biblical language. Ricoeur argues that the metaphors and narratives found in the Bible are closely related to the more abstract, second-order discourse of theology: "At this level religious discourse is reinterpreted in conceptual terms with the help of speculative philosophy."[6] In particular, Ricoeur has stressed the close link between the conceptual discourse of Rahner and Thomas Aquinas on the incomprehensibility of God and the clash of metaphors and narratives in the Bible:

> Where theology comes to grips with analogical concepts, it does at its own level what religious discourse already does with limit expressions, and what creative language does in a still more basic way when it uses models and metaphors.[7]

Ricoeur laments that it was

> an unfortunate turn of events for thirteenth-century theology when it broke its ties with biblical theology in order to elaborate the quaestio without the lectio, the 'science' of theology outside of the work of 'interpreting' the Scriptures.[8]

Ricoeur challenges theologians to confront the conceptual language of philosophical theology with the originating language of the biblical traditions. This project will be a main focus of this investigation. I will reflect on the originating language of Scripture and the conceptual language of two contemporary philosophical theologians in relation to each other.

I will begin by examining the perspectives of the biblical wisdom tradition on the activity of God and Lady Wisdom in human life. The purpose of this section is not to undertake original

---

[5]Charles E. Carlston, "Proverbs, Maxims, and the Historical Jesus," JBL 99(1980):105.

[6]Paul Ricoeur, "Philosophy and Religious Language," JR 54 (1974):73.

[7]Paul Ricoeur, "'Response' to Karl Rahner's Lecture: On the Incomprehensibility of God," JR 58 Supplement (1978):S131.

[8]Ibid., S129.

historical or exegetical research, but rather, in light of recent scholarship, to explore the sapiential themes that have particular relevance for the concerns of contemporary Christology.

The historical survey of the biblical wisdom tradition leads to the issue of hermeneutics, the question of how to understand, interpret and apply the sages' heritage today. In the third section of the first chapter, I will use the work of Hans-Georg Gadamer and Paul Ricoeur to articulate the hermeneutical issues involved in this project.

Gadamer's hermeneutics accords a central role to Bildung, the formation of an interpreter through encounters with the classic texts and works of art of a tradition.[9] The entire discussion in Gadamer's Truth and Method is an exploration of how the process of Bildung occurs. Gadamer's discussion of Bildung offers a way to understand the process of formation in wisdom of the ancient sages. For the ancients, training wisdom was the formation of the student's powers of judgement and discernment through the confrontation with a tradition.

Ricoeur's work on metaphor and narrative illumines the use of images and metaphors by the wisdom writers, and his insistence upon the link between the first-order religious discourse of the Bible and the second-order conceptual discourse of philosophical theology provides a link between the biblical tradition and the theologies of Rahner and Pittenger.

The two central chapters of this investigation will study the work of Rahner and Pittenger as contemporary representatives of the tradition of Logos Christology who are related to the perspectives of the wisdom tradition. Since Pittenger is especially dependent upon the philosophy of Alfred North Whitehead, the third chapter will begin with a discussion of Whitehead's cosmology and its relation to the wisdom tradition. Each chapter will first discuss the thinker's understanding of the presence of God in all human experience and then the relationship between this general presence of God and the specific revelation of God in Jesus Christ.

The interpretation of the biblical tradition's witness to Jesus Christ and the interpretation of contemporary human experience are both projects that take place within the medium of language. The transition from the Bible to contemporary philosophical theology involves a shift in the use of language, and both Rahner and Pittenger were aware of the special demands that Christology places upon language. Both the second and third chapters will

---

[9]Hans-Georg Gadamer, Truth and Method, (New York: Crossroad, 1982), 10-19.

examine the theologians' respective understandings of the role of religious language in Christological claims and the relation of philosophical and dogmatic language to the language of the Bible.

The third chapter will conclude with a critical evaluation of Rahner and Pittenger. The tradition of Wisdom or Logos Christology, including its contemporary representatives Rahner and Pittenger, seems open to suspicion from three angles: political theology, feminist theology, and the awareness of pluralism. The concluding chapter will study these three problematic areas in contemporary theology. Discussion of these areas of concern will illustrate the contribution that the wisdom tradition can make to contemporary theological reflection.

CHAPTER I

THE ORIGINS OF WISDOM CHRISTOLOGY

Wisdom Christology arises from the influence of the wisdom tradition upon New Testament authors and later Christian theologians. The first chapter will begin by exploring the roots of the wisdom tradition in Israel. The teachers of wisdom reflected upon the patterns found in experience in hope of understanding the ordering power at work in creation. The sages combined a fundamental trust in the intelligibility of experience with a sharp sense of human limit.

The sages personified the ordering power of creation in the figure of Lady Wisdom, who appears both as a gracious woman who lures her followers with promises of life and fulfillment and also as a scolding prophet who threatens disaster on those who reject her call for justice.

The books of Job and Qoheleth challenged the confidence of the earlier wisdom tradition in the intelligibility of experience and confronted their readers with the paradox of a world order established by God but hidden from human comprehension.

The later books of the wisdom tradition, Ben Sira and the Wisdom of Solomon, relate the universal activity of Lady Wisdom to specific revelatory events in the history of Israel. Ben Sira identifies Lady Wisdom with the Torah, and the Wisdom of Solomon portrays Lady Wisdom as leading the people of Israel out of Egypt.

The second part of this chapter will examine the influence of the wisdom tradition upon the New Testament's interpretation of Jesus. The Synoptic tradition places many wisdom sayings on the lips of Jesus, thereby presenting him as a teacher of wisdom. Occasionally Jesus is explicitly associated with Lady Wisdom. 1 Corinthians 8:6, the prologue of John, and the hymn in Colossians 1:15-20 present Christ as the ordering power of creation, thus according him the role of Lady Wisdom in holding together the order of the universe. This part of the chapter will examine the relation between Jesus and the wisdom tradition in the Synoptic tradition, the Pauline tradition, and John.

This chapter will conclude by reflecting upon the language of the wisdom trajectory in light of the work of Gadamer and Ricoeur. The hermeneutical philosophies of Gadamer and Ricoeur argue that the meaning of texts is not limited to the historical circumstances of their composition and first reception. Classic texts have the power to open up transforming visions of the world in

1

widely different settings and in widely different times. The concern of Gadamer with formation and play offers analogies to the wisdom tradition, and Ricoeur's discussion of the role of language illumines the use of language by the biblical writers. Their reflections on hermeneutics offer a transition from the biblical writers to the twentieth-century theologians.

The vision of Christ as the Logos, the incarnation of Lady Wisdom is of crucial importance for the Christologies of Rahner and Pittenger. Both theologians place the prologue of John at the center of their Christological reflections. Both relate the Christ-event to the ordering power of the evolutionary process of the universe, and both see the revelation of God in Jesus Christ as the decisive key to understanding the activity of God throughout all experience.

For both Rahner and Pittenger there is a dialectic of similarity and difference in the relation between the Christ-event and the universal activity of God in all creation. For both theologians, the Christ-event is in continuity with the entire cosmic process and thus is similar to God's universal activity; however, both also stress the unique and definitive presence of God in Jesus Christ, and thus the dissimilarity between this event and the universal activity of God in creation. The biblical roots of this dialectic of similarity and dissimilarity are to be found in the New Testament's identification of Jesus Christ with the figure of Lady Wisdom.

Three areas of contemporary theological discussion pose a sharp challenge to the usefulness of the wisdom tradition. Political and liberation theologians have accused the wisdom tradition of supporting the status quo and not offering an adequate basis for a critical stance in society. Feminists have decried the subordination of Lady Wisdom to Yahweh in the Hebrew and Jewish tradition and have lamented the Christian substitution of the masculine "Logos" for the feminine "Sophia" as the name for the divine in Christ and the ordering power of creation. Moreover, in light of the contemporary awareness of pluralism in the encounter with other world religions, the claim of universal and definitive significance for Jesus Christ appears problematic. Each of these three areas poses a challenge to the biblical wisdom trajectory, and also to the theologies of Rahner and Pittenger. In addressing these concerns, the work of Rahner and Pittenger can help develop a retrieval of the biblical trajectory of Wisdom Christology.

The purpose of the first chapter is to introduce the main elements of the wisdom tradition which are of importance for contemporary Christology. It is not my aim to undertake original exegesis, but rather to review recent biblical scholarship in order to prepare the later comparison of the wisdom trajectory with Rahner and Pittenger and the confrontation of the wisdom tradition with the concerns of political and liberation theology, feminism, and pluralism.

Wisdom in Israel

Two sides of the biblical wisdom tradition will be important for this investigation: the articulation of the presence of God in all experience and the correlation of God's universal presence with special historical revelations.[1] This study will begin by examining the role of God in ordinary experience. First I will explore the views of order and limit in Proverbs, Job, and Qoheleth; then I will turn to the personification of the ordering principle of the universe as Lady Wisdom in Proverbs and Job; I will conclude by examining the correlation between the universal activity of Lady Wisdom and the historical events of the people of Israel in Ben Sira and the Wisdom of Solomon.

Wisdom: Order and Limit

The goal of the wisdom tradition of ancient Israel was to discern the right word and action (or silence and non-action) for the right time.[2] In this project the sages balanced a fundamental trust in the gracious presence of a justice-loving world-order with an acute sense of human limits. The order implanted by God

---

[1]On these two aspects of the wisdom tradition, see Collins, 42-55. Recent years have seen an outpouring of literature on the wisdom tradition. For a survey of recent scholarship, see Dianne Bergant, What Are They Saying About Wisdom Literature? (New York: Paulist Press, 1984). A representative variety of viewpoints may be found in four collections of essays: James L. Crenshaw, ed., Studies in Ancient Israelite Wisdom (New York: KTAV Publishing House, 1976); John G. Gammie et al., eds., Israelite Wisdom: Theological and Literary Essays in Honor of Samuel Terrien (Missoula, Mont.: Scholars Press, 1978); M. Gilbert, ed., La Sagesse de l'Ancien Testament (Gembloux, Belgium: Editions J. Duculot, 1979); M. Noth and D. Winton Thomas, eds., Wisdom in Israel and in the Ancient Near East (Leiden: E.J. Brill, 1960).

[2]On discerning the proper time, see Gerhard von Rad, Wisdom in Israel, trans. James D. Martin (Nashville: Abingdon Press, 1972), 138-143; and James L. Crenshaw, "The Problem of Theodicy in Sirach: On Human Bondage," JBL 94(1975):47-64.

in the world enables humans to reflect upon the patterns in ordinary experience.[3] Insight into this order leads to happiness and success. Fools misunderstand the order of the world, neglect its demand for justice, and thereby deceive themselves and eventually destroy themselves.[4] The sages reflected upon everyday experience accessible to all. Unlike the prophets, who based their appeals on a special call from God, the wisdom teachers made no claim to have received a specific, extraordinary revelation from God. As Walter Brueggemann put it: "The wise teacher affirmed that authority for life is discerned in experience."[5] The teacher of wisdom could urge pupils to cooperate and obey (e.g. Prov 1:8, 4:1-2), but only by appealing to the pupils' own enlightened self-interest:

> My son, do not forget my teaching,
> let your heart keep my principles,
> for these will give you lengthier days,
> longer years of life, and greater happiness (Prov 3:1-2).[6]

The sages based their appeals on the practical consequences of wise speech and action for enriching future experience.[7]

---

[3]Von Rad, 74-96; Walther Zimmerli, "Concerning the Structure of Old Testament Wisdom," in Studies in Ancient Israelite Wisdom, 175-207; James L. Crenshaw, Old Testament Wisdom: An Introduction (Atlanta: John Knox Press, 1981), 19, 54-55, 66.

[4]Klaus Koch, "Is There a Doctrine of Retribution in the Old Testament," in Theodicy in the Old Testament, ed. James L. Crenshaw (Philadelphia: Fortress, 1983), 57-87; Hans Heinrich Schmid, Gerechtigkeit als Weltordnung: Hintergrund und Geschichte des alttestamentlichen Gerechtigkeitsbegriffes, Beiträge zur historischen Theologie 40 (Tübingen: J.C.B. Mohr, 1968).

[5]Walter Brueggemann, "Scripture and an Ecumenical Life-Style," Int 24(1970):11. John L. McKenzie offers a similar judgement in "Reflections on Wisdom," JBL 86(1967):3-4; see also J. Coert Rylaarsdam, Revelation in Jewish Wisdom Literature (Chicago: University of Chicago Press, 1946; Midway Reprint, 1974), 47-73.

[6]All biblical translations will be from The Jerusalem Bible, ed. Alexander Jones (Garden City, N.Y.: Doubleday & Co., 1966), unless otherwise noted.

[7]Philip Johannes Nel argues that the motivation of the sages rests upon four types of argument: (1) the "reasonable character" of the wisdom admonition, appealing to one's reason; (2) "its dissuasive character in which the final consequences and results of one's behavior are illuminated"; (3) "its explanatory character," which looks to observation as the basis of credibility and authority; and (4) "its promissory character." Nel argues that the

Fundamental to this appeal was a faith in the basic intelligibility and regularity of relationships with people and with God. Each word or action has an effect which either benefits or harms the speaker or doer. This is not an extrinsic, juridical decision by God but a basic order of life which can be discerned and verified through experience.[8]

In expressing these relationships the sages used declarations, admonitions, and questions.[9] Declarations often took the form of analogies and metaphors:

Clouds and wind and no rain,
a man who boasts about a non-existent gift (Prov 25:14).

A north wind produces rain,
and gossip a look of rage (Prov 25:23).

Cold water on a tired throat,
good news from a distant country (Prov 25:25).

As the heavens are high and the earth is deep,
the mind of a king is unsearchable (Prov 25:3).[10]

Often the Hebrew text has no copula, and the proverb simply juxtaposes two clashing images, inviting the reader to discern both the point of similarity and the conclusion to be drawn. In the similarity between the two images we find an indication of the broader order of the universe.[11] A proverb arises from a certain insight into a particular situation or series of events but then reaches out beyond its origin, promising guidance and illumination for future decisions. Often the proverb gives no explicit advice and states no explicit rule. Rather, it calls attention to the similarity between different phenomena and invites the hearer to

"dominant dogmatic premise" is "that of the created order which in no way contradicts wise thought." Nel, The Structure and Ethos of the Wisdom Admonitions in Proverbs, BZAW 158 (Berlin: Walter de Gruyter, 1982), 86-88.

[8]Von Rad, 90; Koch, 57-64.

[9]On this classification, see Rudolf Bultmann, The History of the Synoptic Tradition, trans. John Marsh (revised ed.; New York: Harper & Row, 1976), 70.

[10]Translations by William McKane, Proverbs: A New Approach, Old Testament Library (Philadelphia: Westminster Press, 1977), 250-251.

[11]Von Rad, 120.

grasp the relationship and draw the proper consequences for behavior. Thus the function of the proverb, as Thompson argues, is philosophical in the broad sense of expressing the "regularity in the natural order or in human relations."[12]

Many of the proverbs have no explicit religious reference. The lists of proverbs (e.g. Prov 10-29) alternate easily between experiences of the world and experiences of God (e.g. Prov 16:7-11). There appears to be a close connection between understanding the patterns of everyday life and understanding the ways of Yahweh. As von Rad comments, the interweaving of secular and religious experience suggests that "the experiences of the world were for her [Israel] always divine experiences as well, and the experiences of God were for her experiences of the world."[13] In reflecting on the order in human life the Hebrew sage always maintained, whether implicitly or explicitly, faith in God who maintained and supported this order.

However, the confidence in the regularity and intelligibility of the world order found an abrupt counterpoint in the sages' acute sense of human limits. The relationship between act and consequence can never be fully fathomed. In the unpredictability of events we experience our own contingency and dependence upon God.[14] While the sages sought to generalize from experiences and establish insights of lasting validity for generations to come, they also recognized that in this world "nothing of absolute value can be affirmed. What is experienced on any given occasion has always shown itself to be in some way conditioned and relative."[15] We can make plans, but it is God who secures our footsteps (Prov 16:9). The sages warn that claims to wisdom and understanding are inherently dangerous:

---

[12]Thompson, 69; see also John J. Collins, "Proverbial Wisdom and the Yahwist Vision," Semeia 17(1980):1-17.

[13]Von Rad, 62; see also Crenshaw, Old Testament Wisdom, 92.

[14]E.g. Prov 16:1-3, 25; 20:24; 21:31; see Collins, "Proverbial Wisdom," 11-13.

[15]Von Rad, 139. Murphy notes that the freedom of Yahweh always transcended and qualified the regularity of the order of the world. Roland E. Murphy, "Wisdom--Theses and Hypotheses," in Israelite Wisdom, 36.

Do not think of yourself as wise (Prov 3:7).

Neither wisdom nor prudence, nor advice,
can stand in Yahweh's presence (Prov 21:30).

You see some man who thinks himself wise?
More hope for a fool than for him (Prov 26:12)!

Occasionally the sages could juxtapose two directly contradictory proverbs one after the other, thus recognizing the limited validity of either point of view (Prov 26:4-5). This dual perspective requires the student of wisdom to discern the proper time for the proper word and action. While proverbs promise us wisdom and insight, no proverb can tell us when to apply it. There is a proper time for action and waiting, for speech and silence; but no one else can tell us what the time is. We must discern it for ourselves. One proverb may be more fruitful for practical action or non-action at one time, and another contradictory proverb may be more fruitful at another time. As Crenshaw comments: "The decision as to what is better is really a discerning of the appropriate time."[16]

Alongside common-sense proverbs whose meaning is evident we find hidotham, obscure sayings or riddles (Prov 1:7) whose interpretation is enigmatic. The numerical sayings of Proverbs 30:15-31 may have originally been riddles which teased the mind of the hearer into searching for a common element among dissimilar phenomena.[17] Von Rad has noted the playful character of riddles:

The riddle is, after all, in the last resort, playing at discovering the truth. One person hides or disguises the truth, the other brings it out of concealment into the light.[18]

The playfulness of the riddles and the juxtaposing of contradictory viewpoints suggest a gamelike quality of hiding and seeking in the search for wisdom. The world order is always present, but we cannot always discern the connection between events, and thus at times the world order is hidden from our understanding:

---

[16]Crenshaw, "Problem of Theodicy in Sirach," 53.

[17]R.B.Y. Scott, The Way of Wisdom in the Old Testament (New York: Macmillan Publishing Co., 1978), 55; Crenshaw, Old Testament Wisdom, 32; Von Rad, 37; McKane, 267.

[18]Von Rad, 37.

To conceal a matter, this is the glory of God,
to sift it thoroughly, the glory of kings (Prov 25:2).

The sages' sense of limit and of the hiddenness of wisdom
found its most radical expression in the critical questions of Job
and Qoheleth. Both books give rise to problems of interpretation;
the theme that is of importance for this investigation is their
paradoxical affirmation of a world order which humans cannot
comprehend.[19] Qoheleth affirms that there is a right ordering of
events by God but denies that humans can understand God's activity:

[God] has made everything beautiful in its time; also he has
put eternity into man's mind, yet so that he cannot find out
what God has done from the beginning to the end (Eccl
3:11).[20]

---

[19]On Qoheleth, see James L. Crenshaw, A Whirlpool of Torment:
Israelite Traditions of God as an Oppressive Presence (Philadel-
phia: Fortress, 1984), 77-92; idem, Old Testament Wisdom, 126-48;
Robert Gordis, Koheleth--The Man and his World: A Study of Eccle-
siastes (3rd ed., augmented; New York: Schocken Books, 1968); J.A.
Loader, Polar Structures in the Book of Qoheleth, BZAW 152 (Ber-
lin: Walter de Gruyter, 1979); and James G. Williams, Those Who
Ponder Proverbs: Aphoristic Thinking and Biblical Literature,
Bible and Literature Series, no. 2 (Sheffield, England: Almond
Press, 1981). On Job, see Robert Gordis, The Book of God and Man:
A Study of Job (Chicago: University of Chicago Press, 1978); Emil
G. Kraeling, The Book of the Ways of God (New York: Charles
Scribner's Sons, 1939); Marvin H. Pope, Job, Anchor Bible, vol. 15
(Garden City, N.Y.: Doubleday & Co., 1965); Claus Westermann, The
Structure of the Book of Job: A Form-Critical Analysis, trans.
Charles A. Muenchow (Philadelphia: Fortress, 1981); and Gustavo
Gutiérrez, On Job: God-Talk and the Suffering of the Innocent,
trans. Matthew J. O'Connell (Maryknoll, N.Y.: Orbis, 1987).

[20]Translation of RSV. The meaning of hā`olām has vexed
translators, partly because its use in this context is unique in
the Hebrew Bible. The New American Bible translates "the timeless"; the Jerusalem Bible proposes: "he has permitted man to consider time in its wholeness." Scott translates: "he has put in
their minds an enigma." R.B.Y. Scott, Proverbs. Ecclesiastes,
Anchor Bible, vol. 18 (Garden City, N.Y.: Doubleday & Co., 1965),
220. Lys translates the word as "la notion du temps total." D.
Lys, "L'Etre et le Temps. Communication de Qohèlèth," in La
Sagesse de l'Ancien Testament, 255. Crenshaw translates the word
as "ignorance," but notes that "'eternity' is also possible" (Old
Testament Wisdom, 134).

Qoheleth tests the traditional relationship of act and consequence against his own experience and is confounded by its apparent absence.[21] The wise do not appear to benefit from their wisdom, nor do the foolish suffer from their folly (Eccl 6:8; 7:15). Qoheleth shares the empirical approach of the earlier sages, but he is sceptical about any conclusions, including his own:

I have put all this to the test by wisdom, claiming to be wise; but wisdom has been beyond my reach. Reality lies beyond my grasp; and deep, so deep, who can discover it (Eccl 7:23-24)?

Qoheleth's enigmatic language has given rise to two main schools of interpretation: those who stress the negative aspects of the book, and those who see a more positive perspective on life.[22] The positive side of Qoheleth's quest appears in his affirmation that everything is "beautiful in its time" (3:11) and in the divine imperative of joy. The proper response to the inscrutability of the cosmic order is to find joy in one's work and in one's family (5:17-19; 8:15; 9:1, 7-10).

Job, like Qoheleth, continues the empirical approach of the earlier sages. He rejects the claims of his friends who defend the perspective of the earlier wisdom tradition:

I can reflect as deeply as ever you can,
I am in no way inferior to you.
And who, for that matter, has not observed as much (Job 12:3)?

Job accuses his friends of pleading the case of God with lies (13:7) because they rigidly apply the act-consequence formula to Job's life and thus falsify his experience. However, Job's own search for wisdom seems to collapse in failure. Like Qoheleth, he cannot discern the connection between act and consequence. There seems to be no reason for his suffering.

Speaking from the whirlwind, God accuses Job of "obscuring my designs with empty-headed words" (38:2), but God nowhere repeats

---

[21]Gese comments on the _Beziehungslosigkeit_ which baffles Qoheleth. Hartmut Gese, "The Crisis of Wisdom in Koheleth," in _Theodicy in the Old Testament_, 144-45.

[22]For the former viewpoint, see Crenshaw, _Old Testament Wisdom_, 126-148; and _Whirlpool of Torment_, 77-92. For a defense of the latter, see Gordis, _Koheleth_, 112-132.

the friends' charges that Job has sinned.[23] Instead, God shifts the context of the discussion from an anthropological to a cosmological focus. Passing over human suffering in silence, God recounts the wonders of the natural universe, denying that these can be judged from the perspective of one human life. God's speeches seem to suggest an analogy between the order and harmony in the natural world, which humans only partially comprehend, and the order and harmony in the moral order, which is also only partially comprehensible to humans.[24]

After Job repents in dust and ashes, God praises him for having spoken "truthfully" about God (42:7). Job's anguished questions and "empty-headed words" which obscure God's designs (38:2) were more faithful to the experience of God than the conventional wisdom of the friends. But then God proceeds to act in accord with the friends' theology of punishment and reward by rewarding Job and threatening the friends! The instability of the conclusion leaves the reader with no clearly defined, reliable pattern to impose on future experience. Nonetheless, God's preference for Job's honest and painful questions does validate Job's demand that claims about God be tested in concrete human experience. It should be stressed that Job and Qoheleth do not simply depart from the older wisdom tradition. Even in their searching critiques, they continue the empirical method of reflection, they affirm the ordering power of God in the world, and they develop, albeit with painful intensity, the earlier sages' awareness of the difficulty of understanding the ways of God.[25]

Lady Wisdom:
Hidden and Revealed

The sages' search for an understanding of human experience became in time a quest for the ordering principle behind all creation. The sages personified the primordial world order as

---

[23]Gordis notes the significance of this divine silence as a rejection of the friends' traditional theology (Book of God and Man, 117).

[24]Ibid., 133; von Rad, 225; Roland E. Murphy, "Wisdom and Creation," JBL 104(1985):6.

[25]Murphy underlines the distinction between "doctrine and style" made by Qoheleth: "He dissented from traditional wisdom at several points, but he never ceased to be a sage. He constantly employed the experiential tests of wisdom (Eccl. 2:1-3; 7:23)" ("Wisdom and Creation," 7).

Lady Wisdom, a feminine figure who appears variously as threatening (Prov 1:20-33), inviting (Prov 8-9), and hidden (Job 28).

Lady Wisdom first appears in Proverbs 1:20-33 as an ominous, threatening figure. She is the harsh and demanding critic of the normal folly and heedlessness of the human race. She "cries aloud in the street; in the markets she raises her voice" (1:20), suggesting a universal appeal in the precincts of everyday life.[26] As Trible observes, Lady Wisdom begins by appealing to all, but she ends with only a solitary listener who "will dwell secure and will be at ease from dread of evil" (1:33).[27] Far from affirming the normal condition of humankind, Lady Wisdom makes an urgent and threatening warning to heed her call before catastrophe strikes.

In Proverbs 8 Lady Wisdom repeats her threats but balances these with gracious promises and a welcoming invitation to enjoy her delights.[28] The poem consists of three sections: Lady Wisdom

---

[26]Trible reviews various interpretations of this passage and describes Lady Wisdom as "a poet who preaches, counsels, teaches, and prophesies." Phyllis Trible, "Wisdom Builds a Poem: The Architecture of Proverbs 1:20-33," _JBL_ 94(1975):509. Trible analyses the passage as a "chiasmus of four concentric circles converging on the center of the poem," which is the "announcement of derisive judgement" (pp. 511-518). Kayatz describes the passage as a Weisheitspredigt and notes the similarities to prophetic forms of address. Christa Kayatz, Studien zu Proverbien 1-9, Wissenshaftliche Monographien zum alten und neuen Testament, no. 22 (Neukirchen-Vluyn, Netherlands: Neukirchener Verlag, 1966), 119.

[27]Trible, 518.

[28]There has been much debate over how Wisdom should be characterized. Von Rad views her as "the self-revelation of creation" (pp. 144-66). Murphy questions whether "the lyrical description of Proverbs 8 is adequately captured by the term 'order'" and argues, against von Rad, that "She is, then, the revelation of God, not merely the self-revelation of creation" ("Wisdom and Creation," 9). Von Rad, himself, however, had made a similar judgement on Wisdom: "wisdom is truly the form in which Jahweh makes himself present and in which he wishes to be sought by man." Gerhard von Rad, Old Testament Theology, trans. D.M.G. Stalker (2 vols.; New York: Harper & Row, 1962), I, 444. Kayatz stresses the Egyptian influence on Lady Wisdom, comparing her to Maat: both exist before creation, both appear as a divine child at play, as lover and beloved, giver of life and safety, as the effective power in the rule of the king (pp. 86-87). For a similar view, see H.H. Schmid, Wesen und Geschichte der Weisheit, BZAW 101 (Berlin: Alfred Topelmann Verlag, 1966), 159. McKane, however, challenges this conclusion (p. 344). Lang has interpreted Lady Wisdom as

calls humans with promises of riches and honor (8:1-21); she
describes her own playing at the creation of the world (8:22-31);
and she renews her call with promises and threats (8:32-36).[29]
As in Proverbs 1, she makes her appeal not in the sacred space of
the temple but in the profane space of the city, crying out at the
city gates.[30] She declares her concern for political matters and
her accessibility outside the borders of Israel by claiming:

> By me monarchs rule and princes issue just laws;
> by me rulers govern, and the great impose justice on the
> world (Prov 8:15-16).

The central section, which describes Lady Wisdom's relation
to Yahweh and creation, raises a difficult philological question.
The Hebrew text reads:

YHWH qānāni rē'shith darkô (8:22).

It is disputed by scholars whether qānāni should be
translated as "created" or "found," "acquired." Even in antiquity
there was no agreement: the Septuagint translates ektisen (created), while Aquila, Symmachus, and Theodotion translate ektēsato
(acquired). Von Rad argues that "qānā means 'acquire' (by
creating)."[31] However, Bruce Vawter opposes this translation,
maintaining that "in no single instance in the OT or in relevant
cognate literatures are we compelled by the evidence to ascribe to

---

"personified school-wisdom." Bernhard Lang, Frau Weisheit:
Deutung einer biblischen Gestalt (Düsseldorf: Patmos, 1975), 147-
84. More recently, Lang has argued that Wisdom is "an Israelite
goddess redefined" as the personification of the wisdom teaching
and, more specifically, of the book of Proverbs. Bernhard Lang,
Wisdom and the Book of Proverbs: A Hebrew Goddess Redefined (New
York: Pilgrim Press, 1986), 126-38.

[29]On the structure of the poem, see Patrick W. Skehan,
"Structures in Poems on Wisdom: Proverbs 8 and Sirach 24," CBQ
41(1979):365-379; Jean-Noël Aletti, "Proverbes 8,22-31. Etude de
structure," Biblica 57(1976):25-37.

[30]On the sociological significance of the city gates, see
Lang, Wisdom and the Book of Proverbs, 22-33.

[31]Wisdom, 151-52. So also McKane, 223, 352-53; Scott argues
that the verb here means "possessed" in the sense that "Yahweh
'possessed' wisdom as an attribute or faculty integral to his
being from the very first" (Proverbs. Ecclesiastes, 68, 72).

the verb qānā in any of its forms the sense 'create.'"[32]
According to Vawter, "in Job 28 and Proverbs 8 Yahweh is not the
creator of wisdom but its discoverer."[33] Vawter argues convincingly that it is the prior expectations of exegetes rather than
the Hebrew text itself that inclines them to translate qānāni
as "created me."

Even if Vawter's argument is not accepted, it is clear that
Lady Wisdom has a special relation to creation. She appears as
the rē'shith darkô, the "head" or "model" of Yahweh's ways and
works.[34] She describes herself as playing at the creation of the
world:

> I was by his side, a master craftsman ('amôn),
> delighting him day after day,
> ever at play in his presence,
> at play everywhere in his world,
> delighting to be with the sons of men (Prov 8:30-31).

The translation of 'amôn has also been much disputed, being
variously amended and understood as either "master workman" (RSV)
or "pet, darling."[35] In either translation Lady Wisdom appears
to have her own proper role and not to be simply an attribute of
God; yet she speaks in a manner characteristic of Yahweh, offering
life and threatening death to those who refuse her (8:35-36).
Lady Wisdom, the ordering power of the universe, is the way in
which humans experience God.[36]

The playful character of riddles and surprising analogies
evidently reflects the playfulness of Lady Wisdom herself. Lady
Wisdom suggests that the created world arises from her playing

---

[32]Bruce Vawter, "Proverbs 8:22: Wisdom and Creation," _JBL_
99(1980):205.

[33]Ibid., 206.

[34]Savignac understands rē'shith as the principle of
Yahweh's creative activity, the best of a series that will follow.
Jean de Savignac, "Note sur le sens du verset VIII 22 dans
Proverbes," _Vetus Testamentum_ 4(1954):429-32.

[35]The latter translation is favored by von Rad (_Wisdom_,
152).

[36]See von Rad, _Wisdom_, 155; Collins, "Biblical Precedent,"
51. Proverbs 3:19 complements this view. Wisdom here is somewhat
ambiguous, for she can be taken as an attribute of either Yahweh
or the earth. As an attribute of the earth she leads humans to a
knowledge of God.

before Yahweh. Johan Huizinga understands this passage to support the conviction that "all is play."[37] Huizinga notes that the verb sahaq, used here, associates laughter and playing, and can also mean "to do something jestingly" and "to dance" and even, on occasion, "to do battle."[38]

The playfulness of Lady Wisdom appears also in her courting of humans. The imagery of wooing runs throughout the descriptions of Lady Wisdom. As von Rad notes, "wisdom personified largely received blood and life from her more sensual opposite, Astarte, the goddess of love."[39] Lady Wisdom threatens as wrathfully as a spurned lover (Prov 1:20-33); she must be searched for as for buried treasure (Prov 2:4); yet she also presents herself (Prov 8:1-10) quite boldly as an alluring alternative to the seductive charms of the "alien woman" of Proverbs 7:6-23. This lovers' game of hiding and seeking is deadly serious, for in it our own lives are at stake (Prov 8:35-36). Huizinga's description of play seems to apply to Lady Wisdom: "Play is a thing by itself. The play-concept as such is of a higher order than is seriousness. For seriousness seeks to exclude play, whereas play can very well include seriousness."[40]

The poem in Job 28 articulates the hiddenness of Wisdom.[41] The poem begins by depicting the dilemma of technological prowess: humans can accomplish physical wonders, tunneling through rocks and extracting precious minerals (28:1-6), even overturning mountains by the roots (28:9). Such engineering feats yield gold and silver and sapphires. While violent action can force physical treasures to come forth from their hiding places in the earth, such activity is completely useless for finding Wisdom. The technological victories of humankind are undermined by the pointed query:

---

[37]Johan Huizinga, Homo Ludens: A Study of the Play-Element in Culture (Boston: Beacon Press, 1955), 212.

[38]Ibid., 35, 41. In II Samuel 2:4 the verb is used of battle, suggesting the identity of play and battle.

[39]Old Testament Theology, I, 444.

[40]Huizinga, 45.

[41]This chapter is generally recognized as an independent unit which does not flow from the preceding dialogue. See Gordis, The Book of God and Man, 100, 278; Pope, xviii.

But tell me, where does wisdom come from?
Where is understanding to be found (28:12)?

The question places in doubt the apparent value of technological successes and launches us on a new and more difficult quest,
but Wisdom is nowhere to be found. She is not "in the land of the
living" (28:13) nor in the deep nor the sea nor the air. Even
Perdition (Abaddon) and Death (Maweth) do not know where Wisdom is
(28:22).

While humans search for her in vain, God alone knows where
she lives (28:23). God's discovery of her took place in illo
tempore, at the time when God set the limits of the world in
creation (28:25-27). In this passage, as in Proverbs 8:22, Wisdom
seems to exist as an entity equiprimordial with God. As Emil
Kraeling argued, Wisdom is "a pre-existent entity, the discovery
of which enabled God to do his creative deeds."[42] Wisdom appears
to be the most valuable treasure in the universe, the secret of
the order of creation, the mystery which gives power over the
natural elements. God's discovery of Wisdom makes possible the
world in which we live, and thus we experience the effects of Wisdom constantly, and yet Wisdom herself is hidden from us. Since
God alone knows the way to Wisdom, it would appear that God wanted
to guard her from all other beings and keep her treasure secret.
It is on this note of unrelieved tension, most scholars feel, that
the original poem ended.[43]

---

[42]Kraeling, 109. As in the case of Proverbs 8:22, there is a
dispute over the translation. Von Rad argues that 28:27 implies
that God created Wisdom (Wisdom, 147). The strongest argument for
von Rad's interpretation is the verb hekînah, which can mean
"established her" or "prepared her" or "directed her." However,
there is a problem with the textual tradition at this verse. Five
Hebrew manuscripts have hebînah ("discerned her"), and this
reading is accepted by Pope and Dhorme as harmonizing better with
the other verbs in the sentence (Pope, 183; E. Dhorme, A
Commentary on the Book of Job, trans. Harold Knight [London:
Thomas Nelson & Sons, 1967], 413). In this reading there is no
suggestion of God creating Wisdom. Terrien accepts the Masoretic
text but translates hekînah as "prepared it." Samuel Terrien,
Job: Poet of Existence (New York: Bobbs-Merril Co., 1957), 172.
Kraeling also accepts the Masoretic text but denies that this
implies creation. He translates the verb as "set it up (like a
model)" (p. 108).

[43]Dhorme, 413-14; Kraeling, 109; Pope, 183; Terrien, 174-75;
von Rad, Wisdom, 148-49. Rowley, however, defends the verse as
part of the original poem. H.H. Rowley, Job, Century Bible (London: Thomas Nelson & Sons, 1970), 234.

However, the present text continues with an oracle from God:

And [God] said to man,
'Wisdom? It is fear of the Lord.
Understanding?--avoidance of evil' (28:28).

Whatever the literary pre-history of the poem may have been,
this verse plays an important role in the present text. It is the
only direct communication from God to humans in the poem, and the
only such communication in the entire book of Job prior to chapter
38. The oracle challenges humankind's exaltation of technological
prowess (28:1-11) and proposes instead "fear of the Lord." The
phrase, on its most literal level, suggests that humans should be
afraid of God; it also suggests a recognition of human limit: the
only wisdom available to humans is that God alone knows the dwelling place of Wisdom. Fear of the Lord also has a more positive
meaning in the alternate translations, "reverence" or "piety."[44]
Gordis translates the phrase as "to be in awe of the Lord."[45]
The elements of reverence and awe, complemented by the last
verse's admonition to "depart from evil" suggest that what is
needed is not only the recognition of human limits but also acceptance. Gordis comments:

> What is available to man, therefore, is not transcendent
> Wisdom, the key to the universe and the meaning of life, but
> practical Wisdom (without the definite article) which ex-
> presses itself in piety and moral behaviour.[46]

By refusing to reveal cosmic Wisdom, the oracle re-directs
human efforts to less ambitious goals. The oracle of Job 28:28
resembles the speeches of God in chapters 38-42 in not resolving
the question of where Wisdom and true understanding are to be
found. Both oracles seem rather to undermine any human claim to
have found true Wisdom; they are messages from God which turn
against themselves and undercut any attempt to explain reality
from God's point of view. In both oracles the paradox of the
revelation of a Wisdom that remains hidden takes the place of any
rational maxim that could be drawn from the story. The perspective of the book of Job recalls the recognition of the ancient
Babylonian sage:

---

[44]William Gesenius, A Hebrew and English Lexicon of the Old
Testament with an Appendix Containing the Biblical Aramaic, trans.
Edward Robinson, eds. Francis Brown et al. (Oxford: Clarendon
Press, 1980), 432.

[45]Book of God and Man, 280.

[46]Ibid., 101.

The will of a god cannot be understood,
the way of a god cannot be known.
Anything of a god [is difficult] to find out.[47]

The oracles may also be compared to the experience of Socrates, who concluded:

> But the truth of the matter, gentlemen, is pretty certainly this: that real wisdom is the property of God, and this oracle is his way of telling us that human wisdom has little or no value.[48]

The descriptions of Lady Wisdom in Proverbs 8 and Job 28 appear directly contradictory. In Job 28 Wisdom is hidden from everyone except God, and God does not reveal her hiding place. In Proverbs 8 Lady Wisdom herself seeks out humans with promises of life and happiness. The inclusion of both perspectives in the Hebrew Bible suggests a dialectic of concealment and disclosure and the inadequacy of either perspective alone to articulate the human experience of Lady Wisdom.

Ben Sira and the Wisdom of Solomon

The critical challenges of Job and Qoheleth did not mark the end of the wisdom tradition in Jewish life. On the contrary, the following centuries witnessed continued literary activity by sages such as Ben Sira and the author of the Wisdom of Solomon.

Ben Sira has a keen sense of the emptiness of human pursuits (40:1-11; cf. Job 7:1-9; 14:1-12; Qoh 1), and he, like Qoheleth and Job, is very aware of the dilemma of a hidden order; Ben Sira affirms that everything is properly ordered by God, but denies that humans can understand what God is doing:

> For the Lord's deeds are marvellous,
> though hidden from mankind (11:4).

> It is impossible to fathom the marvels of the Lord. When a man finishes he is only beginning, and when he stops he is as puzzled as ever (18:6-7).

---

[47]W.G. Lambert, Babylonian Wisdom Literature (Oxford: Clarendon Press, 1960), 266.

[48]Apology 23A, trans. Hugh Tredennick, Plato: The Last Days of Socrates (Baltimore: Penguin Books, 1967), 52.

You must not say, 'What is this? What is that?'
All things have been created for their proper functions
(39:21).

You must not say, 'This is worse than that',
for everything will prove its value in its time (39:34).

Nonetheless, Ben Sira is far more confident of proclaiming
Wisdom's characteristics than Qoheleth and Job were. Ben Sira
begins a process of relating the universal activity of Lady Wisdom
to the specific historical revelations to the people of Israel.
In chapter 24 Lady Wisdom describes her origins:

I came forth from the mouth of the Most high,
and I covered the earth like mist (24:3).

There is a strong analogy to the word of God in creation in
Genesis 1:1 and to the mist of Genesis 2:6.[49] The relation of
Lady Wisdom to God differs from that in Proverbs 8:22 or Job
28:27, for she clearly acknowledges that God created her (24:8-9).
However, her role in creation appears somewhat similar to the
earlier poems. Ben Sira emphasizes Wisdom's ruling prerogatives
in her act of walking around the vault of the sky and the depths
of the seas (24:4-6). Lady Wisdom, the primordial ordering power
of creation, rules over the entire universe.

Ben Sira goes on to relate the universal, cosmic rule of Lady
Wisdom to the Torah and the temple in Jerusalem. She looked for a
dwelling-place, and God directed her:

Pitch your tent in Jacob,
Make Israel your inheritance (24:8).

Ben Sira interprets the Torah as one privileged revelation of
the primeval world order which is present everywhere and always
(24:23-24).[50] Lady Wisdom also associates herself with Israel's
journey through the wilderness: "My throne was in a pillar of
cloud" (24:4). The pillar of cloud recalls the divine guidance of
Israel through the desert (e.g. Exod 13:21; 14:19; Neh 9:12, 19).
This image, which Exodus 13:21 had used of God, is here trans-

---

[49]On the relations between these passages, see Gerald T.
Sheppard, Wisdom as a Hermeneutical Construct, BZAW 151 (Berlin:
de Gruyter, 1980), 23-26.

[50]Torah and Wisdom also appear to be identified in Sir 17.
See ibid., 72-83.

ferred to Lady Wisdom, suggesting that it is through Wisdom that humans experience God's guiding presence.[51]

Thus Ben Sira proposes a correlation between the presence of God, the universal cosmic activity of Lady Wisdom, and the specific historical experiences of Israel. Sheppard argues that in Ben Sira Wisdom functions "as a hermeneutical construct to interpret the Torah as a statement about wisdom and as a guide to Israel's practice of it."[52] The Torah reveals the benefits of Lady Wisdom; and thus Ben Sira, aware of the diversity of Israel's traditions, uses the figure of Lady Wisdom to interpret the Torah. From one perspective, this may be understood as a legitimation of Wisdom by an appeal to the canonical Torah;[53] but from the opposite angle the wisdom tradition is interpreting the Torah on its own terms. Thus von Rad comments that Ben Sira is

> endeavouring to legitimate and to interpret Torah from the realm of understanding characteristic of wisdom. . . . It [the Torah] is the primeval order inherent in the whole world appearing in a new guise. In this provenance lies its worth.[54]

In the "Hymn of the Fathers" (chapters 44-50) Ben Sira presents the great figures of Israel's history as examples of people who followed the guidance of Wisdom. Ben Sira looks to historical individuals as models who show clearly to all nations the benefits of Lady Wisdom. Later nations remember their names and their glory to show "that it is good to follow the Lord" (46:10). Enoch "was taken up, an example for the conversion of all generations" (44:16). Through Noah, Abraham, and Isaac blessings came to all humanity (44:17-26). Solomon's fame reached beyond Israel to "the distant islands" (47:16) and his mind "ranged the earth," filling it "with mysterious sayings" (47:15). Ben Sira regards the historical traditions of Israel as a paradigm for all the world, in effect as "an educational picture book."[55]

---

[51]In a similar vein Philo would later interpret the cloud which separated the Israelites and the Egyptians in Exodus 14:20 as a symbol of both Wisdom and salvation. Philo, Quis Rerum Divinarum Heres, 42. See Sheppard, 32.

[52]Sheppard, 118.

[53]So K. Hruby, "La Torah Identifiée à la Sagesse et L'Activité du Sage dans la Tradition Rabbinique," Bible et vie chrétienne 76(1967):67-68.

[54]Wisdom, 245-46.

[55]Ibid., 257.

19

Burton L. Mack, while noting the absence of Lady Wisdom herself from the Hymn of the Fathers, nonetheless insists on her importance for the hymn. The Hymn of the Fathers itself is preceded by a hymn on creation (42:15-45:33), suggesting the schema: "wisdom-in-creation/wisdom-in-the-social-order."[56] Mack argues that Ben Sira is seeking a firm basis for the social order of Second Temple Judaism.[57] Through contact with Hellenistic paideia, the sage learned

> that a nation's history could be read in order to disclose its logos. With this discovery, the sage could take up the history as paradigmatic and understand it as elucidation of the principle that constituted and ordered the social structure itself.[58]

The description of Lady Wisdom and the correlation of her universal cosmic rule with specific historical events were continued and developed by the Wisdom of Solomon. While the Wisdom of Solomon differs in significant respects from the older wisdom literature, it remains true that, as Collins notes, "its fundamental assumptions about reality are in clear continuity with the Hebrew wisdom tradition."[59]

In the first chapter Wisdom is described as a spirit friendly to humans and is closely associated with "that which holds all things together" (1:7). Lady Wisdom has a role both in ordering the universe and in making humans righteous (e.g. 7:21-8:1). She is also associated with "avenging Justice" (1:8) and with "a

---

[56]Burton L. Mack, Wisdom and the Hebrew Epic: Ben Sira's Hymn in Praise of the Fathers (Chicago: University of Chicago Press, 1985), 161.

[57]Ibid., 152.

[58]Ibid., 162.

[59]John J. Collins, "The Root of Immortality: Death in the Context of Jewish Wisdom," HTR, 71(1978):186. The Wisdom of Solomon accepts the belief in immortal happiness that Ben Sira had rejected (ibid., 177-192). The work was also heavily influenced by Hellenistic thought. See James M. Reese, Hellenistic Influence on the Book of Wisdom and Its Consequences, Analecta Biblica, no. 41 (Rome: Biblical Institute Press, 1970). The work also bears similarity to some aspects of apocalyptic thought. See John J. Collins, "Cosmos and Salvation: Jewish Wisdom and Apocalyptic in the Hellenistic Age," HR 17(1977):121-142. See also David Winston, The Wisdom of Solomon, Anchor Bible, vol. 43 (Garden City, N.Y.: Doubleday & Co., 1979).

jealous ear that overhears everything" (1:10). As in Proverbs 8, Lady Wisdom seeks out humans and offers them the choice of life or death. In relating to Lady Wisdom, to the ordering power of the universe, humans are relating to God.[60]

There has been much debate over how the Wisdom of Solomon's presentation of Wisdom should be characterized.[61] In her relation to the world Lady Wisdom is the principle of order and unity, ordering all things well (8:1), rewarding the righteous and punishing the impious (1:4, 10; 7:27). Being one in herself yet manifold (7:27), she pervades all things (7:24) and renews all things (7:27). Lady Wisdom has converse with God, being initiated into the mysteries of divine knowledge (8:4); she lives with God, sitting beside God as a consort on a throne (9:4). God has no secrets from her, and she is the chooser (hairetis) and artificer (technitis) of God's works (8:4). Lady Wisdom appears to be the form in which God is revealed in the world:

For she is a reflection of eternal light,
and a spotless mirror of the working of God,
and an image of his goodness (7:26).

Thus in coming to know Wisdom humans can know something of God, seeing as in a spotless mirror. It is significant for the later study of the Gospel of John that the Wisdom of Solomon presents Wisdom as parallel to Word (9:2).[62]

There are clear affinities between the Wisdom of Solomon and contemporary Hellenistic philosophy. The increased explicitness and prominence given to the cosmological description of Lady Wisdom in the Wisdom of Solomon may be understood in relation to contemporary philosophies. The Logos or pneuma of the Stoics was described in terms very similar to Lady Wisdom; both are viewed as the principle of order which pervades and permeates the universe.[63] There has been much debate over what direct sources lie

---

[60]Collins, "Cosmos and Salvation," 125.

[61]See C. Larcher, Etudes sur le Livre de la Sagesse (Paris: Librairie Lecoffre, 1969), 362-414.

[62]Dey has assembled a list of passages in Hellenistic Jewish texts where Wisdom and Word are equivalent. L.K.K. Dey, The Intermediary World and Patterns of Perfection in Philo and Hebrews, SBL Dissertation Series 25 (Missoula, Mont.: Scholars Press, 1975), 8.

[63]See A.H. Armstrong, An Introduction to Ancient Philosophy (London: Methuen & Co., 1947), 122; and P. Merlan, "Greek Philosophy from Plato to Plotinus," in The Cambridge History of Later Greek and Early Medieval Philosophy, ed. A.H. Armstrong (Cam-

21

behind the Wisdom of Solomon.[64] The general eclecticism of the age points to an interplay of varied crosscurrents of thought.

The final section of the Wisdom of Solomon, the "Book of History" (chs 10-19), recounts the stories of Genesis and Exodus as typical examples of Wisdom's ever-present activity in the world. Individual characters are not named but are presented as types of righteous individuals. The history of Israel is used to elucidate the experience of all peoples.[65] Even miracles appear as a "retuning or refashioning of nature," not as exceptions disrupting the cosmic order.[66] The Book of History has an acute sense of the power of evil in the world. A "nation of oppressors" has power over a "holy and blameless race" (10:15). The ordinary course of history appears as radically corrupted by idolatry:

> Everywhere a welter of blood and murder, theft and fraud, corruption, treachery, riots, perjury, disturbance of decent people, forgetfulness of favors, pollution of souls, sins against nature, disorder in marriage, adultery, debauchery. For the worship of unnamed idols is the beginning, cause, and end of every evil (14:25-27).[67]

Despite the corruption and confusion of the course of history, the sage nonetheless affirms the goodness of the structure of the world, proclaiming to God, "Being just yourself, you order all things justly" (12:15). The punishment of the wicked is accomplished through the activity of Lady Wisdom or of God. In the final chapters of the work there is a sudden shift from the activity of Lady Wisdom (10:1-11:1) to that of God (11:4- 19:22). Lady

bridge: Cambridge University Press, 1967), 124.

[64]Goodrick sees a dependence upon Stoicism in general and sees all other influences as mediated through Stoic teaching. A.T.S. Goodrick, The Book of Wisdom (London: Rivingtons, 1913), 410. Larcher suggests that the author of the Wisdom of Solomon used a student's "Introduction to Philosophy" which presented a number of different selections, "morceaux choisis de toute nature" (p. 235). Reese sees the author as drawing from a number of schools, including the Stoics, the Aristotelians, the Epicureans, and the popular religion of hellenized Egypt as expressed in the cult of Isis (pp. 66, 89, 156).

[65]Collins, "Cosmos and Salvation," 127.

[66]Goodrick, 367.

[67]On the critique of idolatry, see Maurice Gilbert, La critique des dieux dans le Livre de la Sagesse: (Sg 13-15) (Rome: Biblical Institute Press, 1973).

Wisdom performs the initial work of delivering the people of Israel, but then the text in 11:4 shifts abruptly to the second person "you," addressing the Lord. Evidently the activity of Lady Wisdom and God are equivalent, for both perform the same activities of leading the holy people with little change in meaning. In one later passage (18:14-15) it is the Logos, personified as a mighty and warlike messenger of God, who intervenes in history, bringing judgement upon the wicked.

The Wisdom of Solomon proposes a coherent theology which is in continuity with the earlier Hebrew wisdom tradition. The work further develops the earlier descriptions of Lady Wisdom, using terms and concepts found in contemporary pagan philosophy. Lady Wisdom, the all pervasive ordering power of the universe, is the image of God's goodness and reveals God to humans. By understanding and accepting this ordering power of the universe, humans are relating to God and become wise and virtuous.

This brief survey has suggested something of the variety of viewpoints found within the wisdom tradition. The search of humans for Wisdom and of Lady Wisdom for humans involves a back and forth movement, resembling at times a game of hide and seek. At times both Lady Wisdom (Prov 1:14-20) and humans (Job 28) are presented as frustrated in their search for one another; at other times Lady Wisdom and humans enjoy delight and fulfillment in their relationship to one another (Prov 8-9; Sir 14:20-27; Wis 6:22-7:21). As Terrien suggests, the playfulness of Lady Wisdom and her delight in God and in humans is the key to her role as a mediator between God and humankind: "Playful Wisdom is the mediatrix of presence."[68]

Wisdom in the New Testament

The wisdom tradition of the Hebrew Bible and Intertestamental Judaism was one important influence on early Christianity. We turn now to the association of Jesus and Wisdom (1) in the Synoptic tradition, (2) in the Pauline trajectory, and (3) in the Gospel of John and the Epistle to the Hebrews. As in the previous section, the aim of this discussion is not to offer original exegesis; its purpose is rather to review recent discussions of the evidence for the association between Jesus and the wisdom tradition.

---

[68]Samuel Terrien, The Elusive Presence: The Heart of Biblical Theology, Religious Perspectives, 26 (San Francisco: Harper & Row, 1978), 357.

Jesus and Wisdom in
the Synoptic Tradition

The Sayings of Jesus

In the Synoptic tradition there are numerous wisdom sayings found on the lips of Jesus.[69] The memory of Jesus as a teacher of wisdom was an important preparation for the eventual interpretation of Jesus as Wisdom incarnate.[70] How many of the Synoptic wisdom sayings can be attributed to the historical Jesus is difficult to determine and is not essential to this investigation.[71] What is clear is that the earliest strands of the sayings tradition present Jesus as a teacher of wisdom.

Many of the wisdom sayings of Jesus demonstrate strong parallels to the wisdom literature of Judaism and the ancient Near East, as well as to the Greek tradition. For example, Bultmann compares Jesus' admonition, "Give to anyone who asks, and if anyone wants to borrow, do not turn away" (Mt 5:42), with the earlier sages' advice:[72]

---

[69]Bultmann finds wisdom parallels for almost every saying in the Sermon on the Mount (pp. 73-108). Carlston counts 102 wisdom sayings of Jesus. Charles E. Carlston, "Proverbs, Maxims, and the Historical Jesus," JBL 99(1980):91. See also Dieter Zeller, Die weisheitlichen Mahnsprüche bei den Synoptikern, Forschung zur Bibel Band 17 (Würzburg: Echter Verlag, 1977), 54-143.

[70]On this issue, see Martin Hengel, The Son of God: The Origin of Christology and the History of Jewish-Hellenistic Religion, trans. John Bowden (Philadelphia: Fortress, 1976), 74.

[71]Bultmann, using the criterion of dissimilarity, questions the historical authenticity of the wisdom sayings (pp. 104-05). Nonetheless, he admitted: "It is quite possible that Jesus took a popular proverb and altered it, and he could certainly have coined a secular proverb himself" (p. 101). Carlston, however, protests that a thorough application of the criterion of dissimilarity "can only prejudice us at the outset against wisdom-motifs in his [Jesus'] teaching which probably cannot be eliminated without violence" (p. 104). For a similar protest against Bultmann's judgement, see Williams, 56.

[72]Bultmann, 106. Other examples cited by Bultmann include Mt 6:19-20, Prov 10:2; 11:4 and Baba bathra 11a; and Mt. 6:34 and Sanh 100b, as well as Egyptian and Arabic and Turkish parallels (p. 107).

He who gives to the poor shall never want,
He who closes his eyes to them will bear many a curse (Prov 28:27).

Do not repulse a hard-pressed beggar,
nor turn your face from a poor man (Sir 4:4).

Carlston compares Matthew 7:13 ("The road that leads to perdition is wide and spacious.") with Bion of Borysthenes of the fourth-century B.C.E.: "The road which leads to Hades is easy to follow."[73] While Jesus warns, "Many are called, but few are chosen" (Mt 22:14), the Greek tradition cautions: "The thyrsus-bearers are many, but the bacchants few."[74] Jesus observes that "No one can be the slave of two masters" (Mt 6:24); according to Plutarch, Alexander the Great rejected Darius' demand that they divide Asia, saying, "The world cannot tolerate two suns nor Asia two kings."[75] Such sayings could be easily multiplied further.

Like Israel's sages, the Synoptic Jesus utters declaratory wisdom sentences, admonitions, and impossible questions.[76] Many of the wisdom sayings of Jesus require no privileged revelation from God but formulate maxims for living based on ordinary human experience accessible to all. Carlston comments on a series of wisdom sayings (Mt 6:24=Lk 16:13; Mt 7:20=Lk 6:43; Lk 12:15 and 16:3): "All of this is self-evident in almost every culture, and most of it was familiar in proverbial form to many before Jesus' day."[77] We have seen the close link between the wisdom tradition and creation in the Hebrew Bible; W.D. Davies stresses that Jesus' ethical teaching in the Sermon on the Mount is grounded in the order of creation:

We find in Jesus an appeal to the order of creation itself as a ground for morality, that is, an appeal to what was prior

---

[73]Cited by Diogenes Laertius, Lives, IV, 19; Carlston, 102, n. 119.

[74]Carlston, 100, n. 101.

[75]Plutarch, Moralia, "Sayings of Kings and Commanders," cited by Carlston, 101, n. 108.

[76]See Bultmann's lists of examples under each category, (pp. 73-79).

[77]Carlston, 101.

to the Law of Moses in time and rooted in the act of creation.[78]

In a similar vein, Richard A. Edwards argues that the beatitudes demonstrate a "wisdom approach" to life; he acknowledges the intertwining of prophetic and wisdom traditions in the beatitudes and woes, but insists:

> Because there is an assumption of a basic point of view about the consequences of an act or state of existence, it is possible to recognize the experience-based orientation of a wisdom saying as its primary characteristic. . . . An act, life, style, or situation will have its appropriate results and these results are placed within the usual eschatological context.[79]

Like the older wisdom tradition, the sayings of Jesus include both world-constructive and world-questioning perspectives. As John Dominic Crossan argues, the establishment of wisdom in proverbs and its undermining in aphorisms and fragments can be seen as points on a continuum of gnomic discourse.[80] The constructive side of Jesus' teaching continues the sapiential themes of giving to the poor (Mt 5:42; Prov 28:27; Sir 4:1), of not putting oneself forward in public (Lk 14:7-11; Prov 25:6-7; Sir 3:17-18), of God's providence (Mt 6:25-33; Sir 11:23), of choosing the right treasure (Mt 6:19-21; Prov 10:2; 11:4), of not judging others (Mt 7:1-2; Wis 12:22), of the rich fool (Lk 12:16-20; Prov 11:28; Sir 11:18-19), and of life as the highest good (Mk 8:37; Prov 3:2; 8:35).

Much recent scholarship has stressed the unsettling, disorienting reversals of expectations that recur in the teaching of Jesus.[81] This side of the sapiential Jesus also finds precedent

---

[78]W.D. Davies, The Setting of the Sermon on the Mount (Cambridge: Cambridge University Press, 1966), 429-30; see also Hans Dieter Betz, "Cosmogony and Ethics in the Sermon on the Mount," in Cosmogony and Ethical Order, eds. Robin W. Lovin and Frank E. Reynolds (Chicago: University of Chicago Press, 1985), 158-76; and Gary A. Tuttle, "The Sermon on the Mount: Its Wisdom Affinities and their Relation to its Structure," The Journal of the Evangelical Theological Society 20(1977):213-30.

[79]Richard A. Edwards, A Theology of Q: Eschatology, Prophecy, and Wisdom (Philadelphia: Fortress, 1976), 61-62.

[80]John Dominic Crossan, In Fragments: The Aphorisms of Jesus (San Francisco: Harper & Row, 1983), 20.

[81]See John Dominic Crossan, In Parables: The Challenge of the Historical Jesus (New York: Harper & Row, 1973); Robert W. Funk, Jesus as Precursor, Semeia Supplements, No. 2 (Philadelphia:

in the earlier sages. For example, Williams considers Jesus and Qoheleth together as representatives of "the aphoristic wisdom of counter-order." According to Williams, both Jesus and Qoheleth accord the individual a central place in their thought, and both call into question their received tradition through the use of disorienting literary paradoxes.[82] Where they differ, according to Williams, is in their evaluation of the values of life. Qoheleth's metaphors are "either pessimistic concerning the values of existence or are negated and stilled in paradox"; Jesus' metaphors, by contrast, are overwhelmingly positive, overturning the present state of affairs for the sake of a gracious future.[83] Tannehill has studied the sayings of Jesus with an eye to their "imaginative shock," their power to "affect our perception of the situation by bringing a new image into play or activating symbols which were recessive, thereby combating perceptions based on other images."[84] According to Tannehill, the paradoxical sayings of Jesus create a deliberate tension within the hearer by mounting "an attack on our natural tendency to put self-protection first."[85]

Jesus and Lady Wisdom

In addition to the wisdom sayings of Jesus there also appear passages in Luke and Matthew which associate Jesus with Lady Wisdom. In Luke 7:33-35 (par. Mt 11:18-19), Lady Wisdom sends envoys, her children, into the world, and they are rejected. Jesus may possess a somewhat more exalted position than John the Baptist due to his title as Son of Man,[86] but he appears, like John, as a

---

Fortress, 1975); Robert C. Tannehill, The Sword of His Mouth, Semeia Supplements, No. 1 (Philadelphia: Fortress, 1975); and Williams.

[82]Williams, 47-63.

[83]Ibid., 60, 63.

[84]Tannehill, 22, 25. Tannehill cites H.R. Jauss and G. Buck on the productive meaning of negative experience (p. 58, n. 14).

[85]Ibid., 71.

[86]On the meaning of "the Son of Man," see Geza Vermes, "The Use of Bar Nas/Bar Nasa in Jewish Aramaic," Appendix E in Matthew Black, An Aramaic Approach to the Gospels and Acts, (Oxford: Clarendon Press, 1967); and H.E. Todt, The Son of Man in the Synoptic Tradition (Philadelphia: Westminster, 1965).

child of Lady Wisdom.[87] Luke 11:49-51 (par. Mt 23:34-36) presents Jesus as a prophet and apostle of Lady Wisdom, the culmination of a series of messengers sent by her. Jesus has a climactic position as the final envoy, but he is not identified with Lady Wisdom.[88]

Jesus's lament over Jerusalem in Luke 13:34-35 (par. Mt 23:37-39) is sometimes cited as a wisdom saying.[89] However, Werner Kümmel questions the wisdom associations of the oracle, arguing that "there is no authority anywhere for connecting the wisdom myth with the expectation of the coming Messiah (Matt 23:39)."[90] In Luke 9:58 (par. Mt 8:20) Jesus states, "Foxes have holes, and the birds of the air have nests, but the Son of Man has nowhere to lay his head." This passage does not mention Wisdom explicitly but presents the Son of Man in a setting reminiscent of Philo, who had written: "A sophos has no house or kinsfolk or country, save virtues and virtuous actions."[91] The Philonic parallel suggests an identification of Jesus as a wise person, not as Lady Wisdom herself.

Luke 11:29-32 (par. Mt 12:38-42) presents the Son of Man as a "sign to this generation." Jesus is greater than Solomon or Jonah, but again he is not identified with Lady Wisdom. Robinson inter-

---

[87]See R.G. Hamerton-Kelly, Pre-Existence, Wisdom, and the Son of Man: A Study of the Idea of Pre-Existence in the New Testament (Cambridge: Cambridge University Press, 1973), 30; James Robinson, "Jesus as Sophos and Sophia: Wisdom Tradition and the Gospels," in Aspects of Wisdom in Judaism and Early Christianity, ed. Robert Wilken (Notre Dame, Ind.: University of Notre Dame Press, 1975), 5; and Felix Christ, Jesus Sophia: Die Sophia-Christologie bei den Synoptikern (Zürich: Zwingli Verlag, 1970), 63-80.

[88]Robinson, 5; see also G.N. Stanton, "On the Christology of Q," in Christ and Spirit in the New Testament, ed. Barnabas Lindars (Cambridge: Cambridge University Press, 1973), 37.

[89]Bultmann reconstructs an alleged Wisdom-myth based on Proverbs 1:24 as the context of this saying (p. 115). However, there is no clear textual evidence for such a "wisdom-myth" before 1 Enoch 42:1-3; von Rad charges that Bultmann's reconstruction leads to "disastrous distortions" of earlier texts such as Prov 1:20-32 (Wisdom, 160, n. 17).

[90]Werner Kümmel, Promise and Fulfillment (London, 1957), quoted by Stanton, 38.

[91]De Abrahamo 31. The second clause may well be Philo's moralizing addition to an older saying. See Hamerton-Kelly, 29.

prets Jesus here as the final and greatest emissary of Lady Wisdom, the _primus inter pares_.[92] However, since Jonah was not a wisdom teacher, Jesus may also be taken as transcending all categories, both prophet and sage.

Luke 10:22 (par. Mt 11:27) may also come from a sapiential context:

'All things have been delivered to me by my Father; and no one knows who the Son is except the Father, or who the Father is except the Son and anyone to whom the Son chooses to reveal him.'

Robinson sees the "exclusive and reciprocal relation of Father and Son" and the "exclusivity of the mediation of salvation" as conclusive evidence that Jesus and Lady Wisdom are here being identified.[93] Robinson's argument succeeds in showing the tendency of the Synoptic tradition to give Jesus greater and more exclusive significance in revelation and salvation than an ordinary wisdom teacher would possess. One may question, however, whether the passage implies an outright identification of Jesus and Lady Wisdom. There is no explicit evidence for the Son to be identified with Lady Wisdom.[94] The original emphasis of Luke 10:22 and Matthew 11:27 need not have been sapiential. Thus in Luke, Jesus appears as a child of Lady Wisdom, the last and greatest of her representatives.[95]

Two themes in particular are striking in Luke's presentation of Lady Wisdom: her playfulness and her subversiveness. In Luke

---

[92]Robinson, 5; so also Hamerton-Kelly, 30.

[93]Robinson, 10.

[94]Bultmann, for example, considers Mt 11:27 to be a Hellenistic revelation saying in contrast to and originally separate from the wisdom saying in Mt 11:28-30; he cites a parallel from Akhnaton's Hymn to the Sun: "No other knows thee save thy Son Akhnaton, Thou hast initiated him into thy plans and thy power" (p. 160). Davies views Mt 11:25-30 as typical of Jewish eschatology and compares it with the Qumran scrolls (p. 207).

[95]Luke has probably preserved the perspective of Q on this issue. See Jack Suggs, _Wisdom, Christology, and Law in Matthew's Gospel_ (Cambridge, Mass.: Harvard University Press, 1970). For differing viewpoints on Q, see Robinson, 5-16; William Beardslee, "The Wisdom Tradition in the Synoptic Gospels," _JAAR_ 35(1967):237; and Ulrich Wilckens, "Sophia," in _Theological Dictionary of the New Testament_, VII, ed. Gerhard Friedrich (Grand Rapids, Mich.: Wm. Eerdmans Co., 1971), 515-16.

7:33-35 Lady Wisdom playfully sends two messengers who adopt dia-
metrically opposed styles of life; yet she is justified by both.
Jesus's taunt in Luke 7:32 accuses his hearers of not "playing the
game," of being "spoilsports" because they refused either to dance
to a pipe-tune or cry to a dirge. In Luke 11:49-51 Lady Wisdom
sends prophets and apostles who are troublesome critics of their
generations. Her messengers are in opposition to the ruling powers of their ages and as a result are rejected, persecuted, and
put to death.

In Matthew there are textual changes in two passages that
substitute Jesus in place of Wisdom. Matthew 11:18-19 (par. Lk
7:33-35) ends the last line with "apo tōn ergōn autēs" instead of Luke's "apo pantōn tōn teknōn autēs."[96] Matthew
23:34-36 (par. Lk 11:49-51) omits the opening phrase, "Therefore
also the Wisdom of God said," and substitutes, "I" (i.e., Jesus).[97] Suggs interprets the difference between the two Gospels
as a deliberate alteration of Q by Matthew in order to identify
Jesus with Lady Wisdom.[98] Suggs also cites the invitation found
in Matthew 11:28-30 as further evidence of the identification of
Jesus and Wisdom.[99]

Suggs's analysis of Matthew's redactional tendency does establish that Matthew very probably did substitute Jesus for Wisdom
in passages from Q. However, it is not entirely clear that Mat-

---

[96]Suggs argues that the Lukan version was found in Q originally because (1) the final saying was probably attracted to its
present place in Luke by the presence of children (paidia) in the
parable (Lk 7:32), and (2) the textual tradition contains numerous
cases of "children" in Matthew (p. 35, n. 9).

[97]It is again probable that Luke's version was that of Q.
Luke's use of the aorist eipen strongly suggests that the Wisdom
of God was not here originally identified with Jesus; if Jesus
were the speaker referring to himself, one would expect the present tense legei. See Suggs, 18, and Hamerton-Kelly, 31.

[98]Suggs, 57-60.

[99]Ibid., 77-81. Many scholars have followed D.F. Strauss in
seeing a relation between this passage and the wisdom tradition,
particularly Sir 6:23-28; 51:23-27. Strauss had also posed the
question of whether the identification of Jesus and Wisdom might
not have been a stage leading to the Logos Christology of John.
See Hans Dieter Betz, "The Logion of the Easy Yoke and of Rest
(Matt. 11:28-30)," JBL 86(1967):11; cf. also Bultmann, 160; and
Krister Stendahl, The School of Saint Matthew and Its Use of the
Old Testament (Lund: CWK Gleerup, 1967), 141-42.

thew actually portrays Jesus as the incarnation of Lady Wisdom. Matthew nowhere attributes to Jesus the cosmological role characteristic of Lady Wisdom. Marshall D. Johnson has directly challenged Suggs's conclusions, noting that the only people who mention Jesus's "wisdom" in Matthew are the unbelieving Nazarenes in a passage that comes from Mark (Mt 13:54).[100] Johnson observes that the deeds of Christ in Matthew 11:2 are also the deeds of his disciples in 10:2-16: healing, teaching, preaching. However, the disciples are not incarnations of Lady Wisdom. Thus he concludes that Matthew 11:19 presents an analogy, not an identification, of Jesus and Lady Wisdom.[101] Turning to Matthew 23:34-36, Johnson draws precisely the opposite conclusion from Suggs: "it would seem that Matthew deliberately avoids any identification of Jesus with Wisdom."[102] Johnson conjectures that Matthew's readers would not have known or investigated the source and suggests that Matthew drops mention of "Wisdom" because he is not very interested in Wisdom speculation.[103]

Johnson succeeds in casting doubt upon Suggs's conclusions. However, his own interpretation minimizes the association of Jesus and Wisdom more than is warranted. While Suggs is too eager to posit a fully developed Wisdom Christology in Matthew, Johnson is too reluctant to admit the functional equivalence of Jesus and Wisdom in passages such as Matthew 11:19 and 23:34-36. Matthew does attribute to Jesus the functions of Lady Wisdom in revelation and in sending prophets and sages. What is lacking in Matthew is the association of Jesus with the ordering power of creation. Matthew does view Jesus as the Son of God who is the ultimate and decisive revelation of the Father.[104] This belief requires that Jesus be related to the Torah and Lady Wisdom, who had previously been accepted as revelatory of God. If Jesus is the only one who

---

[100]Marshall D. Johnson, "Reflections on a Wisdom Approach to Matthew's Christology," CBQ 36(1974):57.

[101]Ibid.

[102]Ibid., 55.

[103]For Johnson, the passage simply expresses the early church's belief that Jesus had sent his followers and that they should be prepared to undergo persecution (p. 55).

[104]For example, Jack Kingsbury's study of Matthew's structure and Christology stresses the title "Son of God" with roots in the Hebrew Bible's traditions of David. Matthew: Structure, Christology, Kingdom (Philadelphia: Fortress, 1975). The title "Son of God" may bear some relation to the righteous man in the Wisdom of Solomon (2:13, 16, 18), but it is not a major focus of the wisdom tradition.

reveals the Father (Mt 11:26-27), then a tension is created: the Torah and Lady Wisdom cannot continue as separate revelations beside Jesus. This tension in the logic of Matthew's Christology could well have provided an impetus toward the explicit attribution of Lady Wisdom's cosmological role to Jesus. However, the Gospel of Matthew itself treats of Wisdom only occasionally and mainly in passages derived from Q; nowhere does Matthew present the cosmological implications of identifying Jesus with Lady Wisdom.

The Pauline Trajectory

1 Corinthians

In 1 Corinthians 1:22-23 Paul proclaims Jesus as the "wisdom of God." The reason for Paul's proclamation may lie in the theology of his opponents in Corinth.[105] The discussion of wisdom in 1 Corinthians 1:10-4:21 indicates that wisdom was a major concern to the Corinthians.[106] The "wisdom of this world" which Paul rejects has been taken by some commentators to be Greek philosophy.[107] However, the importance of wisdom in Hellenistic Judaism suggests that Paul's opponents may have been interpreting Christ within a form of contemporary Jewish theology which is not simply to be

---

[105]The correspondence between Paul and Corinth has been much debated and the sequence of events variously reconstructed. I follow Conzelmann in maintaining the unity of the epistle. Hans Conzelmann, 1 Corinthians: A Commentary on the First Epistle to the Corinthians, Hermeneia, trans. James Leitch, ed. George MacRae (Philadelphia: Fortress, 1975), 4. So also E.-B. Allo, Saint Paul: Première Epître aux Corinthiens (Paris: Librairie Lecoffre, 1934), lxxxv. For differing views, see Walter Schmithals, Gnosticism in Corinth: An Investigation of the Letters to the Corinthians, trans. John Steely (Nashville: Abingdon Press, 1971), 99-100, 156-57; and John Hurd, The Origin of 1 Corinthians (New York: Seabury, 1965).

[106]See Birger Pearson, "Hellenistic-Jewish Wisdom Speculation and Paul," in Aspects of Wisdom in Judaism and Early Christianity, 46. Conzelmann believes that Paul himself introduced the "catchword 'wisdom'" to Corinth (p. 57). However, there is no clear evidence to support this. On the contrary, Paul denies that he came preaching "in persuasive words of wisdom" (2:4). It is more probable that he is taking over the terminology of his opponents and giving it his own interpretation. See Pearson, 56.

[107]E.g. L. Cerfaux, Le Christ dans la Théologie de Saint Paul (Paris: Les Editions du Cerf, 1951), 197.

identified with Greek philosophy.[108] Some scholars, notably Bultmann, Schmithals, and Wilckens, have argued that Paul's opponents
were Gnostics and that "wisdom" is to be understood as the Gnostic
revelation.[109] These scholars all assume that there was already
available in the first century a Gnostic myth of the descent of
the Redeemer who reveals true wisdom. However, the dating of
Gnostic sources casts serious doubt upon this assumption; textual
evidence for Gnosticism is simply lacking for the time of
Paul.[110]

Another alternative for explaining the theology of the Corinthians lies in the writings of Philo and the Jewish wisdom tradition. The similarities between Philo and the Corinthians are
striking.[111] Both place a high value on eloquence as an expression of one's spiritual state; both use the terminology of
teleios, nēpios, pneuma, psyche, and sophos; both view the wise
as "filled," "rich," and as "kings". Paul stresses the separation
between the human sphere and the divine (2:10-12); apparently his
opponents stressed the continuity between the two. Paul emphasizes that Christians have received "the Spirit which is from God"
(2:12); the Corinthians deny that they have received anything
(4:7), apparently maintaining that they had always possessed the

---

[108]See Richard A. Horsley, "Gnosis in Corinth: I Corinthians
8:1-6," NTS 27(1980-81):32-51.

[109]Rudolf Bultmann, Theology of the New Testament, trans.
Kendrick Grobel (2 vols.; New York: Charles Scribner's Sons,
1955), I, 178; see also Ulrich Wilckens, Weisheit und Torheit
(Tübingen: J.C.B. Mohr, 1959); and Schmithals, 36, 124-25, 159.

[110]For a rebuttal of the Gnostic hypothesis, see R. Wilson,
Gnosis and the New Testament (Oxford: Basil Blackwell, 1968), 53-
54; Hengel, 33-35; Robert Grant, Gnosticism and Early Christianity
(New York: Harper & Row, 1966), 68. Gnosticism is a syncretistic
phenomenon; there are certain similarities among Philo, Jewish
wisdom theology, the theology of Paul's opponents, and second-
century Gnosticism. However, Bultmann's discovery of Gnosticism
in Philo or Schmithals's reconstruction of Gnosticism in Corinth
are terminologically vague and confused, since no Gnostic texts
can be dated to the first century. See Rudolf Bultmann, Primitive
Christianity in Its Contemporary Setting, trans. R.H. Fuller
(Cleveland: World Publishing Co., 1970), 163.

[111]See James A. Davis Wisdom and Spirit: An Investigation of
1 Corinthians 1.18-3.20 Against the Background of Jewish Sapiential Traditions in the Greco-Roman Period (Lanham, Md.: University Press of America, 1984); see also Richard Horsley, "Wisdom of
Word and Words of Wisdom in Corinth," CBQ 39(1977):224-39; and
idem, "Gnosis in Corinth," 32-51.

divine spirit.[112] This affirmation of the ontological continuity between God and humankind as part of the natural order is very close to the perspective of Philo.[113]

If the Corinthians were interpreting Christianity from a frame of reference similar to Philo's, it is possible to conjecture how they could have denied the importance of the cross, the uniqueness of Jesus, and the resurrection of the dead. There would be no necessity for a divine Saviour to die for humankind's sins, for all people possess by creation a God-given spirit which unites them to God. Pearson suggests that they may have regarded the cross as the "milk" given to babes which the mature had outgrown.[114] This would explain Paul's fear that the cross of Christ would be emptied of its power if he preached with eloquent wisdom (1:17; 2:1-5). For the Corinthian opponents of Paul, Jesus would be a teacher or guide to the realization of their natural potential. Jesus would be "one manifestation of eternal Wisdom which is the divine in man and in the universe,"[115] but he would not be the unique incarnation of Wisdom, for he manifests what is possible for all humans through the natural order of creation. Thus Jesus may be placed alongside of Paul, Cephas, and Apollos (1:12; 3:4-5).

Finally, the belief in the ontological continuity between God and humankind may have as its temporal correlate the affirmation of present exaltation and fulfillment.[116] Thus the Corinthians could claim to have already achieved transcendence and could deny the resurrection of the dead (15:12). They had already become kings (4:8) and had passed over to a higher level of existence.[117]

Paul reacts from an apocalyptic point of view and emphasizes the discontinuity between God and humankind. If the Corinthians are to be understood against the background of Philo, Paul's response may be understood against the background of the Similitudes

---

[112]See Hamerton-Kelly, 122.

[113]See Erwin Goodenough, By Light, Light: The Mystic Gospel of Hellenistic Judaism (Amsterdam: Philo Press, 1969), 63-64.

[114]Pearson, 52.

[115]Hamerton-Kelly, 123.

[116]Ibid.

[117]Cf. the belief in present exaltation at Qumran (1QH 3:19-23).

of Enoch.[118] In the Similitudes and in 1 Corinthians 2:6 wisdom is a secret plan decided by God before creation. The rulers of this world do not know this wisdom, God's secret plan has been revealed to the righteous who are promised glory and happiness.

For Paul, Christ as "the wisdom of God" is the central, supremely important element in God's secret plan. Paul emphasizes the role of the cross (1:17-18; 2:2), presenting it as the key to the defeat of the rulers of this age (2:8). When Paul refers to Christ as the wisdom of God, he is probably taking a term used by his opponents in a mystical, Philonic sense and reinterpreting it in his own apocalyptic fashion. Paul's main point in 1 Corinthians 1:18-2:16 is that revelation and salvation proceed from a transcendent source that is not accessible to humans through their own powers or through the order of creation. In opposition to the mystical and immanent emphases of the Corinthians, Paul presents an apocalyptic understanding of a secret, hidden wisdom whose center is the cross of Christ.

Paul's presentation of Jesus as the wisdom of God in the first chapters of 1 Corinthians does not appear to draw upon the figure of Lady Wisdom from the sapiential tradition. However, 1 Corinthians 8:6 does give Jesus Christ a mediating role in creation very similar to that of Lady Wisdom in the Wisdom of Solomon and to the Logos and Sophia of Philo.[119] Some scholars judge this verse to be a pre-Pauline formula taken over by Paul.[120] The prepositions eks, eis, and dia suggest a three-fold understanding

---

[118]Hamerton-Kelly, 114-15. The Similitudes are still to be dated to the early first century B.C.E. despite the objections of Milik. See J.T. Milik, "Problèmes de la Litterature Hénochique à la Lumière des Fragments Araméens de Qumrân," HTR 64(1971):375. The main objection to Milik's thoery is the identification of the Son of Man with an historical individual other than Jesus of Nazareth. Moreover, it seems unlikely that a Jewish author would continue to use the term "Son of Man" after Christian use had become widespread.

[119]See Robert Grant, The Early Christian Doctrine of God (Charlottesville, Va.: University Press of Virginia, 1966), 5-6; Richard A. Horsley, "The Background of the Confessional Formula in 1 Kor 8:6," ZNW 69(1978):130-35; Bultmann, Theology, I, 132. A. Feuillet, Le Christ: Sagesse de Dieu d'après les Epîtres Pauliniennes (Paris: Librairie Lecoffre, 1966), 59-85.

[120]E.g. Philip Vielhaur, Geschichte der urchristlichen Literatur (Berlin: Walter de Gruyter, 1975), 32; John G. Gibbs, Creation and Redemption: A Study in Pauline Theology, Novum Testamentum Supplements, 26 (Leiden: E.J. Brill, 1971), 59; Conzelmann, 144-45.

35

of causality which is implicitly philosophical.[121] God the Father is the first and final cause, the origin of creation and the goal of redemption, while Jesus Christ is the instrumental cause of both creation and redemption. Gibbs stresses the repeated distinction between _ta panta_ and _hemeis_ as indicating: "The difference between creation and redemption is that only the latter is moving in accord with the Father's purpose, only the latter is _eis auton_."[122] Hamerton-Kelly and Feuillet both see the distinction as marking a shift "from a cosmological to a soteriological interest."[123] What is striking is the close link between the orders of creation and redemption here established.

Other overtones of the wisdom tradition appear in 1 Corinthians 10:1-4 where Paul interprets the Eucharist in a setting which suggests an implicit identification of Christ and Lady Wisdom. The method of exegesis which Paul uses here is very similar to that of Philo. The emphasis on spiritual food and drink is also a common Philonic motif.[124] Moreover, Philo himself had interpreted the peripatetic rock as referring to Wisdom.[125] The conclusion to which the Philonic parallel points is that Paul is implicitly identifying Christ and Wisdom. While Paul himself does not explicitly interpret the Eucharist as the food and drink of Lady Wisdom, he does attribute to Christ the role that Lady Wisdom had played in Jewish reflection on the Exodus.

---

[121]See Robert Grant, "Causation and 'The Ancient World View,'" _JBL_ 83(1964):32-40; and _idem_, _Early Christian Doctrine_, 6.

[122]Gibbs, 61.

[123]Feuillet, 66; quoted by Hamerton-Kelly, 130, n. 4.

[124]Philo identifies the manna of the Exodus with Wisdom and with the Logos. In interpreting Exodus 16:4, Philo comments: "Of what food can he [Moses] rightly say that it is rained from heaven, save of heavenly Wisdom?" Philo, _De Mutatione Nominum_ 258-60; cited by Peder Borgen, _Bread from Heaven: An Exegetical Study of the Concept of Manna in the Gospel of John and the Writings of Philo_ (Leiden: E.J. Brill, 1965), 14.

[125]"For the flinty rock is the Wisdom of God, which He marked off highest and chiefest from his powers, and from which He satisfies the thirsty souls that love God." Philo, _Legum Allegoriae_ II, 86.

Colossians

The identification of Jesus with Lady Wisdom appears in more developed and explicit form in Colossians 1:15-20.[126] This passage is generally recognized as a hymn taken over from an earlier tradition.[127] The similarities between Lady Wisdom and the hymn's description of Christ are clear.[128] Christ is the "image of the invisible God" (Col 1:15); Lady Wisdom was the image of God's goodness (Wis 7:26); Christ is "the first-born of all creation" (Col 1:15); Wisdom was "acquired" (Masoretic text) or "created" (Septuagint) at the beginning of God's way (Prov 8:22). Christ is the one who "holds all things in unity" (Col 1:17); Lady Wisdom was the mediator of creation (Sir 24:31; Wis 7:21; 8:1, 6) and

---

[126]Authorship of Colossians has been much debated. Kümmel defends the theory of Pauline authorship, while Perrin and Lohse challenge it. See Werner Georg Kümmel, Introduction to the New Testament, trans. Howard Kee (New York: Abingdon Press, 1975), 340-46; Norman Perrin, The New Testament: An Introduction (New York: Harcourt, Brace, Jovanovich, 1974), 121-23; and Eduard Lohse, Colossians and Philemon, trans. William R. Poehlmann and Robert J. Karris, ed. Helmut Koester (Philadelphia: Fortress, 1971), 41. I regard the letter as most probably Deutero-Pauline.

[127]Lohse, 41-42; Vielhauer, 43-44. See also Nikolaus Kehl, Der Christushymnus im Kolosserbrief: Eine motivgeschichtliche Untersuchung zu Kol 1,12-20, Stuttgarter Biblische Monographien (Stuttgart: Verlag Katholisches Bibelwerk, 1967); Franz Zeilinger, Der Erstgeborene der Schöpfung: Untersuchungen zur Formalstruktur und Theologie des Kolosserbriefes (Vienna: Verlag Herder, 1974); Johannes Lähnemann, Der Kolosserbrief: Komposition, Situation, und Argumentation, Studien zum Neuen Testament 3 (Gütersloh, Germany: Gütersloher Verlagshaus Gerd Mohn, 1971); Franz-Josef Steinmetz, Protologische Heils-Zuversicht: Die Strukturen des soteriologischen und christologischen Denkens im Kolosser- und Epheserbrief, Frankfurter Theologische Studien (Frankfurt am Main, Germany: Josef Knecht, 1969).

[128]See W.D. Davies, Paul and Rabbinic Judaism: Some Rabbinic Elements in Pauline Theology (London: S.P.C.K., 1962), 150-152; Jack Sanders, The New Testament Christological Hymns: Their Historical Religious Background (Cambridge: Cambridge University Press, 1971), 75-87; Grant, Early Christian Doctrine, 51; for a differing view, see Jean-Noël Aletti Colossiens 1,15-20: Genre et exégèse du texte: Fonction de la thématique sapientielle (Rome: Biblical Institute Press, 1981), 148-176.

was closely associated with "that which holds all things together" (Wis 1:7).[129]

As Davies notes, the two-fold function of Lady Wisdom in creation and redemption is here being applied to Christ.[130] In identifying Jesus with Lady Wisdom and thus asserting a strong continuity between the orders of creation and redemption, the author of Colossians is developing the implications of 1 Corinthians 8:6 but is modifying the perspective of 1 Corinthians 1-2. If Christ is the power who holds all things together, then the revelatory and salvific event of the death and resurrection of Jesus is in direct continuity with the creative forces of the natural world. Nonetheless, Colossians does retain some of the apocalyptic themes of 1 Corinthians 1-2: the mystery as been "hidden for ages and generations" but now it is manifest to God's saints (Col 1:26).[131] The author decries "philosophy" and "human traditions" (2:8) and proclaims the defeat of the principalities and powers (2:15). Thus the trajectory of Pauline thought involves an intertwining of the apocalyptic and wisdom traditions' perspectives.

The Gospel of John and
the Epistle to the Hebrews

The Background of the
Gospel of John

The Gospel of John presents Jesus as the incarnation of the Logos, a figure closely related to Lady Wisdom. Despite the enormous literature concerning the Fourth Gospel, there is still a large degree of uncertainty regarding the Gospel's composition and authorship.[132] The problems of composition and authorship need

---

[129]See also Philo, Quaestiones in Exodum ii, 117 and De fuga et inventione 101; cited by Sanders, 83, n. 2, 81.

[130]Paul and Rabbinic Judaism, 152.

[131]See Hamerton-Kelly, 177-78.

[132]I will use the traditional designation for the Gospel without thereby adopting any theory of authorship. The traditional attribution of the gospel to John, the son of Zebedee, has been challenged by many critics. E.g. Rudolf Bultmann, The Gospel of John: A Commentary, trans. G.R. Beasley-Murray, eds. R.W.N. Hoare and J.K. Riches (Oxford: Basil Blackwell, 1971), 11, 483-85; and Ernst Käsemann, The Testament of Jesus: A Study of the Gospel of John in Light of Chapter 17, trans. Gerhard Krodel (London: SCM Press, 1968), 1. Schnackenburg offers an "intermediate" solution

not detain us, but the question of the background of the gospel is of some importance for this investigation. Various scholars have proposed a variety of theories on the religious milieu which formed the context for the gospel's language.

Bousset and Bultmann have championed the theory of Gnostic, Mandaean, and Hermetic influence upon John.[133] However, there is no firm textual support for these claims, for no clearly defined form of Gnosticism is known to antedate the New Testament.[134] In particular, Bultmann's theory that John drew upon a Gnostic redeemer myth must be rejected; for, as Martin Hengel argues: "in reality there is no gnostic redeemer myth in the sources which can

suggesting that the evangelist transmitted the teaching of the Apostle John but was also "a theologian in his own right." Rudolf Schnackenburg, The Gospel according to John, vol. 1: Introduction and Commentary on Chapters 1-4, trans. Kevin Smyth (New York: Herder & Herder, 1968), 102. See also Brown, I, lxxxvii-cii. Scholars have proposed numerous theories of sources and redactors without achieving any consensus. Bultmann's theory of three sources and a later "Ecclesiastical Redactor" has been very influential but has not found general acceptance. For differing views, see Eduard Schweizer, Ego Eimi (Göttingen: Vandenhoeck & Ruprecht, 1939) and E. Ruckstuhl, Die literarische Einheit des Johannesevangeliums (Freiburg, Switzerland: Paulus-Verlag, 1951), and James Price, "The Search for the Theology of the Fourth Evangelist," in New Testament Issues, ed. Richard Batey (New York: Harper & Row, 1970). In this investigation I will follow Brown's method of approaching the Gospel in its present order without presupposing a later editor who significantly modified the evangelist's point of view (Brown, I, xxxiv).

[133]See Wilhelm Bousset, Kyrios Christos: A History of the Belief in Christ from the Beginnings of Christianity to Irenaeus, trans. John Steely (Nashville: Abingdon Press, 1970), 245; Bultmann, Theology, I, 164-83; II, 12-14; and John, 23-25.

[134]See G. Van Groningen, First Century Gnosticism: Its Origins and Motifs (Leiden: E.J. Brill, 1967), 99, 104; W.C. Van Unnik, Newly-Discovered Gnostic Writings: A Preliminary Survey of the Nag-Hammadi Find, trans. H.H. Hoskins (London: SCM Press, 1960), 18-20; Brown notes that Bultmann has been accused of circular reasoning: "he presupposes that there was a Gnosticism in the background of John, and then uses John as his main source for reconstructing this Gnosticism" (I, liv). See also James M. Robinson, ed., The Nag Hammadi Library in English, trans. James M. Robinson et al. (San Francisco: Harper & Row, 1977); Kurt Rudolph, Gnosis: The Nature and History of Gnosticism, trans. and ed., Robert McLachlan Wilson (San Francisco: Harper & Row, 1983).

be demonstrated chronologically to be pre-Christian."[135] Similarly, Bultmann's and Reitzenstein's attempts to reconstruct, on the basis of Mandaean texts, the teachings of a pre-Christian Jewish sect founded by John the Baptist are highly conjectural. The late dating of the Mandaean texts (compiled at the earliest about 700 C.E.) and the likelihood of Christian influence upon them cast doubt upon their usefulness as sources for John's Gospel.[136] The theory of Hermetic influence upon John involves writings from the second and third centuries C.E. Again, scholars have attempted to reconstruct early stages of belief in order to explain the background of the Fourth Gospel. C.H. Dodd has presented an interesting list of parallels, but does not posit "any substantial borrowing on one side or the other."[137]

Another possibility is that John was influenced by the thought-world of the community at Qumran. This hypothesis has the advantage of drawing upon texts composed shortly before the Gospel of John. One important similarity between John and Qumran is the modified dualism expressed in the imagery of a struggle between light and darkness.[138] Both John and Qumran see the world as created by God but divided at present into two opposing camps. In the Dead Sea Scrolls the prince of light (also called the spirit

---

[135]Hengel, 33; see also Charles Talbert, "The Myth of a Descending-Ascending Redeemer in Mediterranean Antiquity," NTS 22(1976):418-40.

[136]See Dodd, 138-43.

[137]Ibid., 53; see also 34-35, 50-51. Brown suggests that the similarities may be due to a common heritage, viz. "the combination of Oriental speculation on Wisdom and Greek abstract thought," and he looks to the Wisdom of Solomon as an example of such a combination (I, lix). See also Schnackenburg, who stresses the differences between John and the Hermetic corpus (pp. 136-38).

[138]Brown explains the term "modified dualism": "By dualism we mean the doctrine that the universe is under the dominion of two opposing principles, one good and the other evil. Modified dualism adds the corrective that these principles are not uncreated, but are both dependent on God the creator." Raymond E. Brown, "The Qumran Scrolls and John: A Comparison of Thought and Expression," in A Companion to John: Readings in Johannine Theology (John's Gospel and Epistles, ed. Michael Taylor (New York: Alba House, 1977), 71.

of truth or the holy spirit) is in combat with the angel of darkness (also called the spirit of perversity).[139] In the Gospel of
John Jesus is the light who has come into the world to overcome
the darkness, but the "prince of this world" (14:30) opposes him
and must be overthrown (12:31). There is precedent for this modified dualism in the apocalypse of Isaiah (Is 24-27) and the Book
of Daniel. The wisdom tradition itself knew of an ethical dualism
of the righteous and the wicked,[140] and there is biblical precedent for contrasting light and darkness.[141] However, there is no
Hebrew or Jewish precedent at all for the light versus darkness
terminology to designate opposing forces.[142]

Another theme shared by John and Qumran is the importance of
loving those within the community (1QS I, 10; Jn 13:34; 15:12).
Moreover, John and Qumran both present eschatologies which emphasize the experience of salvation in the present time. Jesus offers eternal life in the present to those who hear his voice (Jn
5:24). H.W. Kuhn has argued convincingly that in many of the

---

[139]See James Charlesworth, "A Critical Comparison of Dualism
in 1 QS 3:13-4:26 and the 'Dualism' Contained in the Gospel of
John," in John and Qumran, ed. James Charlesworth (London:
Geoffrey Chapman, 1972), 78-80.

[140]See John Gammie, "Spatial and Ethical Dualism in Jewish
Wisdom and Apocalyptic Literature," JBL 93(1974):372-77.

[141]E.g., Amos had proclaimed the day of Yahweh as a "day of
darkness and not of light" (6:18). The terminology may have been
used in the traditions of the holy war. See John J. Collins, "The
Mythology of Holy War in Daniel and the Qumran War Scroll: A Point
of Transition in Jewish Apocalyptic," Vetus Testamentum 25(1975):
607; and Peter von der Osten-Sacken, Gott und Belial, Studien zur
Umwelt des Neuen Testaments 6 (Göttingen: Vandenhoeck und Ruprecht, 1969), 81.

[142]Brown, John, I, lxii. Charlesworth notes that Philo frequently uses the symbolism of light derived from the Hebrew Bible,
but in Philo the "light-versus-darkness paradigm is conspicuously
absent" (p. 103, n. 120). Böcher who argues that John's dualism
is closer to Jewish apocalyptic than to Hellenistic or Gnostic
sources. See O. Böcher, Der johanneische Dualismus im Zusammen-
hang des nachbiblischen Judentums (Gütersloh: Mohn, 1965). Kuhn
has argued that the source for Qumran's dualism is Iranian Zoroas-
trianism. K.G. Kuhn, "Die Sektenschrift und die iranische Religion," ZTK 49(1952):312. For a more sceptical evaluation of the
Iranian hypothesis, see Max Wilcox, "Dualism, Gnosticism, and
Other Elements in the Pre-Pauline Tradition," in The Scrolls and
Christianity: Historical and Theological Significance (London:
SPCK, 1969), 85-88.

Hodayoth eschatological salvation is believed to be a present reality.[143]

I give you thanks, O Lord,
For you have redeemed me from the pit
And from Sheol Abaddon you have lifted me up
to the eternal height.[144]

Both John and Qumran do, nonetheless, retain elements of future expectation. The War Scroll describes preparations for a conflict still to come, and John expects the disciples to suffer persecution from the world (15:18-27). The most obvious difference between John and Qumran is that the former focuses on Jesus while the latter focuses on the Law. The Teacher of Righteousness at Qumran is important as the interpreter of the Law, but he is not himself a savior.[145]

The similarities between John and Qumran need not require direct dependence.[146] Schnackenburg and Brown agree that there are some parallels which are closer to each other than anywhere else in late Jewish literature, especially the light-darkness motif.[147] However, there are other important Johannine themes, such as the Logos and the contrast of life and death, which are absent from Qumran.[148] While there are clear points of contact

---

[143]H.W. Kuhn, Enderwartung und gegenwärtiges Heil (Göttingen: Vandenhoeck und Ruprecht, 1966). See also Helmer Ringgren, The Faith of Qumran: Theology of the Dead Sea Scrolls (Philadelphia: Fortress, 1963); and John J. Collins "Apocalyptic Eschatology as the Transcendence of Death," CBQ 36(1974):21-43.

[144]1QH 3, trans. G. Vermes, The Dead Sea Scrolls in English (2nd ed.; Harmondsworth, England: Penguin Books, 1975), 19-20.

[145]See Wilcox, 92-93.

[146]After a detailed comparison of 1QS 3:13-4:26 and the Gospel of John, Charlesworth concludes that John was probably influenced by the Rule, but he admits that "these similarities, however, are not close enough nor numerous enough to prove that John directly copied from 1QS" (p. 103).

[147]Schnackenburg, 131; Brown, John, I, lxiii.

[148]Schnackenburg sees the absence of the latter from Qumran as "perhaps the strongest argument to show that Johannine 'dualism' cannot have been taken over from Qumran" (p. 131).

between the thought-worlds of John and Qumran, it is not certain that John actually knew and used the Qumran literature.[149]

We turn now to the influence of the wisdom tradition upon the Fourth Gospel, beginning with the prologue. Many scholars consider the prologue of John to contain a hymn from the early church which was incorporated and expanded by the evangelist.[150] However, there is no agreement on exactly which verses should be attributed to the early hymn and which to the author of the Gospel.[151] While the exact demarcation of the original hymn is not of decisive importance for our investigation, it is noteworthy that the prologue's origin is probably independent of the Gospel.

The Logos of the prologue recalls God's creation through the word in Genesis 1. The dabar Yahweh of the Hebrew Bible was the dominant form of God's revelation to Israel, in particular to the prophets.[152] In the wisdom tradition the creative and revelatory functions of the dabar Yahweh were assigned to Lady Wisdom (Prov 8, Sir 24:3). There was a close association and functional equivalence between Logos and Sophia in Philo[153] and the Wisdom of Solomon (9:2; 18:14-15).

The Logos of the prologue of John carries much of the significance of these earlier terms. Dodd has documented the close parallels between the prologue and the wisdom tradition and

---

[149]See Matthew Black, "The Dead Sea Scrolls and Christian Origins," in The Scrolls and Christianity, 106.

[150]See Schnackenburg, 72, 224-29; Sanders, 21-25.

[151]For a schema of eight different theories, see Brown, John, I, 22. Most scholars accept vv 1-5, 10-11, 14, and 16 as part of the original hymn; and most agree in assigning vv 6-8, 15, and 17 to the hand of the evangelist. Vv 9, 12, and 18 are disputed.

[152]Dodd notes that "for the Hebrew the word once spoken has a kind of substantive existence of its own" (p. 213). Cf. Is 55:10-11.

[153]Wolfson comments: "Wisdom, then, is only another word for Logos, and it is used in all the senses of the term Logos." Harry Austryn Wolfson, Philo: Foundations of Religious Philosophy in Judaism, Christianity, and Islam (2 vols.; Cambridge, Mass.: Harvard University Press, 1962), I, 258. See also Goodenough, 23; and Burton Lee Mack, Logos und Sophia: Untersuchungen zur Weisheitstheologie im hellenistischen Judentum, Studien zur Umwelt des Neuen Testaments 10 (Göttingen: Vandenhoeck und Ruprecht, 1973), 110.

Philo.[154] These parallels argue strongly that the prologue is using the same patterns of thought as the wisdom teachers and Philo. The Hebrew Bible never says that Lady Wisdom is God, but Lady Wisdom could offer humans the choice of life or death (Prov 8:35), thus appearing to be the way in which humans experience God.[155]

The main body of the Gospel also shows indications of influence from the wisdom tradition.[156] Lady Wisdom is a "pure emanation of the glory of the Almighty" (Wis 7:25); Jesus has glory conferred on him by the Father (8:54), and he manifests this glory to his disciples and shares it with them (17:22). Lady Wisdom is a "reflection of the eternal light" (Wis 7:26); Jesus is the light who comes into the world (3:19; 8:12; 9:5). Lady Wisdom descends from heaven to dwell with humans and offer them life (Prov 8, Sir 24; Bar 3:37-38; Wis 7:27; 9:10); Jesus is the one "who comes from above . . . who comes from heaven . . . whom God has sent" (3:31-34).[157]

The Bread of Life Discourse (6:35-59) presents the Eucharist in a sapiential setting.[158] The discourse begins (6:35) with a

---

[154]Dodd, 274-77. Brown has also argued persuasively that the background of the prologue is to be found in the wisdom tradition (John, I, cxxii-cxxv). Bultmann himself had proposed a similar thesis in 1923. Rudolf Bultmann, "Der religionsgeschichtliche Hintergrund des Prologs zum Johannes-Evangelium," in Eucharister-ion, Festschrift fur Hermann Gunkel, ed. Hans Schmidt (Göttingen: Vandenhoeck und Ruprecht, 1923, 1-26. However, he later modified this theory by positing a pre-Christian Gnostic source which allegedly influenced both the Jewish wisdom tradition and John (John, 22-31). For a summary of various interpretations, see Sanders, 29-57.

[155]Von Rad comments on Prov 8:35: "Only Jahweh can speak in this way"; while insisting on the distinction between Lady Wisdom and Yahweh, von Rad observes that "wisdom is the form in which Jahweh makes himself present and in which he wishes to be sought by man" (Old Testament Theology, I, 444).

[156]Staley has noted the parallels between the structures and themes of the prologue and the main body of the gospel. Jeff Staley, "The Structure of John's Prologue: Its Implications for the Gospel's Narrative Structure," CBQ 48(1986):241-63.

[157]See Talbert, 418-40.

[158]There has been much debate over the unity of Jn 6:35-58. Bultmann takes vv 51-58 as a later addition by an ecclesiastical redactor who intended to change the emphasis of the gospel by adding a sacramental theme to satisfy the Church (John, 209-37).

44

reminiscence of Ben Sira 24:21. Brown points out that even though the Johannine phrasing is the opposite of Ben Sira 24:21, the meaning of both passages is very similar: Jesus's statement in John implies that humans will never seek anything other than his revelation; Lady Wisdom's invitation in Ben Sira means that humans will never have too much wisdom but will always desire more.[159] John 6 presents Jesus in a style very similar to that of the wisdom literature. The repeated use of "I am" (6:35, 48, 51) recalls Lady Wisdom's speaking of herself in Proverbs 8 and Ben Sira 24.[160] The phrase "who comes to me" (Jn 6:35, 37, 44, 45) echoes the wisdom logion in Matthew 11:28 and the invitations of Lady Wisdom in Proverbs 9:5 and Ben Sira 24:19. The promise of life (6:35, 48, 51, 54, 57-58) is also a continuation of the life-giving promises of Lady Wisdom (Prov 8:35-36; Wis 8:13, 17). The threat of death (6:53) finds a parallel in the threats of Lady Wisdom (Prov 1:32; 8:36; Bar 4:1; Wis 1:8, 12, 16; 2:24).

John looks to the manna of the Exodus as a foreshadowing which is surpassed in the Eucharist (6:49, 58). Both Philo and the midrashic tradition had identified manna and Lady Wisdom.[161] By taking the manna as a type of the Eucharist, John is reinforcing the association of Jesus with Lady Wisdom. Both Jesus and Lady Wisdom (Prov 9:5; Sir 15:3; 24:19-21) offer food and drink as symbols of salvation.

Moreover, Lady Wisdom comes to teach humans the truth (Prov 8:7; Wis 7:27). Jesus claims to know the truth and offers it to humans (Jn 8:45, 55); indeed, he claims to be the truth (14:6). Lady Wisdom disciplines her followers so that they might gain

---

Borgen, arguing from parallels to midrashic method, patterns, and terminology, defends the unity of 6:31-59 against Bultmann (Borgen, 25-26, 96-97). Brown accepts Borgen's arguments as persuasive but points out that vv35-50 could be taken as a complete discourse even according to Borgen's midrashic patterns (John, I, 286, 294).

[159]Brown, John, I, 269.

[160]Ibid., I, 538.

[161]Philo, De mutatione hominum 258-60; Legum Allegoriae III, 162, 168; De sacrificiis Caini et Abelis, 86. On Philo's association of Lady Wisdom and the manna, see Paul Beauchamp, "La Cosmologie religieuse de Philon et la lecture de l'Exode par le livre de la Sagesse: le thème de la manne," in Philon d'Alexandrie: Colloque National à Lyon, 11-15 Septembre, 1966, eds. R. Arnaldez et al. (Paris: Editions du Centre National de la Recherche Scientifique, 1967), 210. From the midrashic tradition, see Exodus Rabbah 25:7 and Borgen, 90, 92, 154-55.

understanding and rest and joy (Sir 6:20-30). Jesus "prunes" his disciples so that they may bear more fruit (15:2). Just as Lady Wisdom is rejected by many (Prov 1:24-25; Wis 1:16-2:24), so also Jesus is rejected by this world (6:59-66; 8:42-47; 10:25-26; 15:18-19). Thus there appear strong parallels between the Johannine Jesus and Lady Wisdom. As Brown observes: "the fourth evangelist saw in Jesus the culmination of a tradition that runs through the Wisdom Literature of the Old Testament. . . . In John, Jesus is personified Wisdom."[162]

Wisdom in John

Thus far we have seen that John shows affinities to both the Qumran writings and the wisdom tradition. These two strands of thought share a common ground in the Hebrew Bible's doctrine of creation, but they develop this belief in strikingly different ways.[163] The wisdom tradition generally emphasizes the goodness of the natural world (Wis 1:14) and understands revelation as in basic continuity with humankind's natural powers of reasoning and

---

[162]John, I, cxxii, cxxv. The theory that John was directly dependent upon Philo is less certain. Argyle has argued that John was directly influenced by Philo. A.W. Argyle, "Philo and the Fourth Gospel," Expository Times 63(1951-52):385-86. There are clear parallels in the use of the term Logos, but there are also major differences. John nowhere uses Philo's elaborate allegorical exegesis to harmonize the Hebrew Bible and Platonism, and the evangelist does not share Philo's sophisticated philosophical interests. It appears that Philo and John both drew upon a common stream of thought, but it is not clear that John actually knew Philo. See Schnackenburg, 127-28; Dodd, 54-73.

[163]Von Rad has championed the thesis that the Jewish apocalyptic tradition has its roots in wisdom literature (Theology, II, 306-08; Wisdom, 263-83). Von Rad is correct in noting that both wisdom and apocalyptic literature seek salvation through grasping the laws which govern the world; however, Collins argues that von Rad's theory of direct derivation is weakened by the ambiguity of the term "wisdom" ("Cosmos and Salvation," 121). Muller has shown that the "mantic wisdom" such as we find in Daniel 1-6 is important for the apocalyptic tradition but is not necessarily related to the wisdom of Proverbs and Ben Sira. H.P. Muller, "Mantische Weisheit und Apokalyptik," Congress Volume Uppsal, Supplements to Vetus Testamentum 22 (Leiden: E.J. Brill, 1972), 268-93. See also John J. Collins, "The Court Tales in Daniel and the Development of Apocalyptic," JBL 94(1975):218-34.

as accessible in principle to all peoples.[164] However, the dialectic of disclosure and concealment in the description of Lady Wisdom and the sceptical questioning of Job and Qoheleth raised doubts about any human claims of wisdom. The Qumran writings emphasize the evil of the present age of the world (e.g. 1QH 3) and understand revelation to be an esoteric unveiling of mysteries which are essentially beyond the power of human reasoning (1QS 9-10). The presence of both these influences sets up a tension within the Gospel of John and raises the question of how the wisdom and apocalyptic traditions together influence the portrait of Jesus. In considering the intertwining of these two traditions, I will discuss the Johannine emphasis on the evil of the world, the question of the exclusivity of Jesus as the bearer of salvation, and the significance of the death of Jesus for John.

John presents the world as a place of deceit and unbelief, of misunderstanding and hatred.[165] The Johannine Jesus speaks of the "prince of this world" as an adversary (12:31; 14:30; 16:11; 17:15), and he charges that his opponents are children of the devil (8:44). The sin of the world lies not in its existence but in its hatred of Jesus (15:48) and its rejection of God (3:19; 12:48). The world is not intrinsically evil, as in later Gnostic thought, but it has fallen into alienation from God. God loves the world and sends the Son into the world to save it (3:16-17; 12:47), thus indicating that the world retains the possibility of being saved. Though created in goodness, the world rejects the Logos through which it came to be (1:2-11).

While John's emphasis on the sin of the world is certainly close to Qumran, the wisdom tradition also knew of the fall of the human race (e.g. Wis 2:23-24) and of the power of evil in the world. Lady Wisdom was rejected in Proverbs 1:24-32; in the Wisdom of Solomon the godless make a pact with Death and persecute the righteous man (1:16-2:20; cf. also 14:25-26). Thus the Johannine emphasis on the evil of the world does not contradict the identification of Jesus with Lady Wisdom. It does, however, provide a dialectical challenge to a fundamentally analogical vision of reality and cautions against any direct and simple acceptance of the ordinary experience of humankind.

The pervasiveness of evil in the world raises the question of the availability of revelation and salvation. For the apocalyptic tradition, revelation is an exclusive imparting of secret mysteries to a small group, mysteries which are in radical discontinuity with the present corrupted world. For the wisdom tradition, Lady Wisdom is present throughout all creation, presenting a

---

[164]See Collins, "Cosmos and Salvation," 121-42.

[165]See Käsemann, 34.

choice of life or death to all humans. In presenting Jesus as the incarnation of Lady Wisdom, John would seem to be following the wisdom tradition. However, some passages seem to indicate that the revelation of God in Jesus is not accessible to humans anywhere outside of the encounter with him.

Bultmann has argued the latter interpretation of the Fourth Gospel; he reads John 7:33-34 to mean that "the revelation is not generally available, but presents itself to man only a certain limited time of its own choosing."[166] Other texts in John (6:53; 14:6; 15:5) reinforce the emphasis on the exclusiveness of the revelation in Jesus. Bultmann understands this revelation to be made present in later times by the community who proclaims the kerygma of Jesus Christ, but this preaching itself is historically limited.[167] According to Bultmann's interpretation of John, humans cannot cross from inauthentic to authentic existence without encountering the historically limited proclamation of Christ.

However, there are other passages in the gospel which suggest that revelation is offered to humans outside the person of Jesus and his Church. Much of the question depends on one's interpretation of the prologue. It is here that Bultmann comes close to contradicting his own reading of John 7:33-34, for he admits that "God revealed himself in His creating."[168] In a passage of considerable interest for this investigation, Bultmann comments on 1:4:

> The Prologue, however, affirms that the significance that the Logos has in his incarnate state has been his from the beginning: ēn to phōs tōn anthrōpōn. And to say that he was the light as the Creator, as the zōē, is to say that the possibility of the illumination of existence . . . was inherent in its very origin.[169]

However, Bultmann goes on to argue that the possibility of revelation in creation has been lost and can be regained only through an encounter with Jesus or his Church.[170] Bultmann bases this claim on his interpretation of verse 5; he admits that in the original hymn this verse referred to the pre-temporal Logos and

---

166John, 307.

167Ibid., 308.

168Theology, II, 17.

169John, 44.

170Ibid., 45 and n. 3.

48

that "it had much the same sense as Wis 7:27f."[171] However, Bultmann argues that in the context of the gospel "light" here refers
not to the pre-temporal Logos but to the incarnate Revealer because the "ou katelaben . . . cannot have any other meaning than
that of ouk egnō and the ou parelabon of vv 10f.; i.e. of the
rejection of the incarnate Revealer"; from this Bultmann concludes
that "phainei must then refer to his [the incarnate Revealer's]
revelation."[172]

There are, however, no grounds for presupposing a rigid par-
allelism between vv 4-5 and vv 10-11. Up until v 5 the reader has
no indication whatsoever that any change in the meaning of Logos
or light has taken place. It is perfectly intelligible that the
light in v 5 still refers to the offer of revelation implicit in
creation and that humans reject this offer.[173] Bultmann assumes
that the revelation throughout the cosmos has become a lost possibility. However, the affirmation in the present tense, phainei,
suggests the opposite conclusion: the possibility of the illumination of existence remains open to humans.

The presentation of Jesus as the epiphany of the Logos suggests that the revelation in Jesus is not an esoteric and exclusive imparting of a secret to only a chosen few but rather is a
manifestation of the creative, revelatory, and salvific power
which is at work throughout the entire universe. Dodd and Lightfoot argue persuasively that the key to understanding the prologue
lies precisely in the identification of Jesus with the Logos.
This implies that what is true of the one is true of the other:

The life of Jesus therefore is the history of the Logos, as
incarnate, and this must be, upon the stage of limited time,
the same thing as the history of the Logos in perpetual relations with man and the world.[174]

This implies that 1:4-5 and 1:9-13 may be read in a double
sense as referring to both the historical ministry of Jesus and to
the work of the Logos throughout history. Thus the light which

---

[171]Ibid., 46, n. 1.

[172]Ibid., 46.

[173]Brown notes that John the Baptist is not mentioned until v
6 and that an editor would hardly introduce John the Baptist after
describing the ministry of Jesus (John, I, 26).

[174]Dodd, 285. Lightfoot had offered a similar judgement:
"the Lord's ministry is the relations, written small, of the Logos
with mankind." R.H. Lightfoot, St. John's Gospel: A Commentary
(Oxford: Oxford University Press, 1966), 81.

shines in the darkness (1:4-5) refers primarily to the goodness of the principle of creation; but since Jesus is the incarnation of the Logos, it can also describe his appearance on earth. Similarly, 1:9-13 refer most naturally in the present context to the historical career of Jesus; but since Jesus is the epiphany of the Logos, they may also refer to the perennial work of the Logos, coming to humans with an offer of illumination but often finding rejection.

In light of the identification of Jesus and the Logos, the passages in the main body of the gospel which were cited above can also be read in a double sense. The claim that "no one can come to the Father except through me" (14:6) can refer equally well to the Jesus and to the Logos who is present everywhere. Similarly, we can read the threat of being cut off from the vine (15:5) as applying to being cut off from the Logos. We have seen the relation between Lady Wisdom and the Eucharist; the warning of 6:53 can be taken as a warning about rejecting not only the person of Jesus but also the Logos, especially since Lady Wisdom had also offered bread and wine (Prov 9:5). Moreover, Jesus's threat that he will go away and not be found (7:33-34) need not be restricted to one historical individual, for Lady Wisdom had made exactly the same threat (Prov 1:24-28).

Other passages in John (3:20-21; 10:16; 11:52) reinforce the impression that salvation is possible without an historical encounter with Jesus. Bultmann tries to evade the implication of 3:20-21 that a person can live by the truth before encountering Jesus.[175] However, v 21 implies that a person can indeed live by the truth before coming into the light of Jesus. As Schnackenburg expresses the relation, "those whose actions are in accordance with God will feel themselves drawn to the 'light,' so that their works may be clearly seen."[176]

This suggests that the role of Jesus is to reveal and make manifest the realities of human existence. This need not reduce the Gospel to what Bultmann fears will be "a mythologically embellished moralism"; nor need it reduce the mission of Jesus merely to revealing "what has been decided beforehand," as Bultmann warns.[177] Jesus as the epiphany of the Logos can transform human lives precisely by being the effective presence of the creative, revelatory, and salvific power of the cosmos. If the Logos who is incarnate in Jesus is also present throughout all of history offering life and light to humans, then we do not have a "moralism"

175John, 159.

176Schnackenburg, 408.

177John, 159, 158.

based simply on human efforts. We have seen that the earlier sages viewed wisdom and understanding as gifts coming to humans from Lady Wisdom; in a similar way the Logos of John can offer the gift to humans to "live by the truth" and do what they do in God (3:21). On the basis of a Logos Christology, both Rahner and Pittenger will challenge Bultmann's restriction of the area of grace to the historical proclamation of the Gospel; both will insist that the availability of salvation outside of an encounter with Jesus or the Christian Church in no way implies a Pelagian reliance on the sufficiency of human efforts alone.

The evangelist also tells us that there are children of God scattered throughout the world (11:52). Dodd suggests that this verse probably refers not only to the Jews of the Dispersion but also to those who have not known Jesus but have been given a new birth by the Logos; according to Dodd, these people are probably also the "other sheep not of this fold" (10:16).[178] However, Brown objects to Dodd's reading, suggesting that 11:52 refers to those Gentiles who are destined to become God's children and accept Jesus. Brown does not believe that John could have conceived of someone becoming a child of God apart from receiving the Spirit of Jesus.[179] In favor of Dodd's reading is the implication of John 11:52 that the children of God are already scattered throughout the world. Thus it appears possible that John could allow the possibility of revelation and salvation through the Logos outside of the historically and geographically limited proclamation of Jesus and the Christian Church. This perspective is in harmony with the earlier sages' view of Lady Wisdom calling people of all nations. Given the conflicting tendencies within the Gospel itself, Dodd's reading can hardly be accepted as definitive; however, it is a persuasive interpretation which finds support in the sapiential background of the prologue.

Most of Christian theology has attributed great importance to the death of Jesus as an atoning sacrifice.[180] If revelation and salvation are offered to all through the Logos, one may question what significance the death of Jesus has for John. John's description of the Passion differs considerably from that of the Synoptic Gospels. Where the Synoptics had presented Jesus as

---

[178]Dodd, 282.

[179]John, I, 29, 440.

[180]See Martin Hengel, The Atonement: The Origins of the Doctrine in the New Testament, trans. John Bowden (Philadelphia: Fortress, 1981); for an historical study of different views on the question, see Gustaf Aulen Christus Victor: An Historical Study of the Three Main Types of the Idea of Atonement, trans. A.G. Hebert (New York: Macmillan Co., 1961).

wishing to avoid his death (Mt 26:39; Mk 14:36; Lk 22:42) and as despairing on the cross (Mt 27:46; Mk 15:34), the Johannine Jesus appears calmly in control of the entire drama. There is no agony in the garden (cf. Jn 18:1-11), and Jesus simply declares, "It is accomplished," as he dies (Jn 19:30). In John the death of Jesus paradoxically coincides with his elevation and glorification because it is the moment when he returns to the Father (7:39; 12:16, 23; 13:31-32; 17:15).[181] In an analogous way the Wisdom of Solomon (3:1-5) had presented the death of the just not as a God-forsaken disaster but as a peaceful return to the hands of God where they find blessings and peace.

When Jesus is lifted up, he draws all people to himself (12:31). For John, the death is the fulfillment of Jesus's obedience to the Father, an act which enables him to return to the glory he had before the world began (17:5).[182] Bultmann notes that "John has subsumed the death of Jesus under the idea of Revelation;" Jesus's death by itself "has no pre-eminent importance for salvation," but marks the return of the Son to the Father.[183] John does not present Jesus's death as a vicarious atonement for sin but rather as the completion of his life-work. Dodd notes that the relation between sign and reality is central to John's understanding of the cross. Earlier in the Gospel Jesus has been offering the "signs" of life and light; but the reality of the gift of life looks forward to its manifestation in the death of Jesus:

> But in order that we may pass beyond signs to the reality, the death and resurrection must be actual. . . . The Passion looms in immediate imminence; the event is on the verge of happening, which will manifest in action the reality behind all the signs.[184]

The paradoxical manifestation of the glory of God through the death of Jesus reveals and makes effective the offer of life.

We have seen that John develops the interpretation of Jesus as the incarnation of Lady Wisdom. The prologue presents the Logos in the role of Lady Wisdom, and the main body of the gospel portrays Jesus as performing the functions of Lady Wisdom. The

---

[181]See Käsemann, 19.

[182]See Dodd, 395.

[183]Theology, II, 53.

[184]Dodd, 372.

Johannine themes of the evil of the world and the battle of light and darkness are close to the Qumran scrolls and suggest an interpenetration of wisdom and apocalyptic influences within the gospel. As in the case of the Pauline trajectory, the presentation of Jesus in the Gospel of John draws upon themes from both wisdom and apocalyptic traditions. The apocalyptic stress on the discontinuity between our ordinary experience of this world and the experience of revelation and salvation serves as a counterbalance to the wisdom tradition and a warning against making too smooth a transition from the common wisdom of the human race to the meaning of revelation and salvation.

The Epistle to the Hebrews

The prologue to the Epistle to the Hebrews also portrays Jesus in language that had been characteristic of Lady Wisdom.[185] The Son is the mediator of creation, the one through whom God created the universe (1:2). Hamerton-Kelly compares the opening verses to the role of Lady Wisdom passing into holy souls and making them friends of God and prophets (Wis 7:27).[186] The term apaugasma (radiance, Heb 1:3) had previously been used of Lady Wisdom (Wis 7:25). Lady Wisdom was the image of God's goodness (Wis 7:26); Christ is the "perfect copy" of God's nature (Heb 1:3). Lady Wisdom had been presented as the power reaching throughout creation, "ordering all things for good" (Wis 8:1); Christ sustains all things by his "word of power" (Heb 1:3). Thus the description of Christ in the prologue to the epistle is very closely related to the presentation of Lady Wisdom in the Wisdom of Solomon.[187]

---

[185]Many scholars believe that an older source has been used as the basis for 1:3. See Vielhauer, 44-45; Graham Hughes, Hebrews and Hermeneutics: The Epistle to the Hebrews as a New Testament Example of Biblical Interpretation (Cambridge: Cambridge University Press, 1979), 6, 146, n. 11.

[186]Hamerton-Kelly, 243.

[187]On the epistle's relation to Philo, see R. Williamson, Philo and the Epistle to the Hebrews (Leiden: E.J. Brill, 1970); and Jean Héring, The Epistle to the Hebrews, trans. A.W. Heathcote and P.J. Allcock (London: Epworth Press, 1970), 4.

Hermeneutics and Language

This survey of the biblical wisdom tradition has suggested that there are two complementary processes intertwining in the origins of Wisdom Christology. In the first process, the sages of Israel and Jesus as presented in the Gospels offer proverbs and wisdom sayings which articulate a religious dimension of human experience.[188] This process employs a variety of literary forms, ranging from proverbs and impossible questions to poems of Lady Wisdom, to the wisdom discourse of the Sermon on the Mount. As Thompson has argued, proverbs perform a "philosophical function" by reaching for a sense of the whole, and yet the wisdom tradition turns back critically upon any claim to have understood the whole.[189] Wisdom appears as both hidden and revealed, as accessible to humans through reflection on the patterns of experience and yet as always beyond our grasp. Lady Wisdom offers herself freely to all who will listen (Prov 8), but to think oneself wise is worse than being a fool (Prov 26:12).

The second process relates the universal presence of Lady Wisdom to specific historical events of revelation.[190] Ben Sira and the Wisdom of Solomon interpret the religious heritage of Israel as the work of Lady Wisdom, who is present throughout all human experience. The Wisdom Christology of the New Testament continues the correlation between Lady Wisdom and historical events. By interpreting Jesus as the Wisdom of God, as the Logos through whom all things were made, early Christians were claiming that the religious dimension implicit in all human experience had been revealed, illumined, and expressed in the person of Jesus. In Jesus the early church claimed to have found the key to the mystery of creation, to the structure of the world, and to humankind's relationship to the transcendent creator.

The presence of various and sometimes conflicting claims within the wisdom trajectory forces the seeker of wisdom to a discernment of the proper time for applying or questioning any given perspective. A proverb or larger expression of wisdom arises from an insight into a particular situation and promises guidance and illumination for future thought and action, but the appropriate application of any proverb requires a discernment of the proper time. The sages made active demands upon the acumen of their listeners and thus approach, in their own way, the hermeneutical

---

[188]See Collins, "Biblical Precedent," 42-52.

[189]Thompson, 27-31.

[190]See Collins, "Biblical Precedent," 52-55.

issues of interpretation and application. To understand a proverb is to interpret it and apply it appropriately in ever-changing contexts. For the sages wisdom was to be found not in a static doctrine or theory but rather in proper performance. The poetic descriptions of Lady Wisdom revealing or hiding herself suggest that truth is to be understood as an event of manifestation.

The purpose of this section is to reflect upon the implications of the wisdom tradition for hermeneutics and language. I will turn to the work of Hans-Georg Gadamer and Paul Ricoeur in order to clarify the significance of the biblical wisdom tradition for later interpreters. I will begin by reflecting upon the wisdom tradition in light of the concepts of Bildung (formation) and Spiel (play) in the thought of Gadamer. Then I will explore Ricoeur's reflections on the limit-character of religious language and their applicability to wisdom literature.

Hans-Georg Gadamer

One of the crucial concepts in the work of Gadamer is Bildung (formation).[191] The word has its origins in medieval mysticism, where the human person is called to form and cultivate the image of God in the soul. In the eighteenth century the term came to mean "the properly human way of developing one's natural talents and capacities."[192] For Herder, the term involved "reaching up to humanity"; properly understood, Bildung is not a means to an end but always an end in itself, transcending the "mere cultivation of talents" and denoting the goal of human life.[193] For Hegel, Bildung raises the individual to the universal; the person who is gebildet (formed, cultivated) is detached from immediate purposes and desires and can sacrifice particularity for the sake of the universal. The universal viewpoint is not a fixed, technical concept but rather an openness to other points of view: "To distance oneself from oneself and from one's private purposes means to look at these in the way that others see them."[194] Work is a

---

[191]See Hans-Georg Gadamer, Truth and Method, (New York: Crossroad, 1982), 10-19. As Weinsheimer has noted, Gadamer structures the first third of Truth and Method around Bildung and its linguistic cognates. Joel C. Weinsheimer, Gadamer's Hermeneutics: A Reading of Truth and Method (New Haven, Ct.: Yale University Press, 1985), 68.

[192]Gadamer, 11.

[193]Ibid., 11-12.

[194]Ibid., 17.

form of _Bildung_, for "work is restrained desire . . . by forming the thing it forms itself."[195] By requiring us to sacrifice our particularity, _Bildung_ challenges us to limit ourselves, to rise above our immediate experience by allowing our work and our encounter with objects to shape and form us. Thus _Bildung_ is neither the imparting of a fixed body of knowledge nor the learning of a specific method but rather the forming of a "trained receptivity."[196] The entire project of _Truth and Method_ can be understood as a reflection on the meaning of _Bildung_. The encounter with the classics and the struggle to understand, interpret, and apply them is itself the formation of the interpreter.

In this process Gadamer stresses the priority of the question over the answer and the productive character of negative experience. Following the model of the Platonic dialogues, Gadamer suggests that "the structure of the question is implicit in all experience. We cannot have experiences without asking questions."[197] To ask a question requires the recognition that we do not know, the ability to see what is questionable, and the openness to the possibility of new horizons.[198]

Closely linked to the priority of the question is the productivity of negative experience. The development of our understanding is enriched primarily through experience's power to refute our previous understandings: "every experience worthy of the name runs counter to our expectations."[199] Because experience repeatedly refutes our expectations,

> the experienced person proves to be . . . someone who is radically undogmatic. . . . The dialectic of experience has its own fulfilment not in definitive knowledge, but in that openness to experience that is encouraged by experience itself.[200]

Thus experience involves a destruction of our illusions and makes us aware of our own finitude: "The experienced man knows the

---

195[Ibid.](), 13.

196[Ibid.](), 17.

197[Ibid.](), 325.

198[Ibid.](), 325-30.

199[Ibid.](), 319.

200[Ibid.]()

limitedness of all prediction and the uncertainty of all plans."[201]

The goal of the wisdom tradition of ancient Israel can be understood as a process of _Bildung_, formation through being shaped by a tradition. The seeker of wisdom is advised: "Make the wise your companions and you grow wise yourself" (Prov 13:20). The ancient sages shared Gadamer's ideal of the _gebildet_ person who does not yield to immediate desires or emotions but seeks a more universal viewpoint before speaking or acting:

A man who can control his tongue has knowledge, a man of discernment keeps his temper cool (Prov 17:27).

Make friends with no man who gives way to anger, make no hasty-tempered man a companion of yours (Prov 22:24).

You see some man too ready of speech? More hope for a fool than for him (Prov 29:20).

Again and again the sages advise their hearers to restrain their desires (e.g. Prov 5, 7; Sir 6:2-4) and to submit to discipline (Prov 4:13; 12:1; 15:32; Wis 6:17). The apprenticeship to Lady Wisdom involves a strict discipline which can be compared to a yoke (Sir 6:23-31); the service of the Lord is an "ordeal" which requires testing and humiliation (Sir 2:1-5).

For the sages the learning of wisdom is not a fixed doctrine but a process and performance perfected through example and experience:

Do not underrate the talk of old men, after all, they themselves learned it from their fathers; from them you will learn how to think, and the art of the timely answer (Sir 8:9).

The sages also recognized the productive value of negative experience. The sense of the limits of all wisdom undercuts any claim of human self-sufficiency and cautions us not to consider ourselves wise (Prov 3:7) and thus to remain open to new points of view. As von Rad put it, the sages believed that "experience . . . teaches that you can never be certain. You must always remain open for a completely new experience."[202] The inclusion of Job and Qoheleth within the tradition implies a sense of the value of negative experience and of the critical questions that arise

---

[201]_Ibid._, 320.

[202]_Wisdom_, 106.

from it. Nonetheless, the wisdom tradition did not collapse under the impact of Job and Qoheleth but continued in the work of Ben Sira and the Wisdom of Solomon. As von Rad observes, there is in the wisdom tradition "an oscillation between grasp of meaning and loss of meaning," a dialectic between the earnest search to learn the patterns of experience and the recognition that no conclusions are certain in all instances.[203]

Gadamer's point of entry into the process of _Bildung_ is through the concept of _Spiel_ (play) as "the clue to ontological explanation."[204] Gadamer considers first play in the work of art (Section I), then the play of question and answer in conversation with history (Section II), and finally the play of language with us (Section III). Gadamer asserts that our experience of art involves a truth-claim: "Art is knowledge and the experience of the work of art is a sharing of this knowledge."[205] The experience of the work of art shapes and transforms us; the truth of art is not something we possess; it is not an object which belongs to a subject but rather an event to which the subject belongs, an event which the subject does not control. Gadamer's description of the experience of truth in art bears an analogy to the experience of Lady Wisdom, who is playfully present in human experience and in the cosmos but who is never controlled and dominated by human effort.

Gadamer wants to free the concept of play from the categories of subjectivity. What happens to us in play and in the experience of art is that we lose ourselves. For the game to be played, it must be taken seriously: "One who doesn't take the game seriously is a spoilsport."[206] This experience resists being broken apart into the categories of subject and object, for "the mode of being of the game does not permit the player to behave toward the game as to an object."[207] The players play the game only when they do not stand over against an object but allow themselves to be caught up in the the to-and-fro movement of the game.

Gadamer sees play as the mode of being of the work of art. The work of art only exists when it is experienced; and yet the experience of art is not adequately understood as the experience of an object by an autonomous, evaluating subject. To experience

---

[203]Ibid.

[204]Gadamer, 91.

[205]Ibid., 87.

[206]Ibid., 92.

[207]Ibid.

the work of art, the subject must let go and surrender to the aesthetic experience. The work of art is what is played by the players it plays.

In the work of art play undergoes a transformation into structure (Verwandlung ins Gebilde). This transformation detaches the play from any particular subject or moment of time and allows it to become repeatable and permanent. In the example of a play (Schauspiel), the play is not to be found in the subjective consciousness of either the playwright or the actors or the audience. The detachability of the play from any particular subject (whether playwright, performer, or spectator) is analogous to the process of Bildung. When people undergo Bildung, they become gebildet, detached from immediate desires and purposes; when play becomes Gebilde (structure), it is detached from the conditions of its origin and can be repeated in different contexts and different times.

The transformation into structure is itself a transformation into the truth. The work of art confronts us with a representation of reality which makes a truth-claim upon us, and our response is the joy of recognition (which may not always be pleasurable). In recognition "what is familiar is recognized again."[208] What is recognized is known as something; it is re-familiarized and thereby becomes more truly what it is.

The repeatability of the work of art endows with it a temporality which Gadamer terms that of the Fest (festival). A festival exists only in being celebrated. Its perduring through time is a discontinuous series of different celebrations. The festival is repeated over and over again, but always in a different time. "It has its being only in becoming and in return."[209]

The temporality of the Fest is Gadamer's model for understanding the temporality of the aesthetic. A work of art exists only in its representations. Its very being is always to be different. The first performance or first viewing is the first of countless repetitions to be experienced by different audiences. The work of art itself is wholly contemporary with every age in which it is experienced. Yet this contemporaneity is itself a "task for consciousness," requiring the work of interpretation.[210] The reward of this work of interpretation is the re-cognition of

---

[208]Ibid., 102.

[209]Ibid., 110.

[210]Ibid., 113.

our own world; even in the case of works of art from ages past, they enable us to understand our own world.[211]

Von Rad has noted in passing that Gadamer's understanding of play is analogous to the self-understanding of the sages of Israel, but he has not developed this suggestion.[212] We have seen that there is a playful character to many of the sayings of the wise; number-sayings (e.g. Prov 30:15-31) juxtapose different items, teasing the mind of the hearer into perceiving similarities in difference. Williams has noted that the sayings of the sages include "word play," "image play," and "proverb-play."[213] There is for the sages a playfulness at the heart of creation (Prov 8:30-31) and a playfulness in Lady Wisdom's relation to humans. The search for wisdom can be compared to searching for buried treasure (Prov 2:4; Job 28), a type of game of hide-and-seek. The sages compared the experience of Lady Wisdom to lovers' games of hiding and seeking. At times she must be courted and wooed (Sir 14:20-27); at times she is hidden altogether (Job 28); at times she comes freely, crying out at the city gates (Prov 8); at times she threatens angrily that she will go away and leave us to our own destruction (Prov 1:20-32).

As in the case of lovers' games, this game is deadly serious, for in it our own lives are at stake (Prov 8:35-36). As in the case of Gadamer's play, the play of Lady Wisdom with humans transforms the players. Through the experience of her, humans recognize the world in which they live and come to understand and accept the ordering power of creation, which has been at work throughout human life from the very beginning. Gadamer begins Truth and Method by quoting verses from Rainer Maria Rilke which speak of "being the catcher of a ball thrown by an eternal partner"; in this experience, Rilke continues, "why catching then becomes a power--not yours, a world's."[214] It is interesting to compare Rilke's image of the playful to-and-fro movement between humans and God with the image of Lady Wisdom playing in creation and confronting humans with a challenge.

In Gadamer's terms, a proverb is an insight which undergoes a Verwandlung ins Gebilde, a transformation into structure. A proverb arises from a certain insight into a situation or series of situations. However, by being presented as a proverb, the insight

---

[211]Ibid.

[212]Wisdom, 24, 50.

[213]James G. Williams, "The Power of Form: A Study of Biblical Proverbs," Semeia 17(1980):42-43.

[214]Gadamer, v.

is detached from its original setting and can be interpreted and applied again and again in widely differing settings.[215] The temporality of a proverb, like that of Gadamer's _Fest_, is to be the same precisely by being different each time it is applied. Its continuing meaning is found in its interpretation and application in ever-changing circumstances. A proverb presents us with a truth-claim, but the examples of Job and Qoheleth show us the necessity of critically confronting this truth-claim with our own experience in any given situation.

The playfulness of Lady Wisdom and the dialectic of disclosure and concealment in the descriptions of her suggest that the experience of her is to be understood not as the static possession of an object by a subject but as an event that happens to us and transforms us.

Gadamer argues that when we interpret a work of art we ourselves are being interpreted. In interpreting a proverb or wisdom-poem, it is the meaning of our own lives that is at stake, and thus we ourselves are being interpreted by the text. Gadamer also insists that there is no method which guarantees the success of an interpretation. Tact and taste are necessary to judge whether any particular interpretation is true or whether any truth-claim is justified.[216] In a similar fashion, there is no method for guaranteeing the success of interpreting a proverb. Students of wisdom must grasp the particular circumstances of their time for themselves. The proverbs they have learned can function like Gadamer's classics, forming human judgement and broadening horizons, but no proverb can guarantee its own application in any given situation.

Gadamer's discusssion of _Bildung_ and _Spiel_ leads eventually to the question of language. Language, for Gadamer, is the inescapable medium of hermeneutical experience. "All understanding is interpretation, and all interpretation takes place in the medium of language."[217] The mode of being of tradition is language, and

---

[215]_Ibid._, 99-108.

[216]Gadamer describes tact as "a particular sensitivity and sensitiveness to situations, and how to behave in them, for which we cannot find any knowledge from general principles. Hence an essential part of tact is inexplicitness and inexpressibility" (p. 16). He also comments that the "concept of taste undoubtedly includes a mode of knowing. It is through good taste that we are capable of standing back from ourselves and our private preferences. . . . The decisiveness of the judgment of taste includes its claim to validity" (pp. 34-35).

[217]_Ibid._, 350.

our only path to understanding is through interpretation and application.[218] In this process we are not sovereign over language; Gadamer cautions, "it is literally more correct to say that language speaks us, rather than we speak it."[219] Gadamer concludes, "Language games are where we, as learners--and when do we cease to be that?--rise to the understanding of the world."[220] The sages of Israel were also very aware of the importance of language. Through language-games, proverbs, obscure sayings, and riddles (Prov 1:6), the sages expressed, as von Rad put it, their "right to play with the truth which was inherent in the world."[221]

Paul Ricoeur

Paul Ricoeur has critically appropriated and developed Gadamer's work on hermeneutics.[222] Ricoeur understands religious language as referring to limit-experiences of human existence.[223] Religious language, like poetic language, has the power to redescribe human experience through what Ricoeur, following Ian Ramsey, calls a "disclosure model" of language. A disclosure model, for Ricoeur, employs the sequence "orient-disorient-reorient, without ever perhaps allowing us to make a 'whole' a system of our experience."[224] Such a model views truth not as adequation, as in some forms of linguistic analysis, but as manifestation.[225] The religious text opens up visions of possible ways of being in the world. Ricoeur calls this vision of new possibilities "the world

---

[218]Ibid., 420, 432-33.

[219]Ibid., 421.

[220]Ibid., 446.

[221]Wisdom, 50.

[222]On the relation between Gadamer and Ricoeur, see Josef Bleicher, Contemporary Hermeneutics: Hermeneutics as Method, Philosophy, and Critique (London: Routledge & Kegan Paul, 1980), 217-28; and John W. Van Den Hengel, The Home of Meaning: The Hermeneutics of the Subject of Paul Ricoeur (Lanham, Md.: University Press of America, 1982), 103-07.

[223]Paul Ricoeur, "Biblical Hermeneutics," Semeia 4(1975): 122.

[224]Ibid., 126.

[225]Paul Ricoeur, "Philosophy and Religious Language," JR 54 (1974):72.

of the text."[226] This world is a metamorphosis of the world of everyday reality, a redescription of the possibilities of human existence.

More recently, Ricoeur has developed and modified this perspective in terms of a three-fold mimesis. $Mimesis_1$ describes the "preunderstanding of the world of action, its meaningful structures, its symbolic resources, and its temporal character."[227] This preunderstanding is the basis upon which emplotments can be constructed. $Mimesis_2$ configures the world of $mimesis_1$, transforming it into a story. "With $mimesis_2$ opens up the kingdom of the as if."[228] $Mimesis_2$ leads to a "postunderstanding of the order of action and its temporal features."[229] In the postunderstanding of $mimesis_3$ experience is refigured: "narrative has its full meaning when it is restored to the time of action and of suffering in $mimesis_3$."[230]

The vision of new possibilities for human experience unfolds in language. Language is the central category in understanding religion for Ricoeur, for he insists that any religious experience, no matter what its nature, can only be expressed in language.[231] Moreover, in an age of suspicion, there is no direct way to explain the human subject. Our immediate self-understanding is suspect, and we can only find a more appropriate self-understanding through the interpretation of the language we use.[232]

---

[226]Ibid., 80.

[227]Paul Ricoeur, Time and Narrative, 3 vols., vols. 1-2, trans. Kathleen McLaughlin and David Pellauer; vol. 3, trans. Kathleen Blamey and David Pellauer (Chicago: University of Chicago Press, 1984-88), I, 54.

[228]Ibid., 64.

[229]Ibid., 65.

[230]Ibid., 70.

[231]"Philosophy and Religious Language," 71.

[232]Paul Ricoeur, The Conflict of Interpretations: Essays in Hermeneutics, trans. Kathleen McLaughlin et al., ed. Don Ihde (Evanston, Il.: Northwestern University Press, 1974), 101-03; see also idem, Freud and Philosophy: An Essay on Interpretation, trans. Denis Savage (New Haven, Ct.: Yale University Press, 1970), 494-551.

Ricoeur is especially interested in the power of metaphor and narrative to redescribe reality. He argues that it is the conflict between the two opposed interpretations of a statement that sustains the meaning of a metaphor.[233] Taken literally, the metaphorical utterance is absurd. The literal interpretation self-destructs, thus imposing a metaphorical twist which extends the meaning of the statement. Metaphor suggests "the appearance of kinship where ordinary vision does not perceive any relationship."[234] Thus there is a "creation of meaning," "a new signification which occurs through the tension within the copula in the metaphor."[235] In a metaphor

> 'is' signifies both is and is not. The literal 'is' is overturned by the absurdity and surmounted by a metaphorical 'is' equivalent to 'is like . . .' Thus poetic language does not tell us how things literally are, but what they are like.[236]

Ricoeur challenges the traditional manner of distinguishing literal and metaphorical language, suggesting that there is an initial metaphorical impulse which creates the order of thought and undermines the oppositions between proper and figurative speech.[237] The search for an original, literal, non-metaphorical language is in vain.[238] Ricoeur concludes with a paradox: "There is no discourse on metaphor that is not stated within a metaphorically engendered conceptual network. . . . Metaphor is metaphorically stated."[239]

We have seen that many of the sayings of the wise take the form of metaphor. Much of proverbial wisdom is expressed through a clash of images which open up new ways of seeing the world. Through the juxtaposition of clashing images the hearer is prodded

---

[233]Paul Ricoeur, *Interpretation Theory: Discourse and the Surplus of Meaning* (Fort Worth, Texas: Texas Christian University Press, 1976), 50-53.

[234]*Ibid.*, 51.

[235]*Ibid.*, 52.

[236]*Ibid.*, 68; cf. also Paul Ricoeur, *The Rule of Metaphor: Multi-disciplinary Studies of the Creation of Meaning in Language*, trans. Robert Czerny et al. (Toronto: University of Toronto Press, 1981), 7.

[237]*Rule*, 22-23.

[238]*Ibid.*, 138.

[239]*Ibid.*, 286-87.

to see reality in a different way, to grasp similarities in difference that are not readily apparent. Through this process the hearer is to become better prepared to understand future experience and to act and speak in the world.

Metaphor, for Ricoeur, is closely related to narrative. Where metaphor creates meaning through impertinent attribution, narrative invents a feigned plot which creates a new configuration, bringing together goals, causes, and chance into a temporal unity: "It is this synthesis of the heterogeneous that brings narrative close to metaphor. In both cases, the new thing--the as yet unsaid, the unwritten--springs up in language."[240] Ultimately, both metaphor and narrative are included in "one vast poetic sphere."[241]

If wisdom-sayings often present themselves in the form of metaphors, the poems of Lady Wisdom appear as incipient narratives, and the Wisdom Christology of the New Testament finds the meaning of Wisdom in the plot of the life, death, and resurrection of Jesus. Through the narrative of Jesus, the Gospels reconfigure the world of our experience.

Ricoeur's emphasis on the limit-character of religious discourse also finds application to the wisdom tradition. Ricoeur himself observes that the themes of wisdom discourse

> are those limit-situations spoken of by Karl Jaspers, those situations--including solitude, the fault, suffering, and death--where the misery and the grandeur of human beings confront each other.[242]

For both Gadamer and Ricoeur, the significance of a tradition lies in its ability to be interpreted and applied again and again in widely differing contexts. The meaning of the proverbs, the wisdom-poems, and the Wisdom Christology of the New Testament lies in the possibilities for envisioning the world that they open up. The history of effects of the association of Jesus with Lady Wisdom has been of tremendous influence on later Christological reflection. W.L. Knox has stressed the theological and metaphysical implications of Wisdom Christology:

---

[240]*Time and Narrative*, I, ix.

[241]*Ibid.*, I, xi.

[242]Paul Ricoeur, *Essays on Biblical Interpretation*, trans. Peter McCormick et al., ed. Lewis S. Mudge (Philadelphia: Fortress, 1980), 86.

The divine Wisdom, the pattern and agent of creation and the divine mind permeating the cosmos, was identified with Jesus not as a matter of midrashic exposition which could be used and thrown aside, but as an eternal truth in the realm of metaphysics; for only so could the supremacy of Jesus be asserted as against such potent beings as the rulers of the stars in their course. It is probable that Paul was entirely unaware that his letter [Colossians] would produce this effect: whether he realized it or not, he had committed the Church to the theology of Nicaea.[243]

The hermeneutical work of Gadamer and Ricoeur suggests that the importance of a text or series of texts lies in their ability to disclose new possibilities of human existence. As Gadamer insists, to understand is always to understand differently. The interpretation of Jesus as the incarnation of Wisdom has played a central role in the history of Christological reflection, especially in the integration of Christology and ever-changing worldviews.

Karl Rahner and Norman Pittenger have both developed interpretations of Christ as the Logos which seek to integrate Christology into a contemporary world-view. Both Rahner and Pittenger are heavily influenced by the tradition of Logos Christology; behind the prologue of John there is the wisdom tradition of Israel. However, neither Rahner nor Pittenger has emphasized the figure of Lady Wisdom or the heritage of the sages of Israel.

It is the relation between the perspectives of the wisdom tradition and the Christologies of Rahner and Pittenger that will hold our attention in the next two chapters. While there are clearly different levels of discourse present in the language of the sages and the philosophical theologies of Rahner and Pittenger, there is within the wisdom tradition itself an invitation for philosophical reflection and an openness to appropriating new world-views.

---

[243]W.L. Knox, St. Paul and the Church of the Gentiles (Cambridge: Cambridge University Press, 1969), 178; quoted by Hamerton-Kelly, 176.

CHAPTER II

THE CHRISTOLOGY OF KARL RAHNER

The New Testament's interpretation of Jesus Christ as the incarnation of Lady Wisdom claims a close relation between the Christ-event and the activity of God throughout all human experience and the entire cosmos. To retrieve and apply this perspective in contemporary theology requires theologians to relate their interpretation of Jesus Christ to current understandings of human experience and the evolutionary process of the world. Both Rahner and Pittenger have developed contemporary Logos Christologies which seek a coherent understanding of the revelation of God in Jesus Christ and the universal presence of God in all human experience and in the cosmos.

While neither Rahner nor Pittenger refer to the wisdom tradition in a major way, both theologians place the central wisdom texts of the New Testament, especially the prologue of John, at the heart of their Christologies. Rahner and Pittenger, like the biblical trajectory of Wisdom Christology relate the specific historical events of the life, death, and resurrection of Jesus Christ to the universal activity of God throughout all creation.

Rahner and Pittenger both develop a sophisticated conceptual philosophical theology in order to accomplish their project. While their conceptual language obviously moves on a very different level from the more metaphorical and poetic biblical texts, the core of their Christological programs is rooted in the New Testament's identification of Jesus Christ as the incarnation of Lady Wisdom.

Rahner explains the relationship between Jesus Christ and the universal presence of God through his ontology of real symbol; Pittenger approaches it through a Whiteheadian aesthetic interpretation of Jesus Christ as the classical instance of God's love. Both theologians articulate a religious dimension of all human experience and establish a correlation between the universal experience of God and the event of Jesus Christ.

The second and third chapters will examine Rahner's and Pittenger's developments of this theme and their relationship to the biblical wisdom trajectory. Each chapter will discuss their explanation of the universal presence of God and their effort to relate this presence to the event of Jesus Christ, and their understanding of the role of language in theology.

The interpretation of Jesus Christ as the incarnation of Lady Wisdom and the correlation between the Christ-event and the universal presence of God has important implications for three areas of contemporary theological debate: political and liberation theology, feminist theology, and pluralism. The biblical wisdom trajectory, Rahner, and Pittenger all receive a sharp challenge from each of these areas of concern, but all have a contribution to make to the current discussion. The fourth chapter will discuss the ways in which the biblical writers, Rahner, and Pittenger address the concerns of justice, of feminism, and pluralism.

I will begin the second chapter by considering Rahner's metaphysical anthropology and his understanding of the implicit experience of God in all human knowledge and moral decisions. Then I will consider Rahner's Christology, in particular his use of the ontology of real symbol to relate the Christ-event to the universal salvific will of God. Finally, I will explore the role of religious language for Rahner, with attention to his discussion of the incomprehensibility of God and the dimension of mystery. At each stage I will consider the relation between Rahner's perspectives and those of the biblical wisdom tradition.

The Religious Dimension of Ordinary Experience

Metaphysical Anthropology:
The Openness to Revelation

Early in his life Rahner developed a philosophy of religion based upon a creative dialogue with Thomas Aquinas, Immanuel Kant, Joseph Maréchal, and Martin Heidegger.[1] From this early philosophical work, set forth in Spirit in the World and Hearers of the Word, Rahner went on to develop an all-embracing theological vi-

---

[1]On the philosophical background of Rahner's thought, see Anne Carr, The Theological Method of Karl Rahner, American Academy of Religion Dissertation Series, No. 19 (Missoula, Mont.: Scholars Press, 1977), 10-57; Peter Eicher, Die anthropologische Wende: Karl Rahners philosophischer Weg vom Wesen des Menschen zur personalen Existenz, Dokimion, No. 1 (Freiburg, Switzerland: Universitätsverlag, 1970), 13-48; Otto Muck, The Transcendental Method, trans. William D. Seidensticker (New York: Herder & Herder, 1968), 27-204; Louis Roberts, The Achievement of Karl Rahner (New York: Herder & Herder, 1967), 7-44.

sion of God, humankind, and the world.[2] His philosophical studies, which centered on metaphysical anthropology, provided the background for his anthropocentric method in theology, his use of the ontology of real symbol in Christology, and his understanding of religious language.

The problem that Rahner confronts in Hearers of the Word involves the relation between philosophy and theology. Rahner poses the question: how are humans, through our essential structure, oriented toward fulfillment through God's free, historical revelation and through it alone?[3] To answer this question Rahner seeks to show (1) how listening for a revelation from God belongs to humanity's essential constitution and (2) how humans must look specifically to human history as the place of a possible revelation. In conducting his investigation, Rahner brackets the question of whether a divine revelation has in fact occurred and asks simply about the conditions of possibility for humans to receive such a revelation. Thus Rahner claims to be reflecting as a philosopher upon universal human experience; yet he understands philosophy to be a praeparatio evangelii because its final conclusion is to point humans towards a possible revelation. Christian philosophy, for Rahner, is the ontology of humankind's potentia oboedientialis for revelation.[4]

---

[2]Karl Rahner, Geist in Welt: Zur Metaphysik der endlichen Erkenntnis bei Thomas von Aquin, ed. Johannes Baptist Metz (2nd ed; München: Kösel-Verlag, 1957; hereafter cited as GW); English translation: Spirit in the World, trans. William Dych (New York: Herder and Herder, 1968; hereafter cited as SW); Karl Rahner, Hörer des Wortes: Zur Grundlegung einer Religionsphilosophie, ed. J.B. Metz (2nd ed.; München: Kösel-Verlag, 1963; hereafter cited as HW); English translation: Hearers of the Word, trans. Michael Richards (Montreal: Palm Publishers, 1969); partial translation of the first edition of Hörer des Wortes by Joseph Donceel in A Rahner Reader, ed. Gerald A. McCool (New York: Seabury, 1975), 2-65.

[3]HW, 15-44.

[4]Ibid., 15-44. On HW, see Carr, 88-94. Carr argues that HW and GW are actually not philosophy but, as Rahner himself later admitted, "a theology which looks like a philosophy" (p. 4). On the relation of philosophy and theology in Rahner's thought, see also Eicher, 79-93; Klaus P. Fischer, Der Mensch als Geheimnis: Die Anthropologie Karl Rahners, Okumenische Forschungen 5 (Freiburg: Herder, 1974), 209-35; Bert van der Heijden, Karl Rahner: Darstellung und Kritik seiner Grundposition (Einsiedlen: Johannes Verlag, 1973), 65-152.

In _Hearers of the Word_ Rahner investigates humans' question about Being (_Sein_) in order to ground his metaphysics. Like Heidegger, Rahner views the human person as the proper entry-point into the question of Being.[5] In setting out on this path Rahner warns us not to look for the discovery of something essentially new and different. Rahner's metaphysics concerns itself, in Hegel's phrase, with that which humankind "immer schon weiß und gewußt hat."[6] Metaphysics is the systematic reflection upon the question of the meaning of Being, a question which is one with the question about the human person who inquires: "Die Frage nach dem Sein und nach dem fragenden Menschen selbst bilden eine ursprüngliche und ständig ganze Einheit."[7] In ordinary experience we always have some knowledge of Being, but not full recognition and understanding of it. The question of Being can be genuinely asked because there is both a real knowledge and a real lack of knowledge: "Was Sein sei, ist wohl immer schon offenbar und bekannt, aber nich erkannt."[8]

Rahner offers as the first proposition of general ontology the original unity of Being's knowing and being known. In asking the metaphysical question we affirm that Being is fundamentally intelligible because we could not even ask the question without some provisional knowledge of the meaning of Being. Since the Being that we inquire about is the Being in some sense already known, Rahner concludes that Being itself is fundamentally knowable and that every existent has an inner ordering ("_eine innere_

---

[5]For a critique of this procedure, see Florent Gaboriau, _Le tournant théologique aujoud'hui selon K. Rahner_ (Paris: Desclée, 1968).

[6]_HW_, 47; see also _GW_, 47: "Metaphysik ist das begrifflich ausgebildete Verständnis jenes Vorverstehens, das der Mensch als Mensch _ist_." Rahner will later apply this principle to dogmatic theology: "For it is the bitter grief of theology and its blessed task too, always to have to seek (because it does not clearly have present to it at the time) what, in a true sense--in its historical memory--it has always known." Karl Rahner, "Current Problems in Christology," _Theological Investigations_ , vol. I, trans. Cornelius Ernst (Baltimore, Md.: Helicon, 1969), 151 (hereafter cited as _TI_).

[7]_HW_, 53; cf. also _GW_, 71, 129. On the question of Being as the starting point of Rahner's philosophical reflection, see Eicher, 50-52; and Anne Carr, "Starting with the Human," in _A World of Grace: An Introduction to the Themes and Foundations of Karl Rahner's Theology_, ed. Leo J. O'Donovan (New York: Crossroad, 1984), 19-20.

[8]_HW_, 54.

<u>Hinordnung</u>") to being known.[9] This implies, for Rahner, that "Sein des Seienden und Erkennen eine ursprüngliche <u>Einheit</u> bilden."[10] This is the basis for what Rahner calls the "self-presence" (<u>Bei-sich-sein</u>) and the luminosity (<u>Gelichtetheit</u>) of Being. Since Being and knowing arise from a primordial unity, to be is to know and to be known. "Sein ist <u>an sich</u> Erkennen, und Erkennen ist das mit der Verfassung des Seins notwendig mitgesetzte Bei-sich-sein des Seins eines Seienden."[11] The primordial unity of knowing and being known constitutes the very nature of Being.

Rahner notes that this thesis could appear to lead either to German idealism or to pantheism and could seem to jeopardize the very starting point of the investigation.[12] If Being is already known, we cannot truly ask a question about it. From the experience of questioning, Rahner argues that humans do not fully understand Being.[13] Rahner suggests that there are degrees of being present to oneself. There is an analogy of "having Being" (<u>Seinshabe</u>) which reveals itself in the varying degrees to which existents return into themselves and are present to themselves.[14]

All realities, from material entities even to the immanent life of the Trinity, share this fundamental process of expressing themselves, returning to themselves, and thereby possessing themselves. This process realizes itself in two phases: (1) a flowing outward, an <u>emanatio</u> which expresses its essence and (2) a return into itself. The more interior these two phases are, the more profoundly the reality is able to express and understand itself. This is Rahner's interpretation of Aquinas's ontology of the different grades of being.[15] Material reality expresses itself but does not return to itself. Unable to possess itself, it only shows itself to others while remaining hidden to itself. Humans

---

[9]<u>Ibid.</u>, 56.

[10]<u>Ibid.</u>

[11]<u>Ibid.</u>, 59. Rahner's development of the principle of the intelligibility of Being is one of his most significant departures from Heidegger.

[12]<u>Ibid.</u>, 63.

[13]<u>Ibid.</u>, 64.

[14]<u>Ibid.</u>, 65. The shift in language from the first edition to the second is noteworthy: instead of "Analogie des Seins" the later edition reads "Analogie des Seinshabe." On this shift, see Eicher, 185-99.

[15]<u>Ibid.</u>, 66-67.

are able to express themselves by word and deed and return to themselves in a dynamic process of self-expression and self-possession. God, as "pure Being" (reine Sein), is not a static identity of lifeless indifference but rather is the reality of pure self-luminosity, of complete self-expression and self-possession, of absolute "Seinshabe."[16]

This analogical process of "having Being" constitutes for Rahner the Logos-structure of reality. Rahner sees the unity of Being and knowing as the indispensable presupposition for any revelation of God to humankind through a Word. It is only because Being as Logos is fundamentally knowable that the incarnate Logos can reveal God to humans.[17]

The second necessary condition of the possibility of revelation leads us directly to the first principle of Rahner's metaphysical anthropology. For humans to hear the Word of God they must possess an openness (Offenheit) for Being.[18] This is what Rahner means by claiming that the human person is spirit: "Der Mensch ist Geist. Die Transzendenz auf Sein überhaupt ist die Grundverfassung des Menschen."[19]

Rahner develops this assertion by examining human activity in the world, especially human judgements.[20] A judgement affirms

_____

[16]Ibid., 69.

[17]Ibid., 70.

[18]Ibid., 71.

[19]Ibid., 71; see Josef Speck, Karl Rahners theologische Anthropologie: Eine Einführung (Munich: Kösel Verlag, 1967), 88-178.

[20]For a fuller development of this theme, see GW. See also Eicher, 57-64; and Jennifer L. Rike, Being and Mystery: Analogy and Its Linguistic Implications in the Thought of Karl Rahner (2 vols.; Ph.D. dissertation, University of Chicago, 1986), I, 161-202. Rahner here follows closely the work of Joseph Maréchal. Maréchal takes intellectual knowledge, especially judgements of affirmation, as a given fact, a point of departure for metaphysics. For Maréchal, the absolute value of the law of contradiction implicit in every affirmative judgement cannot be simply a convention of the human mind; it requires an implicit inner dynamism of the mind toward an existing absolute. Since the human striving toward the infinite absolute is an a priori condition of possibility for objective judgements, and since humans do in fact make objective judgements, Maréchal claims that humans do possess a real dynamism towards God. Maréchal further argues that a real dynamism requires a real goal. Therefore, Maréchal concludes that

that some real existent is in some particular way. We grasp an object as a thing of this or that type and thus comprehend the particular which is presented to the senses under a general concept. The traditional Thomistic name for this process is abstraction.[21] Etymologically, to abstract means to draw away from, to detach. What is detached from the particular sense object is its "thisness" (_Washeit_), its _quidditas_ or _forma_. In judging we recognize that this _quidditas_ is not restricted to one particular sense object but can be a determinant of other particulars as well. This recognition of the non-restriction, the unlimited character of the _quidditas_ is only possible if our activity of reaching out for the sense object first reaches out for more than the individual object. This "more" must not be thought of as one more object among others. Rather, it is the absolute horizon of all knowable objects, "die Eröffnung der absoluten Weite möglicher Gegenstandlichkeit überhaupt."[22] Our "reaching for more" is the _Vorgriff_, an anticipation of Being, a pre-grasping, a pre-apprehension, a pre-concept. Whenever we know an individual object, we know it in its restriction and its relation to the totality of all possible objects. The _Vorgriff_ is the condition of possibility of abstraction.

The _Vorgriff_ is the a priori dynamism of the human spirit striving beyond individual sense perceptions towards the absolute horizon of all possible objects. Through this dynamism we know the single object as limited, as not completely filling the conscious sphere of what may be known. While the _Vorgriff_ is conscious, it never appears alone to human consciousness. It always appears in the knowledge of a particular object as the condition of the possibility of this knowledge. The _Vorgriff_ is "die _be-_

God's real existence is an a priori condition of possibility of every objective, categorical judgement of the human intellect. This argument provided Rahner with his basic starting point for developing his metaphysical anthropology. Joseph Maréchal, _Le point de départ de la métaphysique: Leçons sur le développement historique et théorique du problème de la connaissance_ (5 vols.; vol. 1: Bruges, Belgium: Charles Beyaert, 1922; vols. 2-5: Brussels: L'Edition Universelle, 1944-49). On Maréchal, see Muck, 27-157; Eicher, 22-33.

[21]_HW_, 76; cf. _GW_, 129-242. For a critical assessment of Rahner's reading of Thomas on abstraction, see Cornelio Fabro, _La svolta antropologica di Karl Rahner_ (Milan: Rusconi Editore, 1974), 123-205.

[22]_HW_, 78.

wußte Eröffnung des Horizontes, innerhalb dessen das einzelne Objekt der menschlichen Erkenntnis gewußt wird."[23]

The Vorgriff is not by itself alone an act of knowledge, but rather only one moment of such an act; and yet we must treat it as some form of knowledge because we have no other model for understanding it.[24] Approaching it as a form of knowledge, we have no choice but to indicate its object. Rahner argues that the object, the "whither" (Worauf) of the Vorgriff must be God, infinite, absolute Being.[25] Thus in every act of human knowledge there is an objective, categorical knowledge through universal concepts and a non-objective, implicit, yet conscious pre-grasp of infinite Being.

According to Rahner, we must be careful not to mistake God for one more object set before the human mind. As the condition of possibility of all knowledge, the Vorgriff never represents an object in itself; the Vorgriff does, however, coaffirm the existence of God because it is the necessary condition of all knowledge of objects, and the existence of God is the necessary condition of the Vorgriff. Thus, through the Vorgriff we continuously transcend all finite reality towards absolute Being. The absolute openness for infinite Being is part of the essential constitution of humankind. There is no domain of Being which is necessarily closed to us, for we are fundamentally oriented to God:

Er ist dadurch allein Mensch, daß er immer schon auf dem Weg zu Gott ist, ob er es ausdrücklich weiß oder nicht, ob er es

---

[23]Ibid., 79.

[24]Ibid., 80.

[25]Rahner briefly considers and rejects two other possible answers to this question (HW, 80-83). The first, that of Kant, claims that the Vorgriff reaches only for the horizon of sense intuition and is limited by space and time. Anything beyond this is outside of the range of human knowledge. The second answer is that of Heidegger. For Heidegger, as Rahner interprets him, the Vorgriff heads for nothingness. Rahner rejects Heidegger's position because the experience of finitude, which is the basis of affirming that nothingness is the end goal, arises only from the Vorgriff's striving toward the infinite. A transcendence towards nothingness would not reveal the finitude of all objects and would not give rise to a negation. Kant's position, Rahner argues, contradicts the very act of its assertion, for in order to know that the totality of human knowledge is finite, we must be able to reach beyond this finiteness.

will oder nicht, denn er ist immer die unendliche Geöffne-
theit des Endlichen für Gott.[26]

Lest the openness of the human person seem to preclude the
necessity or possibility of a supernatural revelation, Rahner
stresses the hiddenness of Being from two angles: that of the
human reaching for more and that of the free God who transcends
necessity. While the transcendence of the human spirit does indeed have an implicit pre-grasp of God, this is always a limit-
experience, a condition of the possibility of the knowledge of
finite objects and not a separate, direct act of cognition. In
and through our abstraction of quiddities we are experiencing God,
but the Vorgriff experiences God as always hidden, as not yet
known.[27]

Moreover, Rahner argues that the God whom the Vorgriff experiences is free. By asking the question of Being, humans implicitly affirm themselves as contingent beings in an intelligible
world.[28] According to Rahner this intelligible contingency excludes the possibility that humans were formed by some impersonal
necessity:

Die notwendige Absolutsetzung einer Zufälligen, die als
solche die Gelichtetheit des Seins bejaht, kann also nur der
gesetze Nachvollzug und die Weiterung (die als gesetze not-
wendig ist) einer freien willentlichen Absolutsetzung dieses
Zufälliger sein.[29]

Rahner insists that freedom is the only possible ground of
intelligible contingency; thus humans must arise from an act of
creative freedom of God. If God is free, then God has the possibility of further revelation.[30] Since the highest expression of
Being is freedom, humankind's relationship to God is interpersonal. Humans can receive an intelligible, interpersonal expression
of God only through empathy, which demands a fundamental attitude
of self-surrender. Empathy enables the lover to receive an interior understanding of the beloved's free act of love. Thus every
experience of interpersonal knowledge is an act of love, for love

---

[26]Ibid., 86.

[27]Ibid., 103-04.

[28]Ibid., 105-08.

[29]Ibid., 111.

[30]Ibid., 112-14.

is the "lamp of knowledge."[31] Authentic knowledge of God can be found only in a person's fundamental act of freedom, which determines a basic attitude towards oneself, one's world, and one's infinite horizon. Rahner concludes his discussion of the hiddenness of Being by laying down the second principle of his metaphysical anthropology: ". . . der Mensch jenes Seiende sei, das in freier Liebe vor dem Gott einer möglichen Offenbarung steht."[32]

Rahner turns next to the place where humans should listen for a possible divine revelation. The human person is spirit, not, however, pure spirit but always spirit-in-the-world. Humans know receptively and discursively, depending upon sense objects in space and time.[33] Humans are historical knowers by nature; we exist as members of a species inseparably bound up with the history of our race. Thus the place where humans must listen for a possible revelation of God is human history.[34] Since God is free, Rahner suggests, all human history reveals God; even when God chooses to be silent, this free silence is revelatory of the God who has chosen not to speak.[35] Thus Rahner proposes his third and final proposition of metaphysical anthropology: "Der Mensch ist jenes Seiende, das in seiner Geschichte auf die möglicherweise im menschlichen Wort kommende geschichtliche Offenbarung Gottes horchen muß."[36] Thus Rahner's metaphysical anthropology leads him to an ontology of the human person's potentia oboedientialis for a possible divine revelation.

The Supernatural Dimension
of Ordinary Experience

Thus far I have examined Rahner's view of the abstract structures of human existence which make possible the experience of revelation. As a Christian theologian, Rahner affirms not only the possibility of revelation but also the reality of God's self-communication in Christ; he further claims that this revelation is not limited in its effects to those who encounter the historical Jesus and the Christian Church but extends throughout all human

---

[31]Ibid., 124.

[32]Ibid., 133.

[33]Ibid., 147-61; see also GW.

[34]HW, 161-72.

[35]Ibid., 133.

[36]Ibid., 200.

experience. Concretely, ordinary human experience is never simply an abstract structure of waiting for a possible revelation or only an implicit metaphysical pre-grasp of Being; all human experience without exception is actively influenced by God's supernatural revelation. The salvific will of God is a universal reality in human life. We turn now to Rahner's understanding of the concrete activity of God in ordinary experience.

Rahner sees God as actively present throughout all human experience, offering revelation and salvation to every person, regardless of the individual's explicit religious self-understanding or lack thereof.[37] While accepting the teaching of Vatican I on the possibility of a natural knowledge of God, he views this as an abstract principle. Concretely, we live in a world always already graced by God: "In the concrete actualization of existence, therefore, there is no knowledge of God which is purely natural."[38] The concept of nature, for Rahner, becomes a "Restbegriff," a remainder concept which refers to a possible order of being which God could have created but in fact did not: "We never have this postulated pure nature for itself alone."[39] The world of our experience is always a world of grace: "The concrete knowledge of God as a question, as a call which is affirmed or denied, is always within the dimension of man's supernatural determination."[40]

The transcendental knowledge of God experiences God as mystery, as "nameless and indefinable, as something not at our disposal."[41] God never appears as one individual existent alongside of other existents, but always as the term of the transcendence of the human spirit. While God can never be experienced directly as an individual existent, God does draw near to us in and through

---

[37]Karl Rahner, "History of the World and Salvation-History," TI, V, trans. Karl H. Kruger (New York: Seabury, 1975), 97-114; idem, "Christianity and the Non-Christian Religions," TI, V, 115-34; idem, "Atheism and Implicit Christianity," TI, IX, trans. Graham Harrison (New York: Herder and Herder, 1972), 145-64; idem, "Theology of Freedom," TI, VI, trans. Karl H. and Boniface Kruger (New York: Seabury, 1974), 178-96.

[38]Karl Rahner, Foundations of Christian Faith: An Introduction to the Idea of Christianity, trans. William V. Dych (New York: Crossroad, 1982), 57.

[39]Karl Rahner, "Concerning the Relationship between Nature and Grace," TI, I, 314.

[40]Foundations, 57.

[41]Ibid., 61.

finite realities. Rahner claims there is a "genuine mediation of immediacy with regard to God."[42] In this mediation the absolute difference between God and finite reality remains, but the finite can point to its ineffable ground.[43]

Rahner refers to the teaching of Thomas Aquinas that "God works through secondary causes."[44] This principle, Rahner notes, means that God is not one more link in a chain of causes. Rather, it is the entire process of the world that reveals God: "The chain [of causes] as a whole, and hence the world in its interconnectedness, . . . this is the self-revelation of its ground."[45] Every specific historical revelation of God, Rahner argues, is to be understood as "the historical concreteness of the transcendental self-communication of God who is already intrinsic to the concrete world."[46] The condition of possibility for any specific experience of God is that immediacy to God in and through the finite "must be embedded in this world to begin with."[47]

Thus Rahner can identify the history of the world and history of salvation and revelation as co-extensive.[48] "Profane history" is ambiguous, allowing different interpretations, but hidden within all profane history is what Rahner calls a "general salvation-and revelation-history":

For by the general history of grace, salvation, and revelation, real salvific activity becomes co-existent with the history of the world and takes place within it at all times and everywhere. For this reason salvation-history is always also the hidden foundation of profane history.[49]

Every finite reality can mediate the presence of God. Insofar as we become present to ourselves through our experience of the world, we become present to God. Thus we have always already encountered God in our ordinary experience, whether or not we were

---

[42]Ibid., 83.

[43]Ibid., 84-87.

[44]Ibid., 86.

[45]Ibid.

[46]Ibid., 87.

[47]Ibid.

[48]"History of the World," TI, V, 103.

[49]Ibid., 108.

explicitly conscious of God. "In this sense the world is our mediation to God in his self-communication in grace, and in this sense there is for Christianity no separate and sacral realm where alone God is to be found."[50]

In describing the encounter with grace, Rahner proposes a phenomenology of the religious dimension of experience by examining limit-situations where we live "on the border between God and the world, time and eternity."[51] Rahner cites the experience of absolute loneliness, the experience of forgiving or sacrificing without personal benefit, and the experience of trying to love God

> when we seemed to be calling out into emptiness and our cry seemed to fall on deaf ears, when it looked as if we were taking a terrifying jump into the bottomless abyss, when everything seemed to become incomprehensible and apparently senseless.[52]

The experience of God, according to Rahner, is deeply unsettling, having "the taste of death and destruction," plunging us into an abyss we cannot master or control; the experience of God is, in Heidegger's word, "uncanny":

> Then is the hour of grace. Then the seemingly uncanny, bottomless depth of God communicating himself to us, the dawning of his approaching infinity which no longer has any set paths, which is tasted like a nothing because it is infinity.[53]

The experience of grace, Rahner warns us, is never something we can claim as a possession. We can only seek it properly by forgetting ourselves.

Rahner develops his understanding of the religious dimension of ordinary experience through his concepts of the formal existential ethic and the fundamental option. By "formal existential ethics" Rahner means that God can and does make concrete moral

---

[50]Foundations, 151-52; see also Karl Rahner, "Nature and Grace," TI, IV, trans. Kevin Smyth (New York: Crossroad, 1982), 180-81.

[51]Karl Rahner, "Reflections on the Experience of Grace," TI, III, trans. Karl-H. and Boniface Kruger (New York: Seabury, 1974), 88.

[52]Ibid., 87.

[53]Ibid., 89.

demands which are not determinable by universal moral principles.[54] By existential ethic Rahner means a moral demand which
cannot "be translated into universal propositions of material
content"; a formal existential ethics examines "the basic elements, the formal structures and the basic manner of perceiving
such an existential-ethic reality."[55] God is intimately concerned with each concrete individual and makes specific moral
claims upon each person. However, this call is never experienced
as a direct, individual object of knowledge alongside of others;
rather, it is an implicit moment of our categorical experience of
the world. Like the Vorgriff, the experience of the formal existential ethic is a "non-objective perception."[56] The experience
of an individual moral demand is always on the level of the "non-
reflective, non-propositional self-presence of the person to itself."[57] Thus it is not sufficient for moral decisions merely to
apply a universal norm; each individual must also be alert to
discern a possible moral demand which is specific to the given
moment.

The individual's experience of God's call is set within the
context of a fundamental decision of a "yes" or a "no" toward
God.[58] The transcendence of the human spirit towards absolute
Being expresses itself in the necessity of a free decision towards
the horizon of all experience. Because God is the transcendental
horizon of human freedom, every individual act is a positive or
negative orientation of the human person towards God. As in the
case of intellectual knowledge, God is never experienced by human
freedom as one categorial reality alongside of others. God is
never simply one of the variety of choices that face us: "God is
present unthematically in every act of freedom as its supporting
ground and ultimate orientation."[59] An act of rejecting God is a
frightening paradox, for human freedom thereby rejects its own
ground of possibility. This "negating freedom" denies God but

---

[54]Karl Rahner, "On the Question of a Formal Existential Ethics," TI, II, trans. Karl-H. Kruger (Baltimore, Md.: Helicon
Press, 1963), 225-29.

[55]Ibid., 229.

[56]Ibid., 230.

[57]Ibid.

[58]"Theology of Freedom," TI, VI, 180-81.

[59]Ibid., 180.

implicitly affirms God as the condition of possibility of it-self.[60]

Human freedom, in making concrete decisions, is fashioning the human person. In choosing our words and actions we are choosing ourselves, and this choice, for Rahner, has eternal significance. Human freedom is "the capacity to do something uniquely final, something which is finally valid precisely because it is done in freedom."[61]

Because our freedom is oriented to our horizon, we can never reflect upon our fundamental stance directly and objectively. Our fundamental "yes" or "no" to God can only be discerned implicitly in and through our specific decisions, and it can never be grasped with direct and certain reflexive consciousness. This is Rahner's understanding of the teaching of the Council of Trent that no one "can know with the certainty of faith, which cannot be subject to error, that he has obtained the grace of God."[62]

In freedom as in knowledge we always experience our transcendental horizon in and through the finite, categorical realities of our world. Our fundamental option is not one choice alongside of others but is rather the inner meaning and unity of the countless individual decisions that we make. Thus Rahner can argue that there is a strict unity between the love of neighbor and the love of God.[63] As the ground of all experience God is encountered "indirectly in a kind of boundary experience as the origin and destination of an act which is objectively directed towards the world."[64] In relating to finite realities, we are implicitly relating to God; thus the specific act of loving our neighbor is itself an implicit act of loving God.

---

[60]Ibid., 181.

[61]Ibid., 186.

[62]Canons and Decrees of the Council of Trent, trans. H.J. Schroeder (Rockford, Il.: Tan Books and Publishers, 1978), 36.

[63]Karl Rahner, "Reflections on the Unity of the Love of Neighbour and the Love of God," TI, VI, 231-49.

[64]Ibid., 244-45.

Wisdom and Rahner: The Religious
Dimension of Experience

The biblical wisdom tradition shares important perspectives and emphases with Rahner. Like Rahner, the ancient sages affirmed that in making judgements about the world we are implicitly experiencing God; they also held that in making moral decisions we are implicitly accepting or rejecting the call of Lady Wisdom. In the wisdom tradition we have seen an awareness of order and limit, descriptions of Lady Wisdom as both hidden and revealed, and a correlation of Wisdom with historical revelation. There are analogies to each of these themes in Rahner.

The sages saw the patterns discernible in human life as revelatory of the activity of Lady Wisdom, the cosmological principle of order in the universe. Murphy notes that the wisdom tradition combines a "stress on experience" with the recognition that "wisdom is from God."[65] This dual perspective challenges any dichotomy between "religious" and "profane" wisdom sayings. According to Murphy, "This distinction is simply not applicable to the wisdom tradition; the Israelite did not feel that his experiential insights were other than a God-given wisdom."[66] Collections of proverbs juxtapose experiences of God and experiences of the world. Von Rad's interpretation of the significance of this procedure is a principle fundamental to Rahner's theological perspective: "The experiences of the world were for her [Israel] always divine experiences as well, and the experiences of God were for her experiences of the world."[67]

The sages combined a trust in the order of creation and an acute sense of the limits of all human understanding of this order. By naming the ordering principle of creation "Wisdom" and by trusting in human insights into experience, the sages were affirming the fundamental intelligibility of human experience in the world. Rahner's principle of the intelligibility of Being and his affirmation of the primordial unity of Being and knowing can be understood as a philosophical development of the ancient sages' trust in the wisdom embedded in creation. For both Rahner and the sages, the intelligibility of the world is the basis for a fundamental trust in experience.[68]

---

[65]"Interpretation of Old Testament Wisdom Literature," 293.

[66]Ibid.

[67]Wisdom, 62.

[68]See Anne Carr, "Theology and Experience in the Thought of Karl Rahner," JR 13(1973):359-76; and Walter Brueggemann, In Man We Trust (Atlanta: John Knox Press, 1972).

However, both the sages and Rahner distrust any simple and direct reading of human experience. Rahner stresses the hiddenness of Being and the ambiguity of profane history; even his examples of the experience of grace are limit-experiences bearing "the taste of death and destruction."[69] For Rahner and for the sages, our experience of Being is a paradoxical coincidence of luminosity and hiddenness, of intelligibility and incomprehensibility. To stress either side of experience to the neglect of the other would be to distort the meaning of human existence and the character of our relationship to God.

The inclusion of Job and Qoheleth within the wisdom tradition and the biblical canon constitutes a jarring counterpoint to the sages' basic trust in the intelligibility of human experience. For Job and Qoheleth the order implanted in the world by God is effective but inscrutable. For both Rahner and the wisdom tradition, human experience involves both understanding and not understanding.

This double perspective found expression in the conflicting portraits of Lady Wisdom as hidden (Job 28) and revealed (Prov 8). In the Hebrew Bible Lady Wisdom is always distinct from God; but, as von Rad argued, she appears as the form in which humans experience God in the world.[70] There is an analogy between the experience of Lady Wisdom as both hidden and revealed and Rahner's description of God as both hidden and revealed in ordinary experience. By presenting Lady Wisdom as the form in which humans experience God, the sages affirmed that the entire created order can manifest God. As von Rad comments, at the center of the wisdom tradition was "the characteristic concept of reality as a force which continually has its effects on men. . . . In these effects of reality Yahweh was at work, ordering and directing."[71] Rahner's interpretation of Thomas Aquinas' theory of secondary causality bears a strong similarity to this perspective. For Rahner, it is the entire process of created reality, "the world in its interconnectedness," which reveals God.[72]

The contrasting perspective of Job 28 finds an analogy in Rahner's emphasis on the hiddenness of God in human experience, even in our experience of grace. In Job 28 God's discovery of Wisdom makes possible the ordering of creation, but humans are

---

[69]"Reflections on the Experience of Grace," TI, III, 89.

[70]Old Testament Theology. I, 444.

[71]Wisdom, 94.

[72]Foundations, 86.

unable to discover her for themselves. Thus humans experience Wisdom constantly but fail to comprehend her. In similar fashion the speeches of God in Job 38-41 call attention to the order in the universe which encompasses and makes possible human life but which surpasses human understanding. Job's anguished cries of anger express the pain of suffering in an incomprehensible world.

In Proverbs 1 and 8 Lady Wisdom confronts humans with a choice of life or death. Since the poems are embedded in a collection of proverbs dealing with various experiences of everyday life, and since humans hear her crying out at the city gates in the midst of secular life, the call of Lady Wisdom is evidently mediated in and through the experiences of ordinary life. The choice of life or death is made in and through decisions about justice, about fidelity in love, about the poor, about speaking and acting in a wide variety of situations. Thus it would appear that the call of Lady Wisdom is not one specific experience alongside of others (as, for example, a prophet's experience of being called). Rather, the poetic descriptions of the call articulate a fundamental challenge of human life which is present whether we acknowledge it or not. While the godless (Wis 2-3) and the adulterous woman (Prov 30:20) deny that they have done anything wrong, in fact they have experienced and rejected the call of Lady Wisdom. In and through the multiple decisions of human life, the sages claimed that we are making one fundamental decision to accept or reject Lady Wisdom; in this decision we are gaining or losing our own selves (Prov 8:35-36). The sages also denied that we ourselves are ultimately the reliable interpreters and judges of our own fundamental decisions: "A man's conduct may strike him as upright; Yahweh, however, weighs the heart" (Prov 21:2; cf. Prov 16:2).

The image of a call coming in and through the everyday experience of the created order of the world bears a clear similarity to Rahner's conceptions of a formal existential ethics and a fundamental option. Rahner develops in more abstract and theoretical fashion the theme of a call implicit in human life, a call which we experience in and through our everyday decisions, a call in response to which we are ultimately deciding our own destiny. Like the sages, Rahner denies that we can discern or judge the decisions we are making with full, reflexive adequacy.

The later stages of the wisdom tradition correlated the experience of Lady Wisdom with the historical revelations to the people of Israel. This process of correlation can be compared to Rahner's interpretation of every specific historical revelation of God as a concrete manifestation of the universal salvific will of God which has always already embedded itself in the entire creative process. According to Rahner, we are disposed by our essential condition to listen for a revelation of God in human history, and yet God's active presence and transforming grace are by no

84

means limited to the specific historical revelations of the Bible. The interpretation of this correlation between God's universal presence and the special biblical revelations leads us into the topic of the next section, the interpretation of Christ in relation to universal human experience.

Christology: Jesus as Real Symbol

Rahner's central category for relating the Christ-event to the universal presence of God in human experience is the "real symbol" (Realsymbol). Rahner interprets the life, death, and resurrection of Jesus Christ as the real symbol of the Logos and as the "real-symbolic cause" of God's universal salvific will.[73] To understand this perspective we turn first to Rahner's ontology of symbol and his application of this theory to relate the Christ-event to universal human experience; then I will discuss his understanding of the relation of Christ to the world-process; finally I will explore the relation between this perspective and the Wisdom Christology of the New Testament.

Christ and the Ontology of Real Symbol

In his article, "The Theology of the Symbol," first published in 1959, Rahner developed his metaphysics of Being into an ontology of symbol.[74] The basic principle of this ontology is:

[73]Foundations, 284; see also Karl Rahner, "The Theology of the Symbol," TI, IV, 221-52. A discussion of the entire range of Rahner's Christological reflections exceeds the limits of this essay. On Rahner's Christology, see Robert Eugene Doud, Rahner's Christology: A Whiteheadian Critique (Ann Arbor, Mich.: University Microfilms, 1977); Otto Hentz, "Karl Rahner's Concept of the Christ-Event as the Act of God in History," (Ph.D. dissertation, University of Chicago, 1977); and idem, "Anticipating Jesus Christ: An Account of Our Hope," in World of Grace, 107-19; Peter Schineller, "The Place of Scripture in the Christology of Karl Rahner," (Ph.D. dissertation, University of Chicago, 1975); and idem, "Discovering Jesus Christ: A History We Share," in World of Grace, 92-106; Joseph H.P. Wong, Logos-Symbol in the Christology of Karl Rahner (Rome: Libreria Ateneo Salesiano, 1984).

[74]"Theology of the Symbol," TI, IV, 221-52; see Maria Elizabeth Motzko, Karl Rahner's Theology: A Theology of the Symbol (Ann Arbor, Mich.: University Microfilms, 1976); and James J. Buckley, "On Being a Symbol: An Appraisal of Karl Rahner," TS 40(1979)453-73.

"all beings are by their very nature symbolic, because they necessarily 'express' themselves in order to attain their own nature."[75] Rahner regards as derivative and secondary the more
common notion of symbol as one reality which points to another
because of some agreement, some similarity between them.

To understand the primordial meaning of symbol Rahner turns
to the metaphysics of Being, in particular to the analogy of having Being. Rahner had earlier argued that beings possess Being to
the degree in which they are able to express themselves and return
to themselves; he had also noted that all beings, including the
triune God, share in this fundamental process.[76] The plurality
of moments in the life of every being is not merely the result of
finitude but is found, in analogous fashion, at the very core of
pure Being itself.[77] For Rahner, "a being is, of itself, independently of any comparison with anything else, plural in its
unity."[78] Every being expresses itself in something other than
itself, returns to itself, and thereby fulfills itself. This
expression which enables the being to constitute itself and know
itself is what Rahner calls a "real symbol." It is only through a
real symbol that a being can know itself and be known by others.
Rahner proposes a second proposition in his ontology of symbol:
"The symbol strictly speaking (symbolic reality) is the self-realization of a being in the other, which is constitutive of its
essence."[79]

This understanding of symbol, which flows directly from the
metaphysics outlined in Spirit in the World and Hearers of the
Word, leads Rahner to his interpretation of the Trinity and the
Incarnation. According to Rahner, the eternal Logos is the real
symbol of the Father, the expression through which the Father
knows and is known, the "other in which he flows out of himself
and possesses himself."[80] As a real symbol the Logos is truly
distinct from the Father and yet is constituted by and united to
the Father. The Logos is first and foremost God's real symbol to
and within God's own self. It is only because of God's inner expression that an external revelation is possible. Rahner applies

---

[75]"Theology of the Symbol," TI, IV, 224.

[76]HW, 65-70.

[77]"Theology of the Symbol," TI, IV, 228.

[78]Ibid., 222.

[79]Ibid., 234.

[80]Ibid., 236-37.

to God the principle that a real symbol is the only means through which a reality can be known by others. It is only because God's eternal Word to humans is truly God's own immanent self-expression that humans can come to know God in the incarnate Word.[81]

Rahner further applies the theology of symbol to the relation between the eternal Logos and the human nature of Jesus. Rahner sees the human nature of Jesus as the real symbol of the Logos, its self-expression in something other than itself.[82] The human nature of Jesus does not remain an external instrument through which the Logos communicates doctrines; it is rather the effective exteriorization of the very reality of the Logos itself.

The eternal God who is immutable can really express the divine self in something other and can become subject to change in so far as God assumes the other reality as God's own. Rahner is careful to purge the analogy of any implication of change when applied to the Trinity. The inner triune life of God is dynamic but immutable. However, the incarnation reveals that God does become subject to change outside of God's self.[83]

In Rahner's view, the humanity of Christ is what arises when the Logos expresses itself in a real symbol. _Spirit in the World_ and _Hearers of the Word_ had argued that the human person is a spirit in the world yet transcending the world, dynamically reaching out for God. This was the only "definition," the only limit that Rahner would put on the human person. This dynamic transcendence which is the essence of the human spirit receives its full actualization in the incarnation. "The incarnation of God is therefore the unique, _supreme_ case of the total actualization of human reality."[84] Human nature assumed by God as God's own reality has "simply arrived at the point to which it always strives by virtue of its essence."[85]

The human person has by nature the possibility of being assumed by God as the material for a divine self-expression. Thus Rahner develops his earlier philosophical definition of the nature

---

[81]_Ibid._

[82]_Ibid._, 237-39.

[83]Karl Rahner, "On the Theology of the Incarnation," _TI_, IV, 109; see also "Current Problems in Christology," _TI_, I, 181; and _Foundations_, 219-23.

[84]"Theology of the Incarnation," _TI_, IV, 110.

[85]_Ibid._, 109.

of the human person by looking at human nature from the perspective of revelation: "If God wills to become non-God, man comes to be, that and nothing else, we might say."[86] The human person is an "abbreviation," a "code-word" for God.[87]

Rahner applies the perspective of the real symbol to anthropology as well, analyzing humans as a unity of body and soul, spirit and matter.[88] The body is the real symbol of the soul, the expression through which the soul constitutes itself.[89] In order to realize itself, the human soul, which is the human substantial form, must express itself through its proper accidents by means of its active, emanating causality. "The giving of the form by the formal cause . . . 'brings about' that which is formed, the actual thing."[90] The soul constitutes a dynamic unity with its faculties; the faculties are accidents really distinct from the soul but are necessary to the soul's self-realization.

Rahner seeks to incorporate his metaphysical anthropology into the heart of his theology. Earlier he had described the human person as "the infinite openness of the finite for God."[91] Now Rahner claims that this is possible only because the eternal Logos could express itself outside of itself. For Rahner, the human person is "forever the articulate mystery of God."[92] The progression of Rahner's thought, moving from philosophical anthropology to the theology of the incarnation, rediscovers anthropology on a theological level; this leads Rahner to claim: "Christology is the end and beginning of anthropology. And this anthropology, when most thoroughly realized in Christianity, is eternally theology."[93] Thus the revelation of God in Jesus Christ manifests the essential, universal structure of humanity.

---

[86]Ibid., 116.

[87]Ibid; see also Foundations, 224-25.

[88]Karl Rahner, "The Unity of Spirit and Matter in the Christian Understanding of Faith," TI, VI, 153-77.

[89]"Theology of Symbol," TI, IV, 247.

[90]Ibid., 232.

[91]HW, 86.

[92]"Theology of the Incarnation," TI, IV, 116.

[93]Ibid., 117.

Rahner also uses the theory of real-symbolic causality to explain the relationship between the Christ-event and the universal salvific will of God. By expressing itself in the life, death, and resurrection of Jesus, God's salvific will constitutes itself as irrevocably present in human history and reveals itself to the human race as unambiguously victorious. What is signified (God's universal salvific will) posits the sign (the life, death, and resurrection of Jesus) and in and through this sign it causes what is signified. In and through the life, death, and resurrection of Jesus God's salvific will "becomes real and becomes manifest as irrevocable."[94] Because Jesus is the real-symbolic expression of God's own self, he is for Rahner the definitive revelation of God. In him God has expressed all that God has to express. The theory of real-symbolic causality allows Rahner to view the Christ-event as constitutive of God's relationship to humankind precisely because it decisively manifests that reality.[95]

Since God's salvific will is always active in human life, Rahner understands Christology to be manifesting and proclaiming a reality which is always already experienced even though it may not be grasped thematically in consciousness. For Rahner the Christ-event is the "absolute climax" of the history of God's revelation.[96] Jesus is the absolute saviour because in him the universal salvific will of God becomes "present in the world historically, really, and irrevocably."[97]

There is in Rahner's Christology a subtle and important dialectic between the uniqueness and absoluteness of God's presence in Christ and the similarity of God's presence in Christ to God's presence in all human life. On the one hand, Rahner repeatedly insists upon the uniqueness of God's presence in Jesus, and yet he also maintains that God's presence in Jesus is in continuity with and thus similar to God's presence in all creation and in all humans. Rahner thus affirms a dialectic of continuity and uniqueness, of similarity and dissimilarity in the relation between the Christ-event and the universal activity of God. Jesus Christ is the absolute and final revelation of God, but he is also an inte-

---

[94]Foundations, 284.

[95]See Hentz, "Rahner's Concept," 156-65.

[96]Foundations, 174.

[97]Ibid., 284.

gral moment in the history of the human race and the evolution of life.[98] Rahner argues:

> in accordance with the fact that the natures are unmixed, basically the active influence of the Logos on the human 'nature' in Jesus in a physical sense may not be understood in any other way except the way this influence is exercised by God on free creatures elsewhere.[99]

In accordance with this principle Rahner applies analogically the formula of Chalcedon to the relation between God and all creation. The relation between the Logos and the human nature of Christ is not an exception to the ordinary relation between God and a creature but is its perfect exemplification. In the incarnation "the ultimate formal determinations of the Creator-creature relationship must also hold in this particular relationship."[100] The fundamental principle of the relation of the Logos to the human nature applies to all creation's relation to God: "Radical dependence upon [God] increases in direct, and not in inverse proportion with genuine self-coherence before him."[101] Thus in Christ "both independence and radical proximity equally reach a unique and qualitatively incommensurable perfection, which nevertheless remains once and for all the perfection of a relation between Creator and creature."[102]

The creative power of God is unique precisely in its ability to call into being a reality which as creature remains wholly dependent upon God but which receives genuine freedom, autonomy, and independence over against God. This paradoxical coincidence of radical dependence and genuine autonomy offers Rahner a perspective for interpreting the relation of the divine and the human in Christ, the relation of grace and free will in human decisions, and the relation of the entire created order to its Creator.[103] In each case Rahner refuses to allow any tension between dependence upon God and genuine creaturely freedom.

---

[98]Ibid., 300-01; see also Karl Rahner, "Christology within an Evolutionary View of the World," TI, V, 157-92.

[99]Foundations, 287; see also "Current Problems in Christology," 163, n. 1.

[100]"Current Problems in Christology," TI, I, 163, n. 1.

[101]Ibid., 162.

[102]Ibid., 162-63.

[103]Ibid., 163-64.

In accordance with this perspective, Rahner approaches each of the issues of Christology with special attention to the similarities between the experience of Jesus and universal human experience, without ever neglecting the uniqueness and finality of the Christ-event. For Rahner the death and resurrection of Jesus form an intrinsic unity. The meaning of the resurrection is neither the resuscitation of a physical body nor the beginning of a new period in the life of Jesus but rather "the permanent, redeemed, final and definitive validity of the life of Jesus."[104]

The horizon for our understanding the resurrection of Jesus is the transcendental hope in the resurrection which is shared by every human person. Rahner claims that each person wants to survive in some final and definitive sense, even though the person may not have an explicit, thematic consciousness of this hope. For Rahner the question about the definitive validity of our own lives is identical with the question of the resurrection.[105] The transcendental hope in the resurrection finds its affirmative answer and its categorical mediation in the testimony of the apostles about Jesus. Thus Rahner argues that the message of the resurrection is neither totally unexpected nor outside the horizon of our experience.[106]

The original resurrection experience was that "Jesus is alive."[107] This experience, which is strictly *sui generis*, is nonetheless to be understood on the analogy of other human experiences "after the manner of our experience of the powerful Spirit of the living Lord."[108] Rahner denies that the experience of the resurrection involved sense experience: "For this manifestation to imply sense experience, everything would have to belong to the realm of normal and profane sense experience."[109] The resurrection experience for Rahner is neither a mystical vision nor a physical sense-experience but rather "the assumption of the fruit of our ongoing history into its final and definitive state."[110]

---

[104]*Foundations*, 266.

[105]*Ibid.*, 268-70.

[106]*Ibid.*, 275.

[107]*Ibid.*, 276.

[108]*Ibid.*

[109]*Ibid.*

[110]*Ibid.*, 277.

In Rahner's view, the historical Jesus claimed that with him there was present "a new and unsurpassable closeness of God which on its part will prevail victoriously and is inseparable from him."[111] The resurrection vindicates this claim of Jesus and reveals him as the absolute saviour, the full and final expression of God's self.

Because human history is a single history, the destiny of one person has significance for others. The life and death of Jesus in their unity are the real-symbolic "cause" of God's salvific will in the sense that "this salvific will establishes itself really and irrevocably in this life and death."[112] Rahner sums up the original experience upon which Christology is founded: "We are saved because this man who is one of us has been saved by God, and God has thereby made his salvific will present in the world historically, really, and irrevocably."[113]

Rahner reads the official Christology of the Catholic Church as a straightforward descending Christology. Its strength is found in its guarding of the uniqueness of the presence of God in Jesus. Its danger is that it tends in practice toward a monophysite piety which allows the humanity of Jesus to be overshadowed by his divinity. Against this danger Rahner stresses that there is no mingling of the natures in Christ. The copula in the communicatio idiomatum does not imply a real identification of Jesus and God but points to a "unique, otherwise unknown and deeply mysterious unity between realities which are really different and which are at an infinite distance from each other."[114]

Rahner offers his own constructive proposal as a "searching Christology." Rahner assumes that non-Christian persons of good will already live in the grace of God; such persons have already responded to Christ with an interior and unreflexive "Yes." A searching Christology seeks to articulate a universal understanding of existence which is implicitly Christian because of antecedent grace; then it seeks to show that the search finds its goal in Jesus Christ.[115] In this endeavor Rahner appeals to three experiences: the absolute love of neighbor, the readiness for death, and

---

[111]Ibid., 279.

[112]Ibid., 284.

[113]Ibid.

[114]Ibid., 290.

[115]Ibid., 294-95.

hope in the future. Each of these experiences implies a search for an absolute saviour.[116]

Rahner proposes a "Christology from below" to complement the classical "Christology from above." Rahner's Christology from below assumes that Jesus understood himself as the absolute saviour and that the resurrection confirmed his self-understanding and manifested him as the mediator of salvation.[117] The absolute event of salvation or the absolute saviour is God's irreversible offer of God's own self to humankind, an offer which affirms and fulfills the human person's essential orientation to God. Rahner claims that this is what the classical doctrine expresses as incarnation and hypostatic union.

The ontic Christological language of the tradition uses categories such as "nature" and "hypostasis" which are derived from the world of things. To avoid monophysite and mythological misunderstandings, Rahner wants to complement ontic Christology with a "consciousness" Christology which translates the traditional ontic language into ontological terms.[118] Rahner claims that the shift from ontic to ontological language in Christology is grounded in the Thomistic principle of the original identity of being and consciousness.[119] Thus every ontic Christological statement can be transposed into an ontological statement.

An ontological Christology views Jesus as existing "in a unity of wills with the Father which permeates his whole reality totally and from the outset."[120] Jesus's fundamental stance is to be given over to God radically and completely.

Rahner's claim that Jesus is the real symbol of God's universal salvific will requires that Jesus Christ be related to the experience of non-Christian religions. Writing from the stance of a Christian dogmatic theologian, Rahner sees the task of the his-

---

[116]Ibid., 295-98.

[117]Ibid., 299.

[118]Ibid., 302-04.

[119]Ibid., 303.

[120]Ibid., 303.

torian of religion as being "to discover Christ a posteriori in non-Christian religions insofar as this is possible."[121] According to Rahner the presence of Christ is found throughout the entire history of salvation, and thus it cannot be absent from non-Christian religions. When a non-Christian attains salvation, the non-Christian religions cannot be understood as not playing a role at all or as playing only a negative role. Non-Christian religions have the possibility and the obligation to awaken a person's relationship to the mystery of existence, however the mystery might be interpreted and concretized.[122]

Christ is present in non-Christian believers and religions in and through the Spirit. To explain the connection between the grace of the Spirit given everywhere and always and the historical event of the incarnation and cross, Rahner uses the scholastic notion of mutual causality. The incarnation and cross are the final cause of the Spirit, the goal of God's universal self-communication. The Spirit's self-communication is always oriented towards the one historical point where it becomes historically tangible and irreversible. Thus the Spirit is everywhere and always the Spirit of Jesus Christ.[123] On the other hand, the Spirit is the efficient cause of the incarnation and cross. The Spirit bears its own goal within itself as an intrinsic entelechy and the Spirit fully realizes its own essence as communicated to the world only in the incarnation and the cross. Because of the presence of the Spirit all faiths have an anticipation of the absolute saviour.[124]

---

[121]Ibid., 312. While this procedure may appear methodologically illegitimate to the historian of religions, it is interesting to note that Eliade comes very close to fulfilling Rahner's request: "One might even say that all hierophanies are simply prefigurations of the miracle of the Incarnation, that every hierophany is an abortive attempt to reveal the mystery of the coming together of God and man. . . . It does not, therefore, seem absurd in the least to study the nature of primitive hierophanies in the light of Christian theology." Mircea Eliade, Patterns in Comparative Religion, trans. Rosemary Sheed (New York: Meridian Books, 1963), 29.

[122]Foundations, 315.

[123]Ibid., 316-18.

[124]Ibid., 318-21.

94

Christ and the World-Process

Rahner's perspective on Christ and creation requires that the Christ-event be related to the entire world-process. Thus Rahner seeks to articulate an "inner affinity," "a sort of similarity of style" between Christology and an evolutionary view of the world.[125] Rahner finds biblical precedent for this approach in Colossians 1:15.[126] Rahner stresses that "the world is something in which everything is related to everything else."[127] The incarnation of the Logos is not a way for God to make "corrections as a kind of afterthought" but rather "appears as the ontologically (not merely 'morally', as an afterthought) unambiguous goal of the movement of creation as a whole."[128] Thus Rahner argues that "Christ has always been involved in the whole of history as its prospective entelechy."[129] In light of this relationship Rahner calls for a mutual interplay between ontology and Christology. On the one hand, Christological statements require "a general doctrine of creation (and the ontology contained in it)"; but on the other hand, Rahner calls for a "retrospective use" of Christology in ontology.[130] Our understanding of creation shapes our interpretation of Christ, but our experience of Christ re-shapes our understanding of the universe. One of the challenges to contemporary theology is to re-think the meaning of the traditional Christological dogmas in light of modern understanding of an evolving world-process. Once again, Rahner's perspective stresses the uniqueness of the Christ-event, but it also establishes the ground of continuity between the Christ-event and God's universal activity.

In approaching this project, Rahner recalls the anthropological starting point and the metaphysical analysis of spirit and matter developed in Spirit in the World and Hearers of the Word. Matter and spirit are two correlated elements never to be found

---

[125]Karl Rahner, "Christology within an Evolutionary View of the World," TI, V, 158; see also Foundations, 178-79. In this project Rahner proclaims his desire not to depend directly upon the work of Teilhard de Chardin, but he admits that some of his conclusions may be similar to Teilhard's theories ("Christology within an Evolutionary View," 159-60; Foundations, 180).

[126]"Current Problems in Christology," TI, I, 164-65.

[127]Ibid., 165.

[128]Ibid.

[129]Ibid., 167.

[130]Ibid., 166.

individually in isolation from each other: "We know what matter and spirit are only by starting from the one man and hence from his one self-realization, and . . . we must conceive of them from the outset as mutually related elements."[131] Rahner claims that natural science, because it abstracts methodically from the human person, does not know matter itself.[132] Matter, according to Rahner, is

> the condition of that otherness which estranges man from himself, which forms the requirement for the possibility of a direct intercommunication with other spiritual existents in space and time--i.e. in history.[133]

Spirit is the human person in the process of self-transcendence, "being lifted out of oneself and being drawn into the infinite mystery."[134]

The relationship between spirit and matter itself has a history, for "matter develops out its inner being in the direction of the spirit."[135] Finite reality has the possibility of real becoming, and this implies a power of active self-transcendence. This self-transcendence is dependent upon the power of God, but it is not simply received passively from God; it is an active empowering of finite reality itself, even to the point of reaching "what is substantially new, i.e. the leap to a higher nature."[136] There is one history of the cosmos, a history which involves matter and spirit inextricably together in a process of "becoming more."[137]

The link between Christ and the evolving process of the universe is to be found in the special role of the human spirit in evolution. The developing history of the cosmos "reaches its proper goal with and in the history of the human spirit."[138] In

---

[131]"Christology within an Evolutionary View," TI, V, 162.

[132]Ibid.

[133]Ibid., 163.

[134]Ibid.

[135]Ibid., 164.

[136]Ibid., 165.

[137]Ibid., 164.

[138]Ibid., 168.

the human spirit "nature does become conscious of itself."[139] The ultimate goal of the entire evolving process is the transcendence of finite reality through the human spirit into the absolute reality of God. In and through the consciousness of the human spirit the cosmos is able to be present to itself and be referred to its ultimate ground. The entire material cosmos becomes "as it were, the one body of the multifarious self-presence of this self-same cosmos and of its orientation to its absolute and infinite foundation."[140] The element of spirit in humans is not a "chance stranger" struggling against Nature but is the result of the cosmos itself pressing forward to self-presence.[141] Nonetheless, for the natural powers of the human person the goal of creation is always "hidden and unattainable": "It can be reached only by accepting the fact of its being hidden and withdrawn."[142]

Rahner seeks to integrate Christology into this developing cosmic process of increasing self-presence and self-transcendence. In this effort Rahner presupposes that "the goal of the world consists in God's communicating himself to it."[143] The cosmic striving for higher levels of consciousness and self-transcendence has been deliberately established by God "as the beginning and first step towards this self-communication and its acceptance by the world."[144] Jesus Christ as Saviour represents the beginning of God's absolute self-communication.[145] Rahner cautions that "beginning" in this context does not imply that God's self-communication "begins in time only with this person."[146] The process of God's self-communication is actually "co-existent with the whole spiritual history of humanity and of the world."[147] Christ has been at work in human history from the very beginning as the final cause, "the moving power of the movement towards the

---

[139]Ibid., 169.

[140]Ibid., 170.

[141]Ibid., 169-70.

[142]Ibid., 168.

[143]Ibid., 173.

[144]Ibid.

[145]Ibid., 174.

[146]Ibid., 175.

[147]Ibid.

goal."[148] What happens in Christ is that the goal of the entire cosmic process, God's self-communication "can be clearly recognized as something irrevocable, and in him it reaches its climax."[149] Christ as Saviour represents both God's self-communication and creation's acceptance. This perspective implies that creation and the incarnation are not two separate acts of God but rather form "two moments and phases" in the one "process of God's self-renunciation and self-expression into what is other than himself."[150] The incarnation is "an intrinsic and necessary element in the process of God's giving himself in grace to the world as a whole."[151] The incarnation represents the beginning of the divinization of the cosmos. While the hypostatic union is a unique event in the person of Christ, it reveals the goal of the entire cosmos. Thus Rahner finds in the hypostatic union an analogical clue to the nature of reality and the meaning of human existence. As always, Rahner maintains both poles of his Christology: continuity and similarity on the one hand, and finality, uniqueness, and absoluteness on the other.

Rahner accepts the Scotist view that the incarnation was the original purpose of God which anticipated the divine will both to create and to redeem.[152] For Rahner this in no way lessens the redemption from guilt and sin effected by the incarnation, but he interprets the divine power of forgiveness which is always present as becoming manifest in Christ:

> properly speaking, it is not Christ's action which causes God's will to forgiveness but vice versa, and this redemption in Christ . . . was already effective from the beginning of humanity.[153]

God's will to pardon and divinize humanity has always already embraced humankind from the beginning of history.

---

[148]Foundations, 195.

[149]"Christology within an Evolutionary View," TI, V, 175.

[150]Ibid., 177-78.

[151]Ibid., 180.

[152]Ibid., 184.

[153]Ibid., 186.

Rahner and Wisdom:
Christ and Creation

Rahner's relating of the Christ-event to universal human experience finds precedent in the Wisdom Christology of the New Testament. In relating Rahner's Christology to the biblical wisdom tradition it is important to be alert to both similarities and differences. While it would be anachronistic to read back later trinitarian speculations or evolutionary theories into the texts of the ancient sages, there are nonetheless both direct historical links and striking similarities between the wisdom tradition of Israel, the Wisdom Christology of the New Testament, and the Christology of Rahner.

The historical connections are borne by the continuous tradition of reading and reflecting upon the wisdom tradition in light of the experience of Jesus Christ. New Testament authors, early church fathers, and medieval theologians all read texts such as Proverbs 8, Ben Sira 24, and the Wisdom of Solomon 6-9 as referring to the revelation of God in Jesus Christ. These texts provided a stimulus for reflection on the relation of Christ to the universal ordering principle of creation and form part of the context for Rahner's cosmic Christology.

The differences between Rahner and the wisdom tradition are obvious and striking. The sages nowhere developed an extensive metaphysics of knowledge or a philosophical theory of human consciousness; they never approached Rahner's vision of a cosmic process of evolution towards greater and greater self-consciousness and self-transcendence. The similarities between Rahner and the wisdom tradition are always similarities in difference.

It is also important to remember and respect the diversity of viewpoints within the wisdom tradition itself. The Hebrew Bible and the Septuagint do not identify Lady Wisdom with God, and so there is no question of interpreting Lady Wisdom in these texts as a real symbol of Yahweh in the immanent, trinitarian sense of Rahner's term. Nonetheless, there is in some texts a certain analogy between the relationship of Lady Wisdom and God and Rahner's concept of real symbol.

We have noted the philological dispute over the translation of Proverbs 8:22.[154] In von Rad's view Lady Wisdom is a creature, not equal to Yahweh, but she is the expression of God outside of God's self, the way humans experience the working of God: "So wisdom truly is the form in which Jahweh makes himself present and

---

[154]Supra, 12-13.

in which he wishes to be sought by man."[155] In Vawter's interpretation, Lady Wisdom in both Proverbs 8 and Job 28 is not a creature or an attribute of God "but rather a possession which [God] (unlike man) has acquired."[156] On this reading the origins of Lady Wisdom are left unexplained; she "comes to Yahweh from without."[157] According to Vawter, Lady Wisdom is not an internally generated expression of God but rather an externally discovered model for God's creative activity. On this reading Proverbs 8:22 means "that Yahweh took possession of a wisdom that he then proceeded to utilize in his work of creation."[158] There can be no question of comparing such an independent figure to what Rahner calls a real symbol of God.

While Vawter's philological arguments cast doubt on von Rad's reading of Proverbs 8:22, von Rad's formulation does capture the significance of Lady Wisdom in Ben Sira and the Wisdom of Solomon. The later Jewish wisdom tradition moves closer in the direction of Rahner's real symbol. In Ben Sira 24:3 Lady Wisdom comes forth from the mouth of the Most High. While she is created by God (24:8), she is an expression of God who reveals God to humans and offers abundant fruits and sweet memories and inheritances (24:19-20). In the Wisdom of Solomon Lady Wisdom is again an expression of God, a "pure emanation of the glory of the Almighty" (7:25). Lady Wisdom is very closely associated with God but never identified as God. However, she does appear as the way God is experienced by humans. The activities of leading and saving the people of Israel in chapters 10-19 are attributed variously to God and Lady Wisdom with little change in meaning.

Philo also views Lady Wisdom or the Logos as an expression or emanation from God, comparable to a ray of light proceeding from the sun.[159] For Philo Lady Wisdom is the expression of God outside of Godself who reveals God to humans.

The influence of the wisdom tradition on the New Testament was particularly important in relating the experience of Jesus Christ to the ordering power of creation and thereby claiming universal significance for the revelation of God in him. Lightfoot's and Dodd's interpretations of John's Gospel provide a direct link between the Wisdom Christology of the New Testament and

---

[155]Von Rad, Old Testament Theology, I, 444.

[156]"Prov 8:22: Wisdom and Creation," 205.

[157]Ibid., 206.

[158]Ibid., 215.

[159]Quaestiones in Genesim IV, 2; see Goodenough, 33.

the Christology of Rahner. Rahner's understanding of Christ as the real symbol of the universal salvific will of God is a development of Lightfoot's reading of John: "the Lord's ministry is the relations, written small, of the Logos with mankind."[160]

The central wisdom-texts of the New Testament (such as 1 Cor 8:6, Col 1:14-20; Jn 1:1-18) establish a very close relationship between the ordering power of creation and the experience of revelation and redemption in Christ. In these texts Christ or the Logos is at work throughout the cosmos from the very beginning of creation, long before the birth of the historical figure, Jesus of Nazareth. The life, death, and resurrection of Jesus reveal, illumine, and make present this universal activity. Grant has commented on the Prologue of John,

> the authentic clue to the meaning of creation has been revealed in Jesus of Nazareth. . . . Since Jesus came from God to give both life and light to men, he obviously manifested God's original purpose of giving life and light; the light and life at the end can be no different from the light and life at the beginning.[161]

This linkage between creation and Christ offers precedent for Rahner's vision of "creation and Incarnation as two moments and two phases of the one process of God's self-giving and self-expression."[162]

Rahner's integration of Christology into an evolutionary world-view clearly moves beyond anything envisioned by the ancient sages or the New Testament writers. And yet there is within the wisdom tradition an interest in the order of the physical universe and an openness to using forms of thought which come from diverse sources. The Wisdom of Solomon made use of Hellenistic philosophy to develop the presentation of Lady Wisdom. Moreover, it was a fundamental principle of the wisdom tradition that there is a close link between understanding the order of the world and the activity of God. King Solomon "spoke of trees, from the cedar that is in Lebanon to the hyssop that grows out of the well; he spoke also of beasts and of birds and of reptiles and of fish" (1 Kgs 4:33). One of Solomon's later admirers claimed to have learned

---

[160]Lightfoot, 81; cf. Dodd, 285.

[161]Early Christian Doctrine of God, 57.

[162]Foundations, 197.

the structure of the world and the properties of the
    elements,
the beginning, end and middle of the times,
the alternation of the solstices and the succession of the
    seasons,
the revolutions of the year and the positions of the stars,
the natures of animals and the instincts of wild beasts,
the powers of spirits and the mental processes of men,
the varieties of plants and the medical properties of roots

from God through Lady Wisdom, "who designed them all" (Wis 7:17-
21). The New Testament's identification of Christ as the power
through whom all things are created and remain in being offers an
invitation to relating the experience of Jesus Christ to the ordering power of creation. By integrating his Christology into an
evolutionary view of the world, Rahner is giving a contemporary,
dynamic interpretation of the New Testament's presentation of
Jesus as Lady Wisdom.

Lady Wisdom appears in various aspects: she is the ordering
power of creation, the principle of intelligibility in the cosmos;
she is the expression of God, the way humans experience God; and
she is specially revealed in historical moments in the experience
of Israel and in Jesus Christ. Rahner's Christology integrates
each of these aspects into his conception of the Logos as the
principle of intelligibility of Being, as the universal revelation
of God, and as unsurpassably and definitively revealed in Jesus
Christ.

Language

In moving from the biblical wisdom tradition to Rahner, there
is a shift in the literary genre and in the level of abstractness
of the discussion. Rahner's theological language is second-order
discourse which seeks to retrieve and interpret the biblical language. As Louis Roberts notes, Rahner's theological method is
fundamentally hermeneutical.[163] Rahner's method begins by as-
suming the truth of the Bible and the fidelity of the defined
teaching of the Catholic tradition to the biblical revelation.[164]

---

[163]Roberts, 7-8.

[164]See Karl Rahner, "The Development of Dogma," TI, I, 39-77;
idem, "Considerations on the Development of Dogma," TI, IV, 3-35;
idem, "What Is a Dogmatic Statement?" TI, V, 42-66; idem, "Exegesis and Dogmatic Theology," TI, V, 67-93; idem, "Theology and
Anthropology," TI, IX, 28-45.

Rahner then asks about the meaning of this tradition for contemporary self-understanding. Crucial to Rahner's method is the claim of continuity in development between the language of the Bible and his own contemporary language. Both the sages of ancient Israel and Rahner stressed the importance of the proper use of language.

I will begin this section by discussing Rahner's understanding of the character of language about God. Then I will examine his view of the role of dogmatic language in Christological claims. Finally, I will explore the relation between Rahner's perspective on language and the use of language by the wisdom tradition.

Language about God

For Rahner the category of mystery and the doctrine of the incomprehensibility of God are crucial to interpreting language about God. Rahner understands every theological statement as "a statement into the mystery."[165] However, Rahner protests against the concept of mystery that was common in Catholic neo-scholastic thought before Vatican II. According to this conception mystery is viewed as "the property of a statement" which is only "provisionally incomprehensible" to human reason.[166] This view distinguishes "truths of natural reason which can be 'seen', 'comprehended' and 'demonstrated'" from mysteries (in the plural) which "can be guaranteed only by a divine communication."[167] Thus for much of the neo-scholastic tradition, ratio serves as the criterion by which a multitude of mysteries can be identified.[168]

In opposition to this understanding of mystery, Rahner retrieves the Thomistic theme of the incomprehensibility of God in the beatific vision. Rahner insists that the perduring incomprehensibility of God is not a "regrettably permanent limitation of

---

[165]Karl Rahner and Karl Lehmann, Kerygma and Dogma, trans. William Glen-Doepel (New York: Herder & Herder, 1969), 96; see also Bacik, 20-47.

[166]Karl Rahner, "The Concept of Mystery in Catholic Theology," TI, IV, 38.

[167]Ibid., 38-39.

[168]Ibid., 40.

our blessed comprehension of God"; rather it is "the very substance of our vision and the very object of our blissful love."[169]
Thus mystery is the final object of the supreme act of knowledge
and constitutes the ultimate fulfillment of the human spirit.
Mystery is "the goal where reason arrives when it attains its
perfection by becoming love."[170] Reason, far from being the criterion for judging mysteries, becomes for Rahner "a defective mode
of a knowledge which is essentially orientated to the mystery as
such."[171]

Ultimately, there is only one mystery which is the reality of
God experienced by the human spirit. In this relationship knowledge is confronted by a fundamental choice: "mystery . . . forces
knowledge either to be more than itself or to despair."[172] Human
knowledge is challenged to acknowledge and accept its own limits
and to surrender to the "sovereign and all-embracing exigence
which cannot be mastered, comprehended or challenged."[173] This
surrender is more an act of love than of knowledge, and so Rahner
affirms that "in Christianity the last word is with love and not
knowledge."[174]

Rahner's concept of mystery imposes a special challenge upon
the proper use of language about God. Since God is experienced as
the infinite horizon of human experience, "the Whither of transcendence," God is always "the nameless, the indefinable, the unattainable."[175] The non-objective "whither" towards which the
human spirit reaches is "a nameless region beyond all categories."[176] The experience of God is always a limit-experience
which is not subject to any further limit: "The ultimate measure
cannot be measured; the boundary which delimits all things cannot
be bounded by a still more distant limit."[177] Thus all human
names and concepts for God must be understood as intrinsically

---

[169]Ibid., 41.

[170]Ibid., 43.

[171]Ibid., 42.

[172]Ibid., 43.

[173]Ibid.

[174]Ibid.

[175]Ibid., 50.

[176]Ibid., 42.

[177]Ibid., 51.

inadequate and must be interpreted in light of the experience of transcendence towards the infinite horizon which is beyond all determination.

> One can only speak correctly of God when he is conceived as the infinite. . . . . All conceptual expressions about God, necessary though they are, always stem from the unobjectivated experience of transcendence as such: the concept from the pre-conception, the name from the experience of the nameless.[178]

In the transcendental experience of God there is a paradoxical coincidence of presence and absence, and thus language about this experience must in some way evoke an awareness of silence. God is always present as the condition of possibility of the knowledge of finite objects; but "the Whither of transcendence is there in its own proper way of aloofness and absence. It bestows itself upon us by refusing itself, by keeping silence, by staying afar."[179] Even in the experience of divinizing grace and the beatific vision, the mystery is not dissolved but intensified. Grace is "the grace of the _nearness_ of the _abiding_ mystery."[180]

Rahner's insistence on the primordial, transcendental character of our experience of God and on the perduring dimension of mystery has far-reaching effects on the use of religious language. For Rahner the conceptual content of a theological statement must be understood as the medium which points to what is beyond anything that is namable. The essential function of a theological statment is mystagogic: "it induces the experience, in grace, of the absolute mystery."[181] Thus the proper use of theological language for Rahner can be understood as a form of _Bildung_. The names and concepts that we predicate of God function properly when they form us and re-orient our lives by opening us to the presence of the nameless mystery. Thus theological language not only speaks of the mystery, "but does it correctly only if it is also a

---

178_Ibid._, 50.

179_Ibid._, 52.

180_Ibid._, 56; see also Karl Rahner, "Thomas Aquinas on the Incomprehensibility of God," _JR_ 58 Supplement (1978):S109-16.

181_Kerygma and Dogma_, 98; on the mystagogic element in Rahner's thought, see James J. Bacik, _Apologetics and the Eclipse of Mystery: Mystagogy According to Karl Rahner_ (Notre Dame, Ind.: University of Notre Dame Press, 1980), 20-47, and Fischer, 365-99.

kind of indication of how to come face to face with the mystery oneself."[182]

Rahner insists on the analogical character of language about God; he notes that "analogy, properly understood, is the basic structure of Catholic theology and hence also of the dogmatic statement."[183] We can only speak of the transcendental experience of God by using "secondary and categorical concepts which are contraries within the realm of the categorical."[184] Thus every statement about God is "dialectical and dipolar."[185] God can be named analogically from created reality because God is its ground, but God is never experienced as one object alongside of others, and thus God "cannot be incorporated into a common and antecedent system with what is grounded."[186]

Analogical language arises from the tension between our transcendental experience of God and our categorical knowledge of individual objects; its meaning is created by the interaction, even conflict between interpretations on these two levels. Thus it is impossible to reduce analogy to univocal language. We cannot translate analogical language into another type of language "which it really means." For Rahner analogical language is more primordial and true than the statements of science and everyday life.[187] Analogy is not only a property of language; it is also the "original relationship in which we are related to the term of our transcendence."[188] This relationship is the ground for all language about God and is also the condition of possibility of our knowledge of finite objects. Thus Rahner can claim that it is actually our analogical understanding of Being that grounds our univocal comprehension of individual objects.[189]

---

[182]Kerygma and Dogma, 98.

[183]Ibid.

[184]Foundations, 71.

[185]Ibid., 72.

[186]Ibid., 73.

[187]See Rike, II, 412-34.

[188]Foundations, 73.

[189]Karl Rahner and Herbert Vorgrimler, Theological Dictionary, trans. Richard Strachan (New York: Herder & Herder, 1965), 18.

Rahner's perspective on analogy is based upon his metaphysics of knowledge. For Rahner the transcendence of the human spirit reaching out for the infinite is the condition of possibility of human knowledge.[190] Only because the _Vorgriff_ reaches out for absolute Being can the human intellect grasp the quiddities of finite beings; every categorical judgement about a particular existent is based upon a transcendental relationship to the infinite horizon which is absolute Being. Since this transcendental relationship is never experienced directly and explicitly as one object alongside of others, it can never be directly and univocally described. Words can evoke some awareness of our transcendental relationship to Being, but they can never present this relationship as a direct of object of knowledge.[191]

There is a strong negative emphasis in Rahner's use of analogy. Rahner accepts the principle of Thomas Aquinas that the height of our understanding of God is to understand that we do not understand:

> Since our mind is not proportionate to the divine substance, that which is the substance of God remains beyond our intellect and so is unknown to us. Hence the supreme knowledge which man has of God is to know that he does not know God, in so far as he knows that what God is surpasses all that we can understand of him.[192]

For Rahner, as for Aquinas, we never comprehend the divine essence either in this life or in the beatific vision in heaven, and so we do not properly comprehend what our words about God mean.[193] Even the knowledge offered by the revelation of God in Christ does not produce God as an empirical object for inspection or as a form which our intellect can comprehend.

The analogical language of Aquinas and Rahner, like the metaphorical language studied by Ricoeur, sets up a tension within the copula. Every true predication of God involves both "is" and "is not." This tension twists and extends the meaning of our statements so that they can be applied to God. Even perfection terms, which are more properly true of God than of created reality, are known to us only through created reality; in predicating them of

---

[190]_HW_, 76-86.

[191]See Rike, I, 161-259.

[192]Thomas Aquinas, _De Potentia_, q. 7, a. 5; quoted by Rahner, "Concept of Mystery," _TI_, IV, 58-59.

[193]Rahner, "Thomas Aquinas on the Incomprehensibility of God," S107-09.

God we can affirm their truth in God but we know their meaning only from creatures. Thus our statements about God have two opposed interpretations, one concerning creatures and a different yet related interpretation concerning God.

Ricoeur has noted both the similarity and the difference between the analogical language of Aquinas, which Rahner accepts, and metaphorical statements:

> It is therefore the res significata that is in excess in relation to the nominis significatio. This splintering of the name and its signification corresponds to the extension of meaning by which words, in metaphorical statements, can satisfy unusual attribution. In this sense, one can speak of an effect of metaphorical meaning within analogy.[194]

There is, of course, no question of simply identifying analogy and metaphor. Ricoeur himself has noted that analogy and metaphor, though very similar, remain distinct predicative operations. Analogy "rests on the predication of transcendental terms, [metaphors] on the predication of meanings that carry their material content with them."[195]

Rahner himself views all language about God as very closely related to poetic language. He suggests that great poetry has "an inner kinship" to Christianity.[196] An openness and sensitivity to poetic language is a presupposition, a prerequisite for hearing the word proclaimed by Christianity.[197] Ideally, "the perfect priest and the perfect poet are one and the same."[198]

---

[194]Rule of Metaphor, 279.

[195]Ibid., 280. In a similar vein, Burrell has noted the "irreducibly metaphorical dimension in analogous expressions" and has argued that even though Aquinas distinguished "obviously metaphorical expressions from those more properly used of God, [he] was not afraid to acknowledge a metaphorical dimension in these latter terms as well." David Burrell, Aquinas: God and Action (Notre Dame: University of Notre Dame Press, 1979), 56-57. McInerny also argues that while there is a real distinction between analogy and metaphor for Thomas, nonetheless in a certain sense analogy may be seen as a kind of metaphor and metaphor may be seen as a kind of analogy. Ralph McInerny, Studies in Analogy (The Hague: Martinus Nijhoff, 1968), 81-84.

[196]Karl Rahner, "Poetry and the Christian," TI, IV, 365.

[197]Ibid., 363.

[198]Karl Rahner, "Priest and Poet," TI, III, 294.

In reflecting on poetic language, Rahner distinguishes "utility words" from "primordial words" (<u>Urworte</u>).[199] Primordial words cannot be defined and limited, for they "always whisper something about everything."[200] Like seashells, they allow us to hear the sound of the "ocean of infinity."[201] Primordial words bring us to the experience of mystery and open us to unfathomable depths of reality. Such words have an essentially religious dimension, for "they are children of God, who possess something of the luminous darkness of their Father."[202] They come to us as "gifts of God, not creations of men."[203]

The same word can function variously as both a utility word and a primordial word. The "water" of the chemist is far different from the "water" of Francis of Assisi or Goethe; according to Rahner, the religious and poetic uses of "water" are more concrete and original and true than the scientific precision of the chemist's H_2O: "the 'water' of the chemist is much rather a narrowed down, technified derivation of a secondary kind from the water of man."[204]

The vagueness of primordial words is essential to their evocative power. They cannot be defined and analysed. "They can only be taken apart by being killed."[205] Primordial words evoke a sense of mystery, an awareness "of the whole in the part and the part in the whole."[206] Rooted in the transcendence of the human spirit for the infinite, primordial words live on the limits of human experience; they are "words of an endless crossing of bor-

---

[199]Ibid., 296.

[200]Ibid., 297.

[201]Ibid., 295-96.

[202]Ibid., 297.

[203]Ibid., 296.

[204]Ibid.; it is interesting to note Whitehead's similar insistence that poetry is more concrete than science. See Alfred North Whitehead, <u>Science and the Modern World</u> (New York: Free Press, 1967), 75-94 (hereafter cited as <u>SMW</u>).

[205]"Priest and Poet," <u>TI</u>, III, 297.

[206]Ibid.

ders," words which open for us a door "into the unfathomable depths of true reality in general."[207]

A primordial word is an efficacious presentation of the reality it evokes: "it brings the reality it signifies to us, makes it 'present', realizes it and places it before us. . . . [S]omething happens: the advent of the thing itself to the listener."[208]

Rahner further suggests that this presentation affects not only the knower but also the object known. Because of the metaphysical principle of being and intelligibility, all realities, according to Rahner, "have a dynamic drive to fulfill themselves by being known."[209] According to the analogy of Seinshabe, existents have being to the degree that they can know and be known. Therefore, "all realities sigh for their own unveiling."[210] The word of the poet is "the sacrament by means of which realities communicate themselves to man, in order to achieve their own destiny."[211]

The words of religious language, like the primordial words of poetry, evoke a sense of our relationship to the whole and call us into the experience of mystery. The function of the word in Christianity is to evoke the incomprehensibility of God and thereby "call us out of the little house of our homely, close-hugged

---

[207]Ibid., 298.

[208]Ibid., 299. Rahner's stress on the quasi-sacramental efficacy of the poetic word refutes Wood's charge that for Rahner "language has an almost negligible impact upon our existential orientation. Language . . . is too lifeless and too remote from the center of our existence to have any creative role in shaping that orientation itself." Charles M. Wood, "Karl Rahner on Theological Discourse," Journal of Ecumenical Studies 12(1975):66. Wood mistakes Rahner's clear distinction between language and transcendental experience for a "fundamental alienation" (p. 66). On the contrary, Rahner finds a power in language which can decisively re-orient our fundamental stance by making present the dimension of mystery which envelopes us.

[209]"Priest and Poet," TI, III, 300.

[210]Ibid.

[211]Ibid., 301. It is interesting to note the similarity of this perspective to Gadamer's claim that realities come to exist more fully when they are re-presented in a work of art (Gadamer, 103).

truths into the strangeness of the night that is our real home."[212]

The Role of Dogmatic Language
in Christology

Rahner's understanding of language about God forms the context for his interpretation of the role and function of dogmatic language in Christological claims. We have seen that Rahner understands the Christ-event to manifest the universal salvific will of God. This claim sets up a special relationship between one segment of finite reality, the life, death, and resurrection of Jesus, and the transcendent horizon of all experience, the "nameless region beyond all categories."[213] This claim makes special demands upon language.

Rahner sees dogmatic language in general as hermeneutical and mystagogical. The Catholic doctrine of the closing of revelation with the end of the apostolic age guarantees the hermeneutical character of later church teaching.[214] The later decisions of the Church's magisterium make no claim to be original revelation but seek to interpret the biblical revelation.

In accordance with his view of mystery, Rahner cautions against understanding this revelation as "the communication of a definite number of propositions, a numerical sum."[215] Revelation is not a set number of truths but rather "a saving Happening" which reaches its climax in Jesus Christ: "God himself has definitively given himself to the world."[216] All dogmatic language is an attempt to interpret this saving event. This event surpasses the capacity of all human language, and so Rahner insists that even dogmatic statements must be interpreted as finite, as unable to "declare the whole of a reality."[217]

---

[212]"Poetry and the Christian," TI IV, 359.

[213]"Concept of Mystery," TI, IV, 42.

[214]"Development of Dogma," TI, I, 48-49; see also "Considerations on the Development of Dogma," TI, IV, 3.

[215]"Development of Dogma," TI, I, 48.

[216]Ibid.

[217]Ibid., 43.

111

Dogmas give a reflexive interpretation to an event which sur-passes all description. Rahner compares this process to a lover who attempts to describe the experience of love: "He 'knows' much more about it than he can 'state'. The clumsy stammerings of his love-letters are paltry and miserable compared to this knowl-edge."[218] Rahner distinguishes "the original, non-propositional, unreflexive yet conscious possession of a reality" from the "re-flexive (propositional), articulated consciousness of this origi-nal consciousness."[219] The two dimensions of consciousness are always found together but are never fused into one. There is no experience without at least some level of explicitly conscious self-reflective awareness; and yet our explicit awareness always arises from a broader, vaguer, and more fundamental non-reflexive experience. There is a constant mutual interaction between the two dimensions of experience. The explicit articulation modifies the originating experience, and the originating experience nour-ishes the ongoing explicit articulation.

Rahner suggests that the early church's experience of Christ was a global, non-reflexive yet conscious experience of a reality which surpasses reflexive articulation:

Christ, as the living link between God and the world . . . is the objective content of an experience which is more elemen-tal and concentrated, simpler and yet richer than the indi-vidual propositions coined in an attempt to express this experience--an attempt which can in principle never be final-ly successful.[220]

The later dogmatic formulations of the church seek to articulate this primordial experience, but they pay a price in the loss of directness of communication; Rahner cautions that

greater reflexive articulateness of a spiritual possession is nearly always purchased at the cost of a partial loss in unhampered communication . . . with the reality given in faith.[221]

Nonetheless, Rahner insists that there is for us no possibility of a "romantic" return to the direct simplicity of the first genera-tion of Christians. Every succeeding generation must grasp the reality through the mediation of tradition. Where Gadamer claims

---

[218]Ibid., 63.

[219]Ibid., 64-65.

[220]Ibid., 65.

[221]Ibid., 67.

112

that "we understand in a different way, if we understand at all,"[222] Rahner maintains that "we must possess this fullness [of the apostolic consciousness in faith] in a different way."[223] To possess this fullness of apostolic consciousness requires an original act of interpretation on the part of each succeeding generation. Rahner assumes that the dogmas defined by the Catholic tradition are faithful to the revelation of God in Christ, but he denies that these dogmas themselves can tell us precisely what they do and do not mean. Dogmas, like all human propositions, call for interpretation.

According to Rahner, every human proposition points beyond itself to a content, but no human proposition can be pinned down exactly to a clear and distinct content: "its reflexive interpretation does not allow us to state adequately and exhaustively all that is concomitantly stated and known in it and all that is not."[224] A proposition is not a fixed "package with sharply defined contents"; it is much more "a kind of window through which a view may be gained of the thing itself."[225] There is always something "more" beyond the unambiguous minimum of the proposition's content which eludes precise definition. Rahner acknowledges what Ricoeur would call a "surplus of meaning" which goes beyond the explicit, reflexive intention of the speaker and illumines the reality described.[226]

---

[222]Gadamer, 264.

[223]"Development of Dogma," TI, I, 67. On the relation between Gadamer and Rahner, see Vincent P. Branick, An Ontology of Understanding: Karl Rahner's Metaphysics of Knowledge in the Context of Modern German Hermeneutics (St. Louis, Mo.: Marianist Communications Center, 1974).

[224]"Development of Dogma," TI, I, 69.

[225]Ibid.

[226]Ibid., 69-70; see also Ricoeur, Interpretation Theory, 45-88. Rahner and Ricoeur both refuse to restrict the meaning of a text to the explicit, conscious intention of the author. Where Ricoeur, following Gadamer, develops a non-romantic theory of hermeneutics, Rahner usually uses the theory of global, non-reflexive consciousness to include more in the "implicit" meaning than the author explicitly intended. However, Rahner also acknowledges that there may be valid implications which the speaker was not aware of even in non-reflexive, global consciousness ("Development of Dogma," 70). As Branick notes, Rahner shares significant emphases with the Schleiermacher-Dilthey school of hermeneutics, but also resembles Gadamer in important ways (Branick, 187-243).

Rahner argues that this human process of understanding occurs in the interpretation of revelation in Christ. In interpreting the language of the Bible and the dogmatic formulations of the tradition "we cannot ignore the irreducible distinction between what is explicitly stated on the hand, and what is co-present in mind and com-municated on the other."[227]

Within this framework of interpretation Rahner posits a process of authentic identity amid genuine development in the history of dogma.[228] Since humans are historical knowers and since God's revelation appears in history, the handing on of the revelation which constitutes traditio necessarily takes place in historical fashion. The dogmatic assertion, like all lasting human communications, remains the same only by changing in relation to different periods: "what is said undergoes a history in the utterance; it is not a mere repetition of the same thing."[229] On the one hand, the process of continued reflection leads to greater articulation of and penetration into the reality so that "the object [of faith] is necessarily displayed ever more fully in its virtualities."[230] However, on the other hand, there is a contrary process at work: "the history of theology is by no means just the history of the progress of doctrine, but also a history of forgetting."[231] It is the intersection and intertwining of these two conflicting tendencies that constitutes the concrete process of traditio.

The language of dogma bears a special relation to Christology, for the principle of the union of the human and the divine in Christ is analogically true of the human word of revelation. A human word can only convey the word of God by remaining a human word: "It is as in Christology: the divinity grows in equal, not inverse, proportion to the humanity."[232]

Applying these perspectives to Christology, Rahner views dogmatic Christological claims as more of a beginning than an

---

[227]"Development of Dogma," TI, I, 72.

[228]"Considerations on the Development of Dogma," TI, IV, 5, 19.

[229]Ibid., 24.

[230]Ibid., 25.

[231]"Current Problems in Christology," TI, I, 151.

[232]"Considerations on the Development of Dogma," TI, IV, 18.

end.[233] The dogmatic formulations of Christology must transcend themselves and serve as "an opening into the immeasurable, a beginning of the illimitable."[234] The incomprehensibility of God functions as a hermeneutical principle for interpreting Christological dogma; we only know God when we know the incomprehensibility of God. This recognition occurs in an experience of limits, "at that point, then, in which comprehension and the determining limits of what is known are jointly transcended in the Incomprehensible and the Unlimited."[235]

Within the Chalcedonian Christological formula itself there is a movement of transcendence at work which leads us beyond any linguistic formulation

> so that through it we might draw near to the ineffable, unapproachable, nameless God, whose will it was that we should find him in Jesus Christ and through Christ seek him.[236]

There is in fact a double hermeneutical principle operative in the interpretation of Chalcedon. First, the dogma of Chalcedon necessarily qualifies its own clear and articulate formulation by transcending itself and leading us into the incomprehensibility of God; secondly, the dogma refers us back to the biblical revelation from which it arose and "never claims to be an adequate condensation of Biblical teaching."[237]

The incomprehensibility of God radically undercuts any human claim on God and leaves the Christian with the unsettling result, in Rahner's words, of being "the true and most radical skeptic."[238] According to Rahner, "no individual truth is really true except in the process . . . in which the truth becomes a question which remains unanswered because it is asking about God and his incomprehensibility."[239] Thus the Christian must admit that "one can hold no opinion to be completely true and no opinion to be

---

233"Current Problems in Christology," TI, I, 149.

234Ibid.

235Ibid.

236Ibid., 150.

237Ibid., 154.

238"Thomas Aquinas on the Incomprehensibility of God," S125.

239Ibid.

completely false."[240] It would seem that Rahner here is laying down a basic hermeneutical principle which tells us how all truth-claims, including the truth-claims of dogma, are to be understood. For Rahner the question of human being, the question which plunges us into the incomprehensibility of God, is more primordial than any answer, even the true answer given by Christology. Even the saving truth of the revelation of God in Christ "becomes a question which remains unanswered because it is asking about God and his incomprehensibility."[241]

Rahner and Wisdom:
The Play of Language

In responding to Rahner's lecture, "Thomas Aquinas on the Incomprehensibility of God," Ricoeur suggested that there is an analogy between the theological doctrine of the incomprehensibility of God in Aquinas and Rahner and the clash of biblical genres of language about God. Ricoeur posed the question: "Is not the incomprehensibility of God already presented [in the Bible] by the mere clash of the opposed ways of speaking of God?"[242] The teachers of the wisdom tradition expressed an awareness of the incomprehensibility of God in their own varied uses of language. We turn now to the analogies between the use of language by the wisdom tradition and by Rahner. I will first examine the incomprehensibility of God as a hermeneutical principle and the dialectic of disclosure and concealment; then I will discuss the role of language in formation for Rahner and the sages.

We have seen that the incomprehensibility of God and the dimension of mystery function as a basic hermeneutical principle for Rahner, offering guidance on how all religious language is to be understood. The sages expressed a similar awareness in the refrain of the wisdom tradition: "The fear of Yahweh is the beginning of wisdom" (Prov 9:10; cf. Prov 1:7; 15:33; Sir 1:14, 27; 32:14; Job 28:28; Ps 111:10). The sages' admonition, "Do not think of yourself as wise" (Prov 3:7), offers the student a clue to how the entire wisdom tradition is to be understood. Von Rad has stressed the mysterious character of God and the world for the wisdom tradition; he comments: "Israel was obliged to remain open . . . to the category of the mysterious."[243] The path of wisdom

---

[240]Ibid.

[241]Ibid.

[242]"'Response' to Karl Rahner's Lecture," S129.

[243]Wisdom, 73.

116

was a "way taken by knowledge along the frontier of the mysterious."[244]

The sages always offered their insights into the patterns of experience and the regularity of the order implanted by God in creation in the context of the limits of human understanding and the incomprehensibility of God. In the Book of Job God prefers the "empty-headed words" of Job which obscure God's designs (38:2) to the clear and consistent theories of Job's friends (42:7). The experience of Lady Wisdom herself is a dialectic of disclosure and concealment expressed by the clash between Proverbs 8 and Job 28. Qoheleth (7:23-24) and Ben Sira (11:4; 18:6-7) both express the dilemma of an order present in the world but hidden from human understanding.

Ricoeur's suggestion that the clash of biblical perspectives articulates the incomprehensibility of God is applicable within the wisdom tradition itself. The conflicting interpretations of the various wisdom books point to the inadequacy of any single formulation of human experience.

The language of Jesus in the Synoptic tradition also implies a sense of the incomprehensibility of God. The "reversal of expectations" which Crossan has emphasized in the parables renders precarious any human explanation of God.[245] Even in the revelation of Christ as the incarnation of Lady Wisdom, there appears to be a dialectic of disclosure and concealment. Paul stresses the tremendous paradox of the wisdom of God appearing in the figure of Christ crucified (1 Cor 1:17-25). While Christ is the wisdom of God, he is not recognized as such either by the "masters of our age" (1 Cor 2:8) or by the Jews and Greeks (1 Cor 1:22-25). Even though Jesus appears as the epiphany of the Logos in the Gospel of John, he is not recognized by the world or even by "his own" (Jn 1:10-11). Rahner's Christology also involves a dialectic of disclosure and concealment. The human nature of Jesus, as the real symbol of the Logos, is the revelation of God to humankind; and yet God remains hidden even in this revelation. The ontology of real symbol implies that there is no direct path to knowledge of any reality, including God. Even God must communicate with humans through the medium of a symbol, a symbol in which God is both hidden and revealed. Rahner acknowledges that the claims of Christology are not unambiguously evident to humans, and so there

---

[244]Ibid.

[245]In Parables, 53-78.

117

can be an explicit, reasoned rejection of the language of Christianity without any guilt.[246] Because God is hidden even in Christ, non-Christians and non-believers can explicitly and reflexively refuse Christ even at the same time that they are implicitly accepting God's offer of grace and love on a non-reflexive, transcendental level.

The incomprehensibility of God and the dialectic of disclosure and concealment force religious language to a paradoxical intersection of affirmation and negation. As we have noted, Ricoeur's study of metaphor has stressed the paradoxical coincidence of "is" and "is not" in metaphors.[247] A similar paradoxical intersection appears in the wisdom tradition and Rahner.

The teacher of wisdom claims both to be and not to be wise. Lady Wisdom both is (Prov 8) and is not (Job 28) revealed in ordinary experience. For the wisdom tradition there is a justice-loving world-order operative in human experience (Prov), and yet there is no evidence of any such order (Job, Qoh). For the Wisdom of Solomon, Lady Wisdom "deploys her strength from one end of the earth to the other, ordering all things for good" (8:1); and yet the world of our experience appears utterly chaotic, ruled by idols and dominated by evil:

> Everywhere a welter of blood and murder, theft and fraud,
> corruption, treachery, riots, perjury,
> disturbance of decent people, forgetfulness of favours,
> pollution of souls, sins against nature,
> disorder in marriage, adultery, debauchery (14:25-26).

Lady Wisdom is manifest in Christ, and yet she is not at all manifest to the many who reject Christ in the Gospel of John and 1 Corinthians.

As we have seen, Rahner's understanding of analogical language about God is also dominated by the paradoxical intertwining of "is" and "is not." The use of analogy as an explicit theme enters Christian theology at least in part through the wisdom tradition, for it is the Wisdom of Solomon which offers the fundamental principle: "through the grandeur and beauty of the creatures we may by analogy (analogōs) contemplate their Author" (13:5).

The paradoxes and metaphors of the ancient sages and the analogical language of Rahner and Aquinas are forms of semantic

---

[246]Foundations, 277; "Atheism and Implicit Christianity," TI, IX, 145-64.

[247]Interpretation Theory, 45-69.

impertinence. They create a tension between opposing meanings which cannot be simply resolved into univocal clarity. They tease our minds into grasping similarities in dissimilarities and into considering how we do and do not understand ourselves, our world, and our God. Both the sages and Rahner believe strongly in the intelligibility of the universe and the possibility of insight into our experience. Yet within the wisdom tradition and within the theology of Rahner there lurk fundamental ambiguities which in principle cannot be completely clarified. Both the sages and Rahner call attention to the inadequacy of language to grasp reality and thus leave their students with the unsettling awareness of their own limits and ignorance.

While language can never fully and adequately describe God, both the sages and Rahner trust that the proper use of language can shape and form humans for a proper response to God. The effect of the recognition of the incomprehensibility of God and the limits of language is to transform the individual and make easier an acceptance of God. The poems of Lady Wisdom, like the primordial words of Rahner, evoke a sense of our relationship to the whole and, in Rahner's words, "whisper something about everything."[248] Though Rahner himself does not mention the word "wisdom" in the context of primordial words, it seems clear from his other examples that wisdom would find a place as one of the great Urworte. As we have seen, primordial words for Rahner have a sacramental function, making present the reality that they represent.

Earlier I suggested that proverbs function like Gadamer's classics by contributing to the process of Bildung. Rahner's theology accords dogmas a similar role. The function of dogmatic language is mystagogical; dogmas are not clear and distinct truths that we can comprehend but are linguistic expressions of a mystery which grasps us and transforms us. Dogmas are for Rahner the verbalized precipitates of grace. Rahner insists upon the necessity of new acts of interpretation to understand dogmas. Simply to repeat a dogma without a renewed effort of interpretation is to lapse into the "history of forgetting" which is part of the history of theology. Dogmas are not neatly packaged contents of truth but windows for viewing and interpreting experience.

While Rahner does not thematize the concept of play, there is a strong play-like movement of to-and-fro that dominates his understanding of religious language. Statements are neither completely true nor completely false.[249] Analogical language lives

---

[248] "Priest and Poet," TI, III, 297.

[249] "Thomas Aquinas on the Incomprehensibility of God," S125.

119

in the to-and-fro movement of affirmation and negation. The dialectic of disclosure and concealment suggests a playfulness about Rahner's God. God is revealed in Christ definitively, finally, and irrevocably; and yet, nearly two thousand years after Christ, God still wills that most of the human race find salvation through non-Christian traditions.[250] Christ is the full revelation, the real symbol of God, and yet people who deliberately reject Christ can still be accepting God. There appears to be a playfulness in God's willing a multitude of religious traditions.

This investigation has suggested strong similarities between the perspectives of Rahner and the wisdom tradition. Rahner himself has noted the pluralism of competing philosophies and worldviews and their effect upon theology.[251] It is to an alternative philosophical theology which also shares many of the perspectives of the wisdom tradition that we next turn.

---

[250]Rahner argues that for every human being, "that which God has intended as salvation for him reached him, in accordance with God's will and by his permission (no longer adequately separable in practice), in the concrete religion of his actual realm of existence and historical condition." "Christianity and the Non-Christian Religions," TI, V, 129.

[251]Karl Rahner, "The Current Relationship between Philosophy and Theology," TI, XIII, trans. David Bourke (New York: Seabury, 1975), 61-79; idem, "Theology as Engaged in an Interdisciplinary Dialogue with the Sciences," TI, XIII, 80-93; idem, "On the Relationship between Theology and the Contemporary Sciences," TI, XIII, 94-102.

CHAPTER III

THE CHRISTOLOGY OF NORMAN PITTENGER

Rahner's theology is one important contemporary retrieval of the tradition of Logos or Wisdom Christology. However, it is not the only contemporary theological perspective to retrieve this tradition and to show similarities to the wisdom tradition. The perspective of God working in and through the order of the universe has been of crucial importance to process thought; and the Christologies of Teilhard de Chardin, Norman Pittenger, and John B. Cobb, Jr. all accord a central place to the cosmological role of Jesus as the Logos or Wisdom.[1]

This chapter will explore the thought of Alfred North Whitehead and Norman Pittenger in light of the wisdom tradition. The form of this chapter will parallel that of the second chapter. I will begin by examining Whitehead's and Pittenger's views of the working of God in ordinary human experience. Then I will discuss Pittenger's interpretation of Jesus Christ, which draws upon both the tradition of Logos Christology and the philosophy of Whitehead. I will conclude by exploring the role of language in religion and dogma for Whitehead and Pittenger. At each stage I will note the similarities and differences between the process thinkers and Rahner, and their relationships to the wisdom tradition.

The Religious Dimension of Ordinary Experience

Whitehead's Metaphysics: A World in Process

Pittenger adopts and adapts the metaphysics of Whitehead in his theology. Since Whitehead's philosophy of organism is of particular importance in shaping Pittenger's understanding of the religious dimension of ordinary experience, it is to Whitehead that we next turn. I will begin with a brief summary of the main principles of Whitehead's philosophy, and then I will discuss

[1]Pierre Teilhard de Chardin, The Phenomenon of Man, trans. Bernard Wall (New York: Harper & Row, 1965), 257-99; The Divine Milieu (New York: Harper & Row, 1968), 113-49; John B. Cobb, Jr. Christ in a Pluralistic Age (Philadelphia: Westminster, 1975); W. Norman Pittenger, The Word Incarnate: A Study of the Doctrine of the Person of Christ (Digswell Place: James Nisbet & Co., 1959; hereafter cited as WI); Norman Pittenger, Christology Reconsidered (London: SCM Press, 1970; hereafter cited as CR).

Whitehead's understanding of the way God affects ordinary experience.

Whitehead views metaphysics as a description of the general characteristics of experience.[2] This description is drawn from one area of experience and is tested by application to other areas. Logical coherence serves as an indispensable test for elucidating its accuracy, but it is not itself part of the description. Logic is a superb instrument; but if it is considered to be an exact and "adequate analysis of the advance of thought, [it] is a fake."[3] The ultimate appeal for verification is not to logic but to the fundamental touchstone of philosophy, "the reaction of our own nature to the general aspect of life in the Universe."[4] Thus Whitehead offers his metaphysics not as a logically demonstrable final system, but as a groping, tentative description, subject to correction and revision.

According to Whitehead's description, reality is constructed of atomic building-blocks called "actual entities." They are the microcosmic pulses of experience which unite to form larger aggregates called societies or nexûs (e.g. trees, houses, people) which comprise the world of our experience. Unlike the inert, imperishable atoms of Democritus, actual entities are vital, transient, complex, and interdependent. They are the "final real things of which the world is made up."[5] Behind them there hides no higher grade of reality. Even God is one more actual entity:

---

[2]Alfred North Whitehead, Adventure of Ideas (New York: Free Press, 1967), 234-35 (hereafter cited as AI). On Whitehead's method, see Charles Hartshorne and Creighton Peden, Whitehead's View of Reality (New York: Pilgrim Press, 1981), 37-58; Victor Lowe, Understanding Whitehead (Baltimore: Johns Hopkins Press, 1966), 325-39; Alix Parmentier, La Philosophie de Whitehead et le Problème de Dieu (Paris: Beauchesne, 1968), 157-93.

[3]Alfred North Whitehead, "Immortality," in Science and Philosophy (New York: Philosophical Library, 1948), 104.

[4]Ibid., 102.

[5]Alfred North Whitehead, Process and Reality: An Essay in Cosmology, eds. David Ray Griffin and Donald W. Sherbourne (corrected ed.; New York: Free Press, 1978), 18, (hereafter cited as PR). On actual entities, see William Christian, An Interpretation of Whitehead's Metaphysics (New Haven, Ct.: Yale University Press, 1967), 17-47; and F. Bradford Wallack, The Epochal Nature of Process in Whitehead's Metaphysics (Albany, N.Y.: State University of New York Press, 1980), 7-46.

God is an actual entity, and so is the most trivial puff of existence in far-off empty space. But, though there are gradations of importance, and diversities of function, yet in the principles which actuality exemplifies all are on the same level.[6]

According to Whitehead, "God's existence is not generically different from that of other actual entities, except that he is 'primordial' in a sense to be gradually explained."[7] Our transient experiences are the ultimate realities.

Whitehead also uses the term actual occasions. This term is often interchangeable with actual entities. However, every occasion is involved in spatio-temporal extensiveness. God is the one non-temporal actual entity who is not an actual occasion.[8]

Actual occasions are the basic units of process. The process in which an actual entity is constituted, in which the many objects of the universe grow together into the unity of a novel one, is called a concrescence. This process itself is, in Locke's phrase, the "real internal constitution" of the actual entity.[9] There is no permanent substance to which transient experiences occur. The process is the formal reality of the actual entity. The principle of process states that "how an actual entity becomes constitutes what that actual entity is. . . . Its 'being' is constituted by its 'becoming.'"[10] When the process is completed,

---

[6]PR, 18.

[7]Ibid., 75. On Whitehead's understanding of God, see Parmentier, 349-444; Christian, 283-381; Laurence F. Wilmot, Whitehead and God: Prologemena to Theological Reconstruction (Waterloo, Ontario: Wilfred Laurier University Press, 1979), 53-70; and Kenneth F. Thompson, Jr. Whitehead's Philosophy of Religion (The Hague: Mouton, 1971), 17-128.

[8]Pols notes that Whitehead usually uses the term "actual occasion" when he wishes to emphasize the "extensiveness" of an actual entity. However, Pols also observes that Whitehead "is not completely consistent, and sometimes uses 'actual occasion' in a context where its scope should include God, e.g. PR [Process and Reality: An Essay in Cosmology (New York: Macmillan Co., 1959)], 113." Edward Pols, Whitehead's Metaphysics: A Critical Examination of Process and Reality (Carbondale, Il.: Southern Illinois University Press, 1967), 4-5, n. 2.

[9]PR, 219.

[10]Ibid., 23. See Martin Jordan, New Shapes of Reality: Aspects of A.N. Whitehead's Philosophy (London: George Allen and Unwin, 1968), 42-62.

the actual entity reaches a state of satisfaction and perishes. In perishing it passes into the state of objective immortality and becomes a datum for the concrescence of other actual entities.

The process of concrescence can be analysed into concrete elements called prehensions.[11] A prehension is a relating, a "grasping" which either carries an object into the real internal constitution of the subject or excludes the object from any such positive contribution. A positive prehension is called a feeling. "Feelings are 'vectors,' for they feel what is there and transform it into what is here."[12] Each actual entity is related to every other actual entity in its actual world by a feeling. The actual world for any given actual entity is that collection of actual entities which are objectified as given data for the initial phase of the concrescence. No two actual entities possess identical actual worlds. The feeling that binds two actual entities may be very vague and insignificant, but no actual entity can simply dismiss another.

It is to be noted that feelings do not imply consciousness. Consciousness is only one form of experience, and the same basic description applies to all forms of experience, to all the various levels of societies that make up our world.

A prehension can be analysed into three elements: "(a) the 'subject' which is prehending . . . ; (b) the 'datum' which is prehended; (c) the 'subjective form' which is how that subject prehends that datum."[13] In a simple physical feeling, the datum is initially prehended as an entire actual entity. This initial datum is then objectified as being the subject of a certain feeling relevant to the prehending subject. This feeling becomes the objective datum for the prehension, and the objectification is the perspective of the initial datum. Objectification selects one component of the initial datum and leaves the other components in relative irrelevance.[14]

---

[11]PR, 220-22. See Paul F. Schmidt, Perception and Cosmology in Whitehead's Philosophy (New Brunswick, N.J.: Rutgers University Press, 1967), 80-98; and Charles Hartshorne, Whitehead's Philosophy: Selected Essays: 1935-1970 (Lincoln, Nb.: University of Nebraska Press, 1978), 125-27.

[12]PR, 87.

[13]Ibid., 23.

[14]Ibid., 86-88. See Jorge Luis Nobo, Whitehead's Metaphysics of Extension and Solidarity (Albany, N.Y.: State University of New York Press, 1986), 19-23.

The subjective form is the reaction of the subject to the objective datum; examples are emotions, valuations, purposes, and conscience.[15] The subjective form provides the immediate novelty of the subject. The initial and objective data may have been very similar for other subjects, but no other subject will have the same reaction. On the one hand, the subjective form expresses the history of the feeling, its origin and purpose, its difficulties and decisions along the way; on the other hand, it re-enacts the feeling of the objective datum. This reproductive reference to the datum is always present in the subjective form, but it never fully determines it.

Each actual entity constitutes itself as a unity of subjective form. An entity is caused insofar as it prehends the actual entities in its past and conforms to them. However, each entity decides for itself _how_ it feels past actual entities and _which_ relevant possibilities it will actualize; thus an entity always reenacts its predecessors with some degree of difference. Thus Whitehead can hold that each entity is _causa sui_. The decision of each actual entity of how to prehend its world and of what possibilities to choose is for Whitehead the locus of freedom and the condition of possibility of embodied novelty in process. This principle of the self-determination of each actual entity prevents Whitehead's metaphysical system of internal relations from collapsing into a monism. For Whitehead there is an element of freedom at every level of processing reality.

The completion of the process of concrescence is the satisfaction of the actual entity.[16] In the satisfaction the many actual entities of the actual world find their respective roles in the final unity of the subject. The integration of feelings proceeds until a concrete unity of feeling is obtained, and one complex, aesthetic satisfaction is reached. The attainment of satisfaction is the final cause of the concrescence, and its achievement terminates the process.[17] The actual entity formally perishes and passes into the state of objective immortality where it will serve as an initial datum for future actual entities.

Every actual entity can be considered both formally and objectively. Process is immanent in the actual entity considered formally; process is transcendent of it considered objectively.[18]

---

[15]_PR_, 24.

[16]_Ibid._, 219.

[17]_Ibid._, 219-20.

[18]_Ibid._, 220.

Its objective aspect begins with its satisfaction and perishing and considers the consequences of the actual entity for future actual entities. As a datum in the concrescences of other actual entities, the actual entity is a superject in the function of objective immortality.[19] All entities of all sorts possess the ability to function as objects. The principle of relativity states that "it belongs to the nature of a 'being' that it is a potential for every 'becoming.'"[20]

This description rejects the notion of an unchanging subject of change.[21] There is no subject which happens to encounter a datum and then reacts to it. According to Whitehead, the feelings encounter a datum and progressively attain the unity of a subject-superject. This unity is the purpose of the feelings. An actual occasion feels as it does in order to be itself. The feelings cannot be abstracted from their final cause, for the final cause constitutes the unity of the feeling. In this sense also an actual entity is causa sui.[22]

The reason for every condition in any process of concrescence is to be found either in other actual entities in the actual world of that concrescence or in the character of the subject of the concrescence. This is the ontological principle.[23] According to this principle, every decision is relative: it is made for some actual entity by some actual entity. Decision does not always involve consciousness; Whitehead uses the term in the etymological sense of a "cutting off."[24] Decision is far from being a mere adventitious afterthought to experience. As we saw above, selection and decision are involved in every simple physical feeling. An actual entity becomes actual because of decisions made by and for it. "'Actuality' is the decision amid 'potentiality.'"[25]

Thus Whitehead's description of the process of the actual world leads to the question of potentiality. Whitehead calls the pure potentials of the universe "eternal objects." They are entities "whose conceptual recognition does not involve a necessary

[19]Ibid., 84-85.

[20]Ibid., 22.

[21]Ibid., 29, 155.

[22]Ibid., 222.

[23]Ibid., 24.

[24]Ibid., 43.

[25]Ibid.

reference to any definite actual entities of the temporal world."[26] They are formative elements of the actual world; this role is described as the "ingression" of the eternal object into the actual entity.[27] An eternal object, in being realized in an actual entity, contributes to the definiteness of that actual entity; it calls forth determination from indetermination; potentiality becomes reality. The eternal object itself is completely neutral as to its particular ingressions; it is indecisive. Without pure potentials, there could be no novelty in the universe, for novel actual things require unrealized potentialities. Without eternal objects the universe would be static and monistic.

Whitehead calls prehensions of actual entities physical prehensions; prehensions of eternal objects are called conceptual prehensions or conceptual feelings. A conceptual feeling is a feeling whose datum is an eternal object; it is the feeling of the eternal object's capacity for being realized as a determinant of process.[28]

The eternal objects are exclusive in their function as determinants. In order to realize one eternal object, an actual entity must reject other eternal objects. The incompatibility of alternatives gives rise to the definite character of the actual world. In order to become this, an actual occasion must reject the possibility of becoming that.[29]

---

[26]Ibid., 44. On the role of the eternal objects in the shaping of Whitehead's metaphysics, see Lewis S. Ford, The Emergence of Whitehead's Metaphysics: 1925-1929 (Albany, N.Y.: State University of New York Press, 1984), 66-94.

[27]Pols notes that the ingression of the eternal objects into actual entities distinguishes them from the Platonic forms, with which Whitehead often identifies them; unlike the forms of Plato, the eternal objects "do not lead another life of which their ingression in actuality is but a reminder" (p. 7). Christian offers an inventory of the various types of eternal objects mentioned by Whitehead (pp. 202-03). For a comparison of Whitehead's eternal objects and Plato's ideas, see Dorothy M. Emmet, Whitehead's Philosophy of Organism (London: Macmillan, 1932), 102-39.

[28]PR, 240. See Christian, 211-15.

[29]PR, 240. For an exposition and critique of the role of freedom for Whitehead, see Pols, 25-142.

In the process of concrescence actual entities function as objects in the self-creation of other actual entities. The eternal objects explain how such objectification is possible.[30] Actual entities are prehended through the mediation of eternal objects which are shared by both the object and the subject. In a simple physical feeling, the re-enaction of the objective datum by the subjective form occurs because one eternal object functions both as a partial determinant of the objective datum and as a partial determinant of the subjective form. Thus the eternal object functions relationally, determining both the definiteness of the objectified actuality and the definiteness of the experiencing subject.[31]

Thus eternal objects, although not themselves actual entities, are formative elements of the actual world. However, the ontological principle states that the only reasons for actual entities are other actual entities. Formative elements cannot "float into the actual world out of nonentity."[32] Whitehead insists repeatedly that apart from things that are actual there is nothing in either fact or efficacy. Thus the eternal objects must exist "somewhere," i.e., in some actual entity. Whitehead locates this "somewhere" in the non-temporal actual entity, in the primordial nature of God.

We have already seen the relevance of the eternal objects for actual entities in the process of concrescence. Relevance for Whitehead expresses "some real fact of togetherness among forms."[33] In accordance with the ontological principle, this togetherness must be found in the formal constitution of some actual entity. The relevance of the timeless pure potentials must express a "fact of togetherness" in the formal constitution of some non-temporal actuality. There can be only one such non-temporal, non-derivative actuality; for it is the necessary condition of all creative process.[34]

The primordial, unfettered, unconditional conceptual valuation of the entire multiplicity of eternal objects is the adjustment of togetherness among the eternal objects; it makes possible the differentiated relevance of the eternal objects to each stage

---

[30]PR, 148.

[31]Ibid., 149.

[32]Ibid., 46.

[33]Ibid., 32.

[34]Ibid., 247.

of the creative process.[35] If there were no ordering, no primordial valuation of pure potentials in the non-temporal actual entity, then there would be a disjunction of eternal objects unrealized in the temporal world. The eternal objects would have no definite, effective relevance to the concrescent process. They would be relatively non-existent for the concrescence. Novelty would be inconceivable and meaningless. Because of the primordial conceptual valuation, the possibilities which transcend the realized temporal world are really relevant to creative advance. The primordial nature of God is the second formative element of the actual world.

The third and final formative element of the universe is creativity. Creativity is not to be confused with God. It is the ultimate of the philosophy of organism.[36] In itself it possesses no character; it cannot be separated from its creatures; it is not itself an actual entity. It is "that ultimate notion of the highest generality at the base of actuality,"[37] "the universal of universals characterizing ultimate matter of fact."[38]

Creativity can only be characterized through its accidental embodiments, and God is its primordial, non-temporal accident. Creativity does not violate the ontological principle; it is not an "external agency with its own ulterior purposes."[39] Nonetheless, it is because of creativity that the actual world has its

---

[35]Ibid., 31. See Christian, 258-79; Nobo, 187-90.

[36]PR, 21. See Parmentier, 275-95. Nobo argues that to be consistent with his own system Whitehead should have listed a fourth and even a fifth formative element in the universe. Nobo argues that the extensive continuum (described in PR) or the Receptacle (described in AI) must be an eternal metaphysical principle because it "is presupposed by the becoming of every actual occasion, but does not itself become" (p. 252). Nobo suggests that "creativity and extension are indissoluble aspects of one ultimate reality--a reality underlying the becoming, the being, and the solidarity of all actual entities" (p. 255). Nobo further claims that there must be an envisagement by the Receptacle or the Ultimate of the possibilities of value which are in the primordial nature of God (p. 309). Nobo argues that this envisagement is a third aspect of the Ultimate and a fifth formative element of the temporal world (p. 317).

[37]PR, 31.

[38]Ibid., 21.

[39]Ibid., 222.

character of creative advance into novelty. Creativity is responsible for the universe's disjunctive diversity, the many, becoming one in a novel, self-experiencing actual entity, which is the universe conjunctively. "The ultimate metaphysical principle is the advance from disjunction to conjunction, creating a novel entity other than the entities given in disjunction."[40] This novel entity in turn becomes part of the disjunctive many as an object for new subjects. Thus there are two movements in the rhythm of creative process: the movement from the many objects to the individual subject and the movement from the satisfied subject back to the objectified many. Efficient and final causation are linked in these two movements: the efficient cause expresses the transition from completed objects to nascent becoming subjects, and the final cause expresses the urge of the subject toward its own satisfaction.

A Metaphysics of Grace:
God in Process

With this brief outline of the basic description of process according to Whitehead's philosophy of organism, we may now investigate more specifically Whitehead's understanding of the presence of God in the process of everyday experience. We return to the process of concrescence and examine the role of God in subjective aim.

Subjective aim is not to be confused with subjective form. The latter, as we have seen, is _how_ a feeling is felt by the concrescing subject. Subjective aim concerns the direction of the concrescence. Every subject must face the question of its final cause; it must decide what sort of entity it will make itself. Even in a simple physical feeling, there is a selection, a decision in the sense of "cutting off," for certain elements of the initial datum are rejected so that one objective datum may be felt by the subject. The adoption of one perspective requires the rejection of other perspectives. The subjective aim is an actual entity's prehension of God's prehension of an eternal object as a relevant possibility for that particular entity.[41]

---

[40]_Ibid._, 21.

[41]_Ibid._, 244. See Thompson, _Whitehead's Philosophy of Religion_, 70-97.

Subjective aim arises from a hybrid physical feeling of God.[42] Whitehead subdivides simple physical feelings into pure and hybrid physical feelings. In a pure physical feeling, the objective datum is constituted by a physical feeling of the initial datum. In a hybrid physical feeling, the objective datum is constituted by a conceptual feeling of the initial datum. In the latter case the conceptual feelings of the objectified actuality and of the concrescing subject will have the same datum but will differ in respect to their subjective forms. We can further subdivide hybrid physical feelings into (1) those that feel the conceptual feelings of temporal actual entities and (2) those that feel the conceptual feelings of God.[43] Thus God is objectified in a concrescent subject by means of the latter's hybrid physical feelings which take God's conceptual feelings as their data.

God's conceptual feelings are prehensions of the eternal objects. The subjective forms of these feelings are valuations which determine the degree of relevance of the eternal objects for each actual occasion. God is not exempt from the principle of relativity; God functions as a superject by offering objectified conceptual feelings as goals for actual entities. God is the "lure for feeling" and the "eternal urge of desire," which establishes the initial phase of each subjective aim.[44] God calls forth novel possibilities relevant to the actual world at its given stage and provides the foundation for meaningful creative advance. God's goal is to achieve the maximum ordered complexity possible in the actual world. The initial phase of the subjective aim is the means through which God works in the world and is present to it.

It must be remembered that subjective aim does not necessarily involve consciousness. Consciousness is merely one form of experience. The same fundamental process of concrescence takes place in all actual entities whether conscious or not.

Whitehead maintains that God's offering of relevant possibilities in the initial phase of subjective aim in no way involves compulsion or infringement upon the freedom of the actual entity. Whitehead vigorously attacks the image of God as a ruling Caesar or a Mesopotamian despot. He sees God in the "brief Galilean vision of humility" that "dwells upon the tender elements in the

---

[42]PR, 246. See Stephen David Ross, Perspective in Whitehead's Metaphysics (Albany, N.Y.: State University of New York Press, 1983), 73-76; for a critique of Whitehead's discussion of the subjective aim, see Pols, 101-25.

[43]Ibid.

[44]Ibid., 344.

world, which slowly and in quietness operate by love."[45] In place of the imperial ruler, Whitehead proposes God the Lover.

As a lover, God proffers Godself to humans as a "lure for feeling," an "object of desire," but leaves humans free to reject this offer. Each actual entity is _causa sui_; it is "its own reason for the decision in respect to the qualitative clothing of feelings. It is finally responsible for the decision by which any lure for feeling is admitted to efficiency."[46]

The subjective form reproduces the feelings of its objective datum but is never fully determined by them. It is novel, unique, and free. The subjective form of the feeling takes the form of a valuation upward or downward. Adversion is valuation upward; in this case the conceptual feeling of the eternal object increases in intensity in the subjective form. Aversion is valuation downward; in this case the importance of the eternal object as felt in the subject is attenuated. Each actual entity is free to cut off the possibilities of optimum development open to it and thus can fail to accomplish the aim God had proposed. Although Whitehead himself did not often use the word, Pittenger suggests that in the case of humans, this is "what religious men call 'sin.'"[47] Sin in this perspective appears to be more a form of lethargy than of wrong willing; sin is more a lack of willing than a positive affirmation of a negative aim.

Rejection of God's lure does not halt the creative advance. God does not combat destructive force with destructive force but rather patiently and tenderly calls the universe forward. God's strength lies in "the overpowering rationality of his conceptual harmonization"; God is "the poet of the world, with tender patience leading it by his vision of truth, beauty, and goodness."[48]

Thus far we have seen that for Whitehead God's loving presence is to be found in the initial goal of each moment of the creative process; God is experienced as the foundation of meaningful novelty and the call to the best possible development and the maximum intensity of feeling. There is another aspect to God's involvement in Whitehead's universe, the transformation of all

---

[45]_Ibid._, 343.

[46]_Ibid._, 88.

[47]Norman Pittenger, _Alfred North Whitehead_ (Richmond, Va.: John Knox Press, 1969), 29.

[48]_PR_, 346.

entities in God's loving presence. For Whitehead this transformation embraces not only humans but the entire actual world. This issue leads us to the question of the nature of evil and Whitehead's fundamental cosmological problem.

For Whitehead the problem of evil is the problem of perishing. The ultimate evil in the temporal world for Whitehead lies in the fact "that the past fades, that time is a 'perpetual perishing.'"[49] The present flees and loses forever its immediacy. Past and present are mutually exclusive. Humans are haunted by the terror of the loss of the past, and yet we refuse to reduce the present to a mere preservation of the past. We desire novelty without loss, but in the temporal world process entails loss. The question asked by religion is "whether the process of the temporal world passes into the formation of other actualities, bound together in an order in which novelty does not mean loss."[50] For cosmology this is the problem of God and the world.

We have already seen the primordial nature of God as the unlimited conceptual realization of the entire multiplicity of pure potentials. In this aspect God is "deficiently actual"; for God's feelings, being merely conceptual, do not possess the fullness of actuality. Moreover, conceptual feelings which are not integrated with physical feelings are not conscious. There is another aspect of God, the consequent nature, which originates with God's physical prehensions of the temporal world. It is "the realization of the actual world in the unity of his nature and through the transformation of his wisdom," "the weaving of God's physical feelings upon his primordial concepts."[51]

The processes of temporal actualities and God are directly inverse. Whereas a temporal actual entity has its origin in physical experience and is motivated by the lure for feeling initially derived from God, God's origin lies in conceptual experience, and God is motivated by the physical experience initially derived from the temporal world.

The consequent nature of God is everlasting. This means that in it there is creative advance without loss. Mutual immediacy is retained amid ongoing process.[52] In this everlasting immediacy whatever can be saved from the temporal world is saved. Those occasions that revolted against the divine call are relegated to

---

[49]Ibid., 340.

[50]Ibid., 340.

[51]Ibid., 345.

[52]Ibid., 346. See Parmentier, 419-38.

133

the "triviality of merely individual facts," but whatever good was
achieved through them is saved.[53] God's consequent nature both
judges and saves the world as it passes into everlasting immediacy. This is "the judgment of a tenderness which loses nothing
that can be saved. It is also the judgment of a wisdom which uses
what in the temporal world is mere wreckage."[54] In addition to
God's "tender care that nothing be lost," God has an infinite
patience which never poses force against force, but indefatigably
responds with love.[55]

The transformation of the temporal world through its reception into the consequent nature of God is inseparably related to
the transformation of God through the derivation of God's consequent nature from the world. The temporal world, transformed and
perfected by its reception into the consequent nature of God, is
the fulfillment of the primordial divine subjective aim. Whitehead expresses this relation in a series of antitheses which appear more perplexing at first sight than they really are. He
himself warns us:

> the apparent self-contradictions depend on neglect of the
> diverse categories of existence. In each antithesis there is
> a shift of meaning which converts the opposition into a con-
> trast.[56]

Whitehead presents his understanding of the relation of God to the
world in a rather playful, paradoxical style:

> It is as true to say that God is permanent and the World
> fluent, as that the World is permanent and God is fluent.
> It is as true to say that God is one and the World many,
> as that the World is one and God many.
> It is as true to say that, in comparison with the World,
> God is actual eminently, as that, in comparison with God, the
> World is actual eminently.
> It is as true to say that the World is immanent in God,
> as that God is immanent in the World.
> It is as true to say the God transcends the World, as
> that the World transcends God.

---

[53]PR, 346.

[54]Ibid.

[55]Ibid.

[56]Ibid., 348.

It is as true to say that God creates the World, as that the World creates God.[57]

In the process of both God and the world Whitehead finds two poles: appetitive vision and physical enjoyment. However, the motion of the two processes is directly converse. God moves from the conceptual to the physical, from primordial, permanent unity to consequent, fluent multiplicity, while the world moves from the physical to the conceptual, from primordial fluent multiplicity to consequent, permanent unity.

In the first antithesis God's primordial nature is seen as permanent and God's consequent nature as fluent, while the world's temporal actuality is seen to be fluent and its everlasting status in God's consequent nature is seen to be permanent. Similarly, in the second antithesis God is seen as primordially one and consequently many, while the world is seen as primordially many and consequently one through its absorption into the divine nature. The temporal actuality of the world is actual eminently in comparison with God's deficiently actual primordial nature, but God's consequent nature, which receives and transforms the temporal world into the kingdom of heaven, is actual eminently in comparison with the temporal world. Neither God nor the world can claim any more priority in creation than the other. God is not before the world but with the world.

Immanence and transcendence are characteristics of all objects. As realized determinants in a concrescence they are immanent; as capacities for determination they are transcendent.[58] The world is an object in the concrescence of God's consequent nature, and God's primordial nature is an object in the concrescence of the temporal world. Thus both are immanent in and transcendent of each other. God's primordial nature "creates" the temporal world by providing the determinate conditions of relevant possibility necessary for creative advance. God's primordial nature is the indispensable primordial datum for the world. The temporal world "creates" God's consequent nature by providing God with the multiplicity which God absorbs into unity. The flux and multiplicity of the world are the data for the consequent nature of God. Both God and the world bring novelty to the other.

The final reconciliation of permanence and flux is the everlasting apotheosis of the world. The final end of creation is "existence in the perfect unity of adjustment as means, and in the perfect multiplicity of the attainment of individual types of

---

[57]Ibid.

[58]Ibid., 239-40.

self-existence."[59] The oppositions between the one and the many and between permanence and process are both overcome in the kingdom of heaven. The opposition between being a means and being as end is overcome because "the sense of worth beyond itself is immediately enjoyed as an overpowering element in the individual self-attainment."[60] Thus pain and suffering are transformed into triumph, and redemption can arrive through suffering. Each actual entity is transformed into "a living, ever-present fact" by being taken into perfect union with every other actual entity in the consequent nature of God.[61]

In this apotheosis there is an unceasing advance into creative novelty without perishing. Actualities have their present lives and pass into novelty without losing the immediacy of their pasts. As each temporal actuality is received into God's nature it is transformed into "a living, ever-present fact," "a complete unity of life in a chain of elements for which succession does not mean loss of immediate union."[62] The connection between the transformed actual entity in the consequent nature of God and the original actual entity in the temporal world is analogous to the connection between the occasions of an enduring personality in the temporal world, but it is even more complete. In both cases each chain of the succession sums all its predecessors. Thus, for Whitehead, the temporal actuality has been transformed without losing contact with its origins in the temporal world.

The apotheosis of the world in the consequent nature of God is subject to the principle of relativity; it becomes an object in the becoming of subjects in the temporal world. This constitutes the fourth and final phase of the universe. Thus far we have seen (1) the primordial conceptual valuation of the eternal objects in the non-temporal actual entity, God, (2) the process of concrescence of the actual entities in the temporal world, and (3) the transformation and everlasting perfection of actuality, and the perfect union of all individual identities in the consequent nature of God. In (4) the final creative phase, the consequent nature of God passes back into the temporal world. This is Whitehead's interpretation of the saying; "For the kingdom of heaven is

---

[59]Ibid., 349.

[60]Ibid., 350.

[61]Ibid. Whitehead is not entirely clear whether an actual entity retains its identity for itself in the consequent nature of God or whether it continues as an ever-present fact only in God's experience.

[62]Ibid.

with us today."[63] The temporal world is transformed in God and passes back into the world. The love in the temporal world is transformed and perfected and returns to flood the world. Each occasion of a temporal society functions as an object not only for others, but for later moments of its own process. Each passing occasion of a person's life is transformed in God and returns to the person as "the inward source of distaste or refreshment, the judge arising out of the very nature of things, redeemer or goddess of mischief."[64]

For Whitehead God's loving presence to the world and the world's transformation in God make possible the creative process of the universe. Whitehead himself was not a theologian and rarely employed the word grace. However, two passages from his writings taken together affirm that one implicit goal of his philosophy was to present a metaphysics of grace viable for the contemporary world:

> More than two thousand years age, the wisest of men proclaimed that the divine persuasion is the foundation of the order of the world, but that it could only produce such a measure of harmony as amid brute forces it was possible to accomplish. This, I suggest, is a plain anticipation by Plato of a doctrine of Grace, seven hundred years before the age of Pelagius and Augustine.[65]

> If we had to render Plato's general point of view with the least changes made necessary by the intervening two thousand years of human experience in social organization, in aesthetic achievements, in science, and in religion, we should have to set about the construction of a philosophy of organism.[66]

For Whitehead the role of Christianity is to have revealed in act, in the life of Christ, what Plato had divined in theory.[67] Thus in proposing his philosophy of organism he is presenting a contemporary metaphysics of grace which seeks to combine the insight of Plato with the revelation of the God of love of Christianity. Whitehead's use of the word grace is, of course, very different from the traditional Christian usage. Whitehead's

---

[63]Ibid., 351.

[64]Ibid.

[65]AI, 160.

[66]PR, 39.

[67]AI, 167.

137

grace, not unlike Pelagius's understanding of the word, is the loving presence of God permeating the natural cosmic process; Augustine's grace was an additional, gratuitous gift of God which could in no way be identified with the creative and sustaining power of God in the natural order.

Wisdom, Whitehead, and Rahner

Whitehead himself seems to have been aware of himself as continuing the project of the wisdom teachers of ancient Israel. In Religion in the Making he writes: "The final principle of religion is that there is a wisdom in the nature of things."[68] He also refers explicitly to the ancient Hebrew wisdom tradition and claims: "The search after wisdom has its origins in generalizations from experience."[69] This statement is very similar to Whitehead's own method of descriptive generalization. Whitehead's metaphysical categories are tentative formulations of the ultimate generalities. The ultimate appeal of the philosophy of organism is not to logic but to our own sense of our relationship to the whole. Whitehead's philosopher is like an aviator, beginning from one area of experience and generalizing from it in a soaring flight of the imagination. Then the philosopher must land, coming back to earth to test metaphysical theories by application to experience.[70]

While the wisdom tradition of Israel never developed a systematic, all-encompassing metaphysical scheme, the ancient sages did begin their reflections by observing experience, and, as Whitehead himself notes, they did proceed to make generalizations from experience. The intimate relation of Lady Wisdom to creation makes clear her universal activity; the sages' claims about Lady Wisdom reach for a sense of the whole. The examples of Job and Qoheleth also make clear the necessity of testing generalizations against the "stubborn facts" of experience. Whitehead himself notes with approval the "keen appreciation of actual fact" of the Hebrew sages, in particular of Qoheleth.[71]

For Whitehead the experience of order is fundamental to our understanding of ourselves and of God. All actual order, he

---

[68]Alfred North Whitehead, Religion in the Making (New York: New American Library, 1974), 138 (hereafter cited as RM).

[69]Ibid., 52.

[70]PR, 5.

[71]RM, 53.

claims, is aesthetic order which arises from the immanence of God in the world.[72] The Wisdom of Solomon had associated Lady Wisdom with the force that holds all things together (1:7); Whitehead calls God the "binding element" in the universe.[73] Lady Wisdom "pervades and permeates all things" (Wis 7:24); Whitehead's God is present throughout the entire universe as the "lure for feeling" and the "eternal urge of desire."[74] As in the description of Lady Wisdom in the Wisdom of Solomon, Whitehead's God appears as an alluring, inviting, persuasive force which is the ordering power of the universe.

Whitehead finds the source of order in the conceptual valuation of the eternal objects in the primordial nature of God. God does not create the eternal objects but coordinates them and renders them relevant to the initial stages of concrescent actual occasions. Whitehead differs from most Christian thinkers by denying that God is the creator of all reality. However, there is an interesting analogy between Whitehead's interpretation of the eternal objects and Vawter's understanding of the role of Wisdom in Proverbs 8 and Job 28. In Vawter's reading, Lady Wisdom resembles Whitehead's eternal objects in that she is not created but discovered by Yahweh and serves as a guiding model for Yahweh's activity of fashioning the world.[75]

We experience the eternal objects in every moment of experience through God's ordering them and making them relevant to the initial subjective aim of each actual occasion. Like the descriptions of Lady Wisdom calling humans in and through everyday activities, Whitehead's God is active whether recognized or not in all types of experience, offering a vision of possibilities. Acceptance of the goal of the subjective aim proposed by God, like acceptance of the call of Lady Wisdom, makes possible greater intensity and harmony of experience; rejection of the goal of the sub-

---

[72]Ibid., 101.

[73]Ibid., 152.

[74]PR, 344. Ford has looked for precedents in the Hebrew Bible for the process view of God as a lure and persuasive agency. However, he neglects the wisdom tradition. His case could be greatly strengthened by reference to passages where Lady Wisdom, acting in place of God, seeks out followers and "lures" them to herself. See Lewis S. Ford, The Lure of God: A Biblical Background for Process Theism (Philadelphia: Fortress, 1978), 15-28. On the role of Lady Wisdom as a lure, see Prov 1:20-33; 8:1-11, 32-36; Sir 24:19-21; Wis 6:13-16.

[75]"Proverbs 8:22: Wisdom and Creation," 205-06.

jective aim, like rejection of Lady Wisdom, harms both the individual and others.

For Whitehead, as for the sages of Israel, we experience a justice built into the order of the universe. Our actions have destructive or constructive consequences which follow naturally. Von Rad has commented that for the wisdom tradition,

> The good man is the one who knows about the constructive quality of good and the destructive quality of evil and who submits to this pattern which can be discerned in the world. Thus, in reality, the good is that which does good.[76]

Similarly, for Whitehead our activities constitute themselves as the context, the actual world for all future occasions. Each action is itself a value with constructive or destructive consequences. Indeed, this is Whitehead's definition of actuality: actual entities make a difference.

Whitehead's vision of a dynamic world in process also finds a certain analogy in the wisdom tradition. While the sages never conceived of modern evolutionary theories, von Rad observes that for the wisdom tradition of Israel "the world was very probably much more of a process than a thing in being."[77] The patterns of experience were never static, unchanging laws. The sages sought to determine the proper time for the application of proverbs. Whitehead notes:

> In scientific investigations the question True or False? is usually irrelevant. The important question is In what circumstances is this formula true, and in what circumstances is it false?[78]

The sages conceived their relationship with Lady Wisdom as a playful to-and-fro movement involving hiding and seeking, giving and receiving, acceptance and rejection on both sides. Lady Wisdom delights in humans (Prov 8:31), and she appears to be hurt and angered by their rejection of her (Prov 1:20-33). Von Rad comments on this relationship:

> The process in which [the Hebrew] found himself was turned to him and his conduct in a relationship of correspondence: it

---

[76]Wisdom, 78.

[77]Old Testament Theology, I, 427.

[78]Alfred North Whitehead, The Function of Reason (Boston: Beacon Press, 1962), 53 (hereafter cited as FR).

was ready to adapt itself to him in blessing and furtherance, but it was also in a position to affect him penally.[79]

Von Rad cites Proverbs 26:27 ("The man who digs a pit falls into it, the stone comes back on him that rolls it") as an example of this natural working out of the consequences of human actions. There is an analogy between this perspective and the cosmology of Whitehead. One of Whitehead's main concerns was to articulate the values that are inextricably embedded in actuality. Whitehead's cosmology is an attempt to overcome any dichotomy between fact and value and to retrieve the sense of values working through the patterns of ordinary human experience. According to Whitehead, each moment of our experience is transformed in the consequent nature of God and flows back into the world as "the inward source of distaste or of refreshment, the judge arising out of the very nature of things."[80]

Like the ancient sages, Whitehead had an acute sense of human limits. The limits and transience of human existence affect philosophy as well as every other human endeavor. Whitehead sees no final conquest of knowledge: "In its turn every philosophy will suffer a deposition."[81] Whitehead was very cautious and modest in making claims for his own metaphysical system. Like the sages, he was open to the possibility of experience correcting and reshaping his generalizations. His insistence on the widest possible sample of experience is an invitation to seek the correcting insights of negative experience: "The ultimate test is always widespread, recurrent experience; and the more general the rationalistic scheme, the more important is this final appeal."[82] Whitehead's caution about his own philosophy did not shake his rationalist faith that there is an intelligible order underlying our experience.

Whitehead comes closest to the perspective of Qoheleth when he describes human experience apart from the hope offered by religion as "a flash of occasional enjoyments lighting up a mass of pain and misery, a bagatelle of transient experience."[83] For Whitehead, as for Qoheleth, the dominant form that human suffering

---

[79]Ibid, 428.

[80]PR, 351.

[81]Ibid., 7.

[82]Ibid., 17.

[83]SMW, 192.

takes is the transience of the realities we experience. What differentiates Whitehead from both Job and Qoheleth most profoundly is Whitehead's trust in the long-term progress in religious insight:

> Religion has emerged into human experience mixed with the crudest fancies of barbaric imagination. Gradually, slowly, steadily the vision recurs in history, under nobler form and with clearer expression. It is the one element in human experience which persistently shows an upward trend.[84]

Given this perspective, Whitehead himself could interpret Job and Qoheleth as critical, questioning moments in a process which leads to greater insight and clearer expression. However, Job and Qoheleth themselves call into question any scheme of human progress in religious vision and confront us with the stark, baffling aporia of the incomprehensibility of God and of human experience. For Job and Qoheleth, the confidence of increased insight into the order of creation can itself be a misleading illusion. Whitehead's philosophy is much closer to the fundamentally positive, world-constructive side of the wisdom tradition than to the world-questioning perspectives of Job and Qoheleth.

Whitehead shares certain emphases with Rahner but has a very different understanding of the relation of God to the universe. Both Whitehead and Rahner view God as actively present throughout all human experience, constantly influencing every person, regardless of the individual's explicit religious self-understanding or lack thereof. Crucial to both thinkers' positions is a distinction between experience and explicit, thematic consciousness. According to both Whiteheadian thought and Rahner's transcendental anthropology, we constantly experience more than we are explicitly conscious of.[85]

For Rahner human experience is an interpenetration of two distinct but inseparable aspects, the transcendental experience of the horizon of Being and the categorical experience of distinct individual objects. Categorical experience can thematize and symbolize transcendental experience but can never adequately capture it in reflexive concepts. Whitehead also interprets experience as an intertwining of two distinct but inseparable modes: the clear and distinct experience of presentational immediacy and the unclear, indistinct, primitive experience in the mode of causal efficacy. By presentational immediacy Whitehead means "what is usually termed sense perception," although he applies his own

---

[84]Ibid.

[85]See Rahner, SW, 387-91; "Theology of Freedom," TI, VI, 178-96; Whitehead, PR, 344-51.

142

"limitations and extensions" to the usual understanding.[86] Presentational immediacy is precise and explicit in consciousness; causal efficacy, on the other hand, is more primitive but also more important. The latter is the "vague, haunting, unmanageable" awareness of the conformation of the present moment to realities in the environment immediately past: "We conform to our bodily organs and to the vague world which lies beyond them."[87] Experience in the mode of presentational immediacy functions as a symbolic reference to the more primitive experience in the mode of causal efficay.

For both Rahner and Whitehead the less distinct and more primordial mode of experience (Rahner's transcendental experience, Whitehead's causal efficacy) relates us directly to our world and to God; for both thinkers the clearer and more explicit mode of experience (Rahner's categorical experience, Whitehead's presentational immediacy) functions as a symbol of the more primordial mode of experience. For both thinkers, religious symbols are attempts to explicitate and make present to reflexive consciousness the presence of God in the primordial mode of experience. However, the relation of God to the world is very different for Rahner and Whitehead. Whitehead's God orders the stubborn facts of past actual occasions and makes relevant a pattern of eternal objects to the receptive phase of a new concrescence, but Whitehead's God does not call into being either the facts of the past, the eternal objects, the new concrescence, or creativity itself. Whitehead's God is not absolute Being, like the object of Rahner's Vorgriff. Rahner's God, on the other hand, is not one actual entity alongside of others in the processing universe but is the transcendent and abysmal source of all that is.

Whitehead and Rahner both explain the implicit presence of God in ordinary experience through theories of abstraction, but they develop their understandings in very different ways. Whitehead's abstraction analyzes the eternal objects which are ordered in the primordial nature of God and made relevant to each moment of creative advance. We experience the primordial nature of God in the relevance of genuinely new possibilities in experience. God is the "ground of all order and of all originality."[88] Rahner, on the other hand, focuses not upon the novelty of new possibilities coming into relevance but upon the abstraction of an unlimited quiddity from a finite object. Rahner argues that the

---

[86]Alfred North Whitehead, Symbolism: Its Meaning and Effect (New York: Capricorn Books, 1959), 21 (hereafter cited as Sym).

[87]Ibid., 43.

[88]PR, 108.

grasp of an unlimited quiddity presupposes a reaching out for absolute Being, which he then identifies with God.[89]

Whitehead's God is not transcendent, incomprehensible mystery in the sense of Rahner's God. Nor is Whitehead's God the ultimate, the absolute source of all being, for Whitehead distinguishes God from creativity and identifies the latter as ultimate.[90] For Rahner finite reality is mysterious to the degree that it participates in the ultimate, all-encompassing mystery which is God. For Whitehead God participates in the all-encompassing mysterious and creative advance of the universe. For Whitehead the ultimate object of awe is the process of passage itself: "It is impossible to meditate on time and the mystery of the creative passage of nature without an overwhelming emotion at the limitations of human intelligence."[91] Whitehead finds the "operative presence" of the passage of nature everywhere: it "must be sought for throughout the whole."[92] While Whitehead's God has a crucial role in the passage of nature, God is not its absolute source or transcendent creator.

Both Rahner and Whitehead understand God to be actively inviting humans, and indeed all forms of reality, to greater levels of intensity of experience and consciousness. Whitehead finds the persuasive invitation of God in the initial goal of an entity's subjective aim and claims that this invitation is found in various forms in each moment of process. Even an entity which is not conscious receives the initial datum of its subjective aim from God and makes its own decision to become what it will be. Rahner sees the entire cosmos in an evolutionary process of pressing forward to greater levels of self-presence. Like Whitehead, Rahner acknowledges that in the processing cosmos "everything is not always already present from the very beginning."[93] The human person is "the being in whom the basic tendency of matter to find itself in the spirit by self-transcendence arrives at the point where it definitely breaks through."[94] This cosmic process becomes conscious of itself in humankind.

---

[89]HW, 76-86.

[90]PR, 21.

[91]Alfred North Whitehead, The Concept of Nature (Cambridge: Cambridge University Press, 1971), 73.

[92]Ibid.

[93]"Christology within an Evolutionary View of the World," TI, V, 166; cf. Whitehead, FR, 24, 29.

[94]Ibid., 160.

On the level of human experience Rahner describes God's call to individual humans in his formal existential ethic. Like the initial datum of Whitehead's subjective aim, the formal existential ethic is not a separate experience unto itself but rather an aspect of the process of decision-making, an invitation which comes from God and proposes God's vision of what this particular human person can become.

Rahner and Whitehead differ in the role they accord to Christ in the cosmic process. For Whitehead the life of Christ is the disclosure in act of what Plato had discerned in theory.[95] The "brief Galilean vision" is a clue to the nature of reality but is not the "climax of the history of the cosmos towards which the entire process has been evolving from the beginning," as Rahner understands the Christ-event to be.[96] Rahner could not accept Whitehead's interpretation of Christ without serious qualification. Rahner could quite easily accept Plato and other non-Christian thinkers as anonymous Christians who were already touched by God's grace and truth. He could also acknowledge large elements of truth in Plato, but he would insist that non-biblical interpretations of God and the world are at least in part objectively mistaken. In Rahner's understanding, the supernatural revelation in Christ is the disclosure not of what Plato's theory had explicitly discerned, but of what Plato had implicitly experienced and incorrectly articulated.

Rahner and Whitehead have very different understandings of the word grace. As we have seen, Whitehead interprets the notion of grace as a description of the universal persuasive activity of God throughout the natural process of the cosmos.[97] Rahner, by contrast, defends the traditional conception of grace as an additional supernatural gift beyond the natural creative activity of God. However, Rahner also interprets the theological concept of nature as a <u>Restbegriff</u>, a remainder concept, an abstraction from our experience which describes a possible world which we never actually encounter. Concretely, for Rahner, we live in a world of grace, a world in which God's supernatural gift of grace is operative at every moment from the very beginning of creation.

---

[95]<u>AI</u>, 167.

[96]"Christology within an Evolutionary View of the World," <u>TI</u>, V, 178.

[97]<u>AI</u>, 160.

Christ as Classical Instance

Pittenger draws heavily upon Whitehead's philosophy in developing his interpretation of Jesus Christ as the classical instance of God's revelation. While he repeatedly professes his respect and admiration for Whitehead's thought, Pittenger insists that Whitehead's philosophy cannot be simply adopted by Christian theologians without adaptation:

> Because of this background in strict philosophy, 'process-thought' must be worked through, not simply 'taken over', by Christian theologians. In a way not dissimilar to that of Augustine with his use of neo-Platonism, or of Thomas Aquinas with his similar use of the newly recovered Aristotelianism of his day, the exponents of 'process-theology' have found in Whitehead's vision of the world material which in their judgement provides a context for Christian faith and a conceptuality with which Christian theologians can work. But it must be adapted to the purpose.[98]

In particular, Pittenger notes the absence of Christology and soteriology from Whitehead's thought,[99] and makes these subjects principal concerns of his own work. Unlike many Whiteheadian thinkers, Pittenger is concerned to call attention to similarities between Whiteheadian and Thomist thought. When challenged on the orthodoxy of Whiteheadian and Hartshornian panentheism, Pittenger quotes Thomas Aquinas as precedent: "In his rule God stands in relation to the whole universe as the soul stands in relation to the body."[100] Pittenger repeatedly refers with approval to Aquinas, citing his views on a variety of issues.[101]

---

[98]Pittenger, Alfred North Whitehead, 45.

[99]Ibid.

[100]Thomas Aquinas, II Sent., dist. 1, q. 1, ad. 1; quoted by Norman Pittenger, Unbounded Love: God and Man in Process (New York: Seabury, 1976), 45; also quoted in idem, The Divine Triunity (Philadelphia: United Church Press, 1977), 95.

[101]See Norman Pittenger, The Christian Understanding of Human Nature (Philadelphia: Westminster, 1964). In this work Pittenger refers favorably to Aquinas on knowledge arising through the senses (p. 45), on human knowledge through signs (p. 45), on grace perfecting nature (p. 59). See also WI, where Pittenger also agrees with Aquinas on the naming of God (p. 38), on the human personality of Jesus (p. 91), and on God as goodness diffusive of itself (p. 148).

Pittenger's concern for the earlier tradition of Christian thought often leads him away from a strictly Whiteheadian position and brings him closer to the perspectives of Rahner. For example, when John B. Cobb, Jr. criticized Pittenger's The Holy Spirit as being inconsistent with Whiteheadian conceptions, Pittenger responds, "I remain convinced that the prior allegiance of an exponent of Christian faith is to the theological tradition he or she inherits and by which he or she tries to live."[102] Pittenger's allegiance to both Whitehead and the Christian theological tradition is a critical one, for he insists that any philosophical or theological claim must be tested in experience, so that it "may be validated, in some fashion or other, by its logical consistency and by its capacity to account for the data which experience provides."[103] Even the definition of what is "orthodox" in traditional Christological speculation must be tested by "the facts of experience and the experience of facts."[104]

In discussing Pittenger's Christology I will examine (1) his view of general and special revelation, (2) his understanding of Jesus Christ as the classical instance of God's revelation, (3) the relation between Jesus Christ and the world-process, and (4) the relation of Pittenger's Christology to the wisdom tradition and to Rahner.

General and Special Revelation

Revelation, for Pittenger, is not the supernatural communication of propositions of divine truth but rather is "a complex of event and its apprehension," an offer of union with God and its acceptance.[105] In this perspective Pittenger is embracing the

---

[102]Divine Triunity, 13. For Cobb's critique, see John B. Cobb, Jr., Review of The Holy Spirit by Norman Pittenger, Religious Education 70(1975):342.

[103]Alfred North Whitehead, 46. On the application of this principle to theology, see Lure of Divine Love, 17, 81.

[104]WI, xiv; Pittenger also makes the positive side of this assertion: the Christian claim "has been verified in experience" (Divine Triunity, 59).

[105]WI, 21. On this point Pittenger notes that he disagrees with Thomas Aquinas, but, without noting it, he is agreeing with Rahner. See Rahner, "Concept of Mystery," TI, IV, 38-40.

view of William Temple that revelation is "the coincidence of divinely guided events and divinely inspired apprehension."[106]

Since God is always and everywhere active in human life, Pittenger finds a "general revelation" of God offered constantly through ordinary human experience.[107] Pittenger is wary of the distinction between "natural theology" and "revealed theology" because it suggests an understanding of revelation as a series of propositions, some of which we can learn ourselves and others of which have to be supernaturally communicated. Pittenger stresses that all our knowledge of God is "the result of God's disclosure of himself to us."[108] Nonetheless, Pittenger does want to distinguish between God's "general" and "special" self-disclosure.

Pittenger largely accepts Whitehead's description of the role of God in ordinary human experience. We experience God as the "lure" of love, a persuasive force that invites us to richer and more intense experience.[109] Following the lead of Whitehead, Pittenger describes God as:

> a reality that is the source of potentiality and the recipient of achievement, a reality that works in the created order to provide aims, and then to accept into itself the good that this actualization accomplished.[110]

While Pittenger generally uses Whitehead's images and categories to describe the relation of God and humankind, he departs from a strictly Whiteheadian perspective on God in important ways. He emphatically embraces Whitehead's view of God as involved in every level of process and as affected by other entities. However, where Whitehead distinguished God from creativity, Pittenger describes God in more traditional terms as the creator of heaven and earth:

---

[106]Ibid., 20-21. Pittenger cites William Temple, Nature, Man, and God (London: Macmillan, 1934), 301-25.

[107]WI, 22.

[108]Ibid., 21.

[109]Lure of Divine Love, 12-22; see also Norman Pittenger, Process-Thought and Christian Faith (New York: Macmillan Company, 1968), 11-54; and W. Norman Pittenger, Rethinking the Christian Message (Greenwich, Ct.: Seabury, 1956), 61-81.

[110]Lure of Divine Love, 64-65.

To think of God as acting in dynamic relation to his creatures not merely as one actor among many, but as the universal creative power which sustains all things, and without
which they could neither be nor act, is true to what our best
knowledge of the world tells us.[111]

As we have seen, Whitehead's God is not the transcendent,
ultimate cause of process but is one factor within the process.
Pittenger, in sharp contrast to Whitehead, accepts the view of
W.R. Matthews that an adequate explanation of the cosmic process
requires "something more" than the process itself: "What is required is some grounding of the whole process in a Reality more
basically real than the process."[112]

Without noting it explicitly Pittenger is here departing from
Whitehead's interpretation of process, in which God is the primordial actual entity but is not an ultimate, transcendent ground
which is "more basically real" than the process. While Pittenger
himself does not call attention to his difference from Whitehead
on this point, this perspective has far-reaching implications for
his theology. While Pittenger continually uses the language and
categories of Whitehead, he transforms their meaning by using them
in the context of a more traditional conception of God.

The general revelation of God in ordinary experience is the
context for Pittenger's understanding of special revelation.
Special revelation does not communicate completely new information, nor is it an absolutely unique form of God's presence in the
world. Special revelation occurs when "God makes a unique, inten-
sive, and peculiarly significant disclosure of himself."[113]

To express the correlation between the universal presence of
God and special revelation, Pittenger turns to Whitehead's understanding of "importance." Events are important when they strike
us with such impact that "they open up new depths for our understanding, illuminate what we have already experienced, and prepare
the way for what we may experience in the future."[114] Importance
shapes our experience of the world by giving us a perspective for
"grading the effectiveness of things about us in proportion to

---

[111]WI, 174.

[112]Ibid., 152.

[113]Ibid., 23.

[114]Ibid.

their interest."[115] An event which is very important becomes definitive for us; it becomes "the key to much else" and has "a quality of decisiveness in our ongoing thought and action; such an event is 'final.'"[116]

Pittenger uses the examples of Bach and Shakespeare to illustrate his point and points to art as an analogy to special religious experiences:

> This or that play, novel, poem, work of art is taken to be marked by such insight, inspiration, and imagination, or such technical skill, that it sets a standard or establishes a criterion by which other work in that field is to be judged. It is unsurpassable because it is definitive.[117]

Pittenger's use of aesthetic experience to interpret special religious revelation follows the example of Whitehead, who sees aesthetic experience as the clue to the underlying order of the universe, the activity of God, and the foundation of moral judgements. Whitehead claims that his metaphysical doctrine finds the foundations of the world in the aesthetic experience. Pittenger follows the example of Whitehead, noting: "Very likely, I am one of those whose orientation is much more aesthetic than ethical."[118]

In developing his interpretation Pittenger stresses that we do not choose which events will be "important" to us. It is the events themselves that strike us with such power to change our self-understanding. Pittenger cites the experiences of a friend bringing out the best in us, of truth bursting upon us, or of having our eyes opened to beauty and goodness. In each of these "we receive the given that comes to us without our seeking it in the first place."[119] In an analogous way, in revelation, whether general or special, "it is God who is prior, God who first moves in upon us. We do not begin on the human level and seek for ourselves and by ourselves."[120]

---

[115]Alfred North Whitehead, *Modes of Thought* (New York: Macmillan, 1938), 15; quoted by Pittenger, *WI* 23.

[116]*CR*, 100.

[117]*Ibid*., 88-89.

[118]Pittenger, *Lure of Divine Love*, 163; see Whitehead, *RM*, 101.

[119]*WI*, 23.

[120]*Ibid*.

Jesus Christ

Pittenger interprets the revelation of God in Jesus Christ as the "classical instance" of God's activity in the world.[121] A classical instance "gives us a criterion by which we may judge all that follows as well as all that has gone before."[122] The special revelation of God in Jesus is not the exclusive or the last revelation of God. Rather, it means that

in this place at this time God acted in such a way that he has given the clue, the key to all that he has done, all that he is doing, and all that he will do in the revelation of himself to men.[123]

In this sense Pittenger claims that what God did in Jesus is final and definitive and of universal significance for all humankind. In this perspective the atonement effected in and through Jesus Christ appears as "at-one-ment": "Jesus is that one in whom God acts focally toward us, in loving revelation and manifestation, calling forth our response."[124] Pittenger adopts Abelard's interpretation of the atonement, complementing it with an ontological grounding. He argues that Abelard is misinterpreted if he is dismissed as "merely exemplarist." According to Pittenger, what Abelard meant was

that in Jesus, God gave us not so much an example of what we should be like but . . . a vivid and compelling demonstration

---

[121]Lure of Divine Love, 114; Process-Thought and Christian Faith, 72-74. On the Christology of Pittenger, see John Arthur Gustavson, Christian Theology in Process Perspective: A Study of Charles Hartshorne's Dipolar Theism and Norman Pittenger's Process Christolgy (Ann Arbor, Mich.: University Microfilms, 1969); David Curtis Minter, Christology in the Thought of Nels F.S. Ferre, W. Norman Pittenger and Paul Tillich (Ann Arbor, Mich.: University Microfilms, 1968); Mary Theresa Rattigan, Christology and Process Thought: The Decisiveness of Jesus Christ in the Thought of Bernard Meland, W. Norman Pittenger, Daniel Day Williams (Ann Arbor, Mich.: University Microfilms, 1973); and Gilbert Lee Sanders, The Christology of W. Norman Pittenger: A Summary and a Critique (Ann Arbor, Mich.: University Microfilms, 1979).

[122]WI, 24.

[123]Ibid.

[124]Lure of Divine Love, 118.

in a concrete event in history that God does love humanity
and will go to any lengths to win from them their glad and
committed response.[125]

The ontological grounding for Abelard's position lies in the
realization that this "love in concrete act is precisely what God
always is and how God always acts."[126] The effect of this demonstration is so powerful that it can transform our lives, opening
up a new vision of reality and drawing us to surrender to God in
love.

Pittenger, like Rahner, sees an essential link between anthropology and Christology. Human beings are "an unfulfilled
capacity for God."[127] Since we are "made towards God," by the
very fact of our creation we are "the potential 'instrument' . . .
for the expression of God."[128] This orientation of the human person to God is the presupposition of the incarnation; it is so
essential that Pittenger can write:

> to say man, in a full Christian theistic meaning of the word,
> is at the same time to say God, or more precisely, to say the
> Word of God, for the Word of God is the undergirding reality
> who sustains man in being and moves through man in expression
> of the divine purpose, however brokenly, imperfectly, and
> sporadically this may be accomplished.[129]

Thus the incarnation of God in Jesus Christ is not an absolutely unique form of God's presence in the world and in human
life. In Jesus Christ "there is full actualization of that image
[of God in the human person], so that he is the Express Image of
God, in human terms and in human experience."[130] By fully actual-
izing a relationship to God which is only partially actualized in
other lives, Jesus reveals "the constant and pervasive activity of
God through his Word in the world and in human life."[131]

---

[125]Ibid., 119.

[126]Ibid.

[127]WI, 179.

[128]Ibid., 181.

[129]Ibid.

[130]Ibid., 181; see also 209, 285.

[131]Ibid., 180.

Pittenger is careful to guard against a Pelagian misunderstanding of this actualization:

> This actualization is both 'from above' and 'from below' . . . it is of God and through the operation of God in his Self-Expressive Word. Yet it is equally important to say that this fulfillment is not arbitrarily imposed from outside of manhood and apart from the consent of manhood.[132]

Like Rahner, Pittenger refuses to allow an opposition between dependence upon God and becoming one's own self. Pittenger accepts the remark of Dean W.R. Inge: "A man is never so truly and intensely himself, as when he is most possessed by God."[133]

Thus the incarnation must be understood in the context of the general revelation of God throughout human experience and the essential orientation of the human person to God. While the event of Jesus Christ is "crucial, definitive, unique," it cannot be absolutely unique, for "the absolutely unique is absolutely unknowable."[134] God's activity in Jesus differs in degree, but not in kind, from the constant divine activity in all human experience. What we discover from this revelation is "that persuasion not compulsion, love not force, is at the heart of the creative process of the universe."[135] Pittenger is quick to add that what is revealed is not in the first place a doctrine or a teaching but a life. He adopts Whitehead's view that "Christ gave his life. It is for Christians to discern the doctrine."[136]

Pittenger, like Rahner, is concerned to retrieve the dogma of Chalcedon as an interpretation of the more concrete and manifold biblical testimony and to restate the meaning of the dogma in terms that can communicate in the contemporary situation. For Pittenger

> the belief that Jesus is truly human and truly divine is the central affirmation of our faith. But the belief that Jesus

---

[132]Ibid., 182.

[133]W.R. Inge, Vale (London: Longmans, Green, 1934), 40; quoted by Pittenger, WI, 99.

[134]WI, 15.

[135]Lure of Divine Love, 102.

[136]Whitehead, RM, 55; quoted by Pittenger, Lure of Divine Love, 102.

Christ is divine was not arrived at as an intellectual exercise but . . . by way of a 'soteriological' experience.[137]

The concern of the early church councils was not to speculate about matters beyond experience but to interpret the significance of the experience of Jesus Christ, to "discern the doctrine" in his life. Thus the "iota" of difference between homoousios and homoiousios involved the pressing existential concern of the reality of the salvation experienced in Christ and the reliability of this experience as an interpretative clue to the whole of reality:

> Furthermore, if the union of God and man in Jesus is not a true, undivided, unconfused, inseparable, unchangeable union, then what guarantee have we that this act of God in Christ is more than an incident or accident in the divine-human relationship?[138]

Like Rahner, Pittenger views the dogma of Chalcedon not as a final conclusion but as an invitation to further reflection. Instead of solving the problem of the interpretation of Jesus Christ, the dogma states the terms in which the problem must be addressed: "If we wish to be true to Christian experience, based as it is upon the Christian event, we must say that here is one who is truly divine, truly human, and yet truly one."[139]

Pittenger fears that the most prevalent interpretations of Chalcedon have neglected the humanity of Jesus and presented a distorted picture of "a God disguised in manhood."[140] Pittenger's concern to stress the full humanity of Jesus leads him to retrieve the work of the Antiochene school of early Christian thought. He argues that Theodore of Mopsuestia and Nestorius have been unfairly accused of having no adequate articulation of the unity of the two natures in Jesus Christ. According to Pittenger, Theodore of Mopsuestia did not propose a "'merely external, accidental' union" of the natures but rather "a real (not 'mere') 'reciprocal relationship,'" which does in fact arise out of, although it is not

---

[137]WI, 83.

[138]Ibid., 85.

[139]Ibid., 88.

[140]Ibid., 89, n. 1; Pittenger is quoting this phrase from W.S. Palmer, Where Science and Religion Meet (London: Hodder and Stoughton, n.d.), 246. See also WI, 100-11.

exhausted in, 'the loving inclination of divine and human selves towards each other.'"[141]

Pittenger argues that the Antiochene terms "eudokia (God's goodwill expressed in the man Jesus) and sunapheia (intimate co-operative union in moral terms)" are not as suspect as the Alexandrian school and its later followers have charged.[142] Drawing upon the Antiochene tradition, Pittenger understands the union of the divine and human natures in Jesus Christ

> after the analogy of personal union such as we know in, say, human marriage or the love of a lover and his beloved. . . . The union of God and man in Jesus is more like what we know of personal relationship, more like what we know too of the 'gracious' quality of such relationship, than it is like anything else.[143]

In Pittenger's Whiteheadian understanding of reality, personal relationships have an ontological importance. Relationships do not "happen" to affect natures and substances which exist independently; relationships are the way in which natures and substances come to be and continue in being in a world of process. Thus, Pittenger argues, it is a fundamental mistake to dismiss a Christology which focuses on relationships as somehow less ontologically real or less orthodox than a Christology which focuses primarily upon natures.

The danger of the Alexandrian school's Christology, Pittenger charges, is that the humanity of Jesus Christ almost inevitably is overshadowed by the divinity: "the refusal to grant a true human

---

[141]WI, 92; Pittenger is here responding to the criticism of Karl Adam that for the Antiochene school the union of the natures is, in Adam's words, "merely external, accidental," or "a mere reciprocal relationship which arises out of the loving inclination of divine and human selves towards each other" (Pittenger's italics). See Karl Adam, The Christ of Faith (New York: Pantheon, 1957), 34; quoted by Pittenger, WI, 92. Pittenger argues that Adam's own positive analogy between the incarnation and loving human relationships is very close to the intention of the Antiochene school (WI, 92). Pittenger is building upon the work of Richard A. Norris, Jr., "The Anthropological Foundations of the Christology of Theodore of Mopsuestia" (dissertation, Library of the General Seminary); F.A. Sullivan, The Christology of Theodore of Mopsuestia (Rome: Gregorianum, 1957); and R.V. Sellars, review of Sullivan in Journal of Theological Studies (1957):341.

[142]CR, 13.

[143]Ibid., 12.

centre to the humanity of Jesus is bound to lead to a serious minimizing of that humanity."[144] Pittenger presses this accusation against a number of contemporary "orthodox" theologians, including H.M. Relton, S.F. Davenport, Leonard Hodgson, and Lionel Thornton.[145] In each case, Pittenger suggests, the fundamental difficulty is a failure to acknowledge the shift in meaning of the word "person" from patristic times to the present. Where contemporary usage understands person as "the organizing centre of the totality of experiences," in the patristic discussions hypostasis did not have psychological connotations but "suggested rather a distinguishable mode of being as well as of energizing or operation."[146] Given the contemporary meaning of the word "person" as "the psychological centre of subjective experience," Pittenger argues that

> the 'person' of Jesus Christ as an historical figure, in his manhood, must necessarily be human. To think of his 'person,' in this sense, as divine would be equivalent to saying, with Apollinarius, that the normal human centre of experience, the psychological ego, was replaced by the divine Word.[147]

In language close to Rahner's Pittenger writes that the incarnation is not an intrusion or a denial of the human person but rather the "crowning and completing of all that is implicit in humanity from its very beginning."[148]

Christ and the World-Process

For Pittenger, as for Rahner, the event of Jesus Christ must be related to the entire world-process. Like Rahner, Pittenger seeks to reinterpret the ancient tradition of Logos Christology within the conceptuality of a modern evolutionary world view. While insisting that the account of Jesus Christ is told in symbolic or poetic language, Pittenger refuses to allow a complete

---

[144]WI, 93.

[145]Ibid., 100-08.

[146]Ibid., 112.

[147]WI, 114.

[148]Ibid., 131; cf. Rahner, "On the Theology of the Incarnation," TI, IV, 109: "The indefinable nature [of the human person] . . . has, when assumed by God as his reality, simply arrived at the point to which it always strives by virtue of its essence."

dichotomy between religious affirmations and scientific discoveries:

> We cannot compartmentalize our worlds. Our philosophical ideas and our scientific discoveries have much to do with the kind of person we are, they help to make us this man in this place.[149]

According to Pittenger, we must interpret Jesus Christ in light of what we know about the rest of reality, and we must interpret the rest of reality in light of the experience of Jesus Christ.[150] Pittenger, like Rahner, calls for a "Christianization" of ontology.

Pittenger embraces the widespread recognition that change and becoming are central to experience and thus are "a basic ingredient in the metaphysical enterprise."[151] While he is heavily influenced by Whitehead and Hartshorne, Pittenger does not want to rely too heavily on any one philosophical description of process.[152] What is central for Pittenger is the fundamental theme of God intimately involved in the entire cosmic process of evolution.

Pittenger notes that the epigenetic interpretation of emergent evolution acknowledges "the appearance of the genuinely new within the ongoing process of evolution."[153] As we have seen, Pittenger, in sharp contrast to Whitehead, further argues that the description of emergent evolution requires some explanation which transcends the process, a "Reality more basically real than the process."[154] Throughout the entire cosmic process there is a nisus or drive which is calling forth new levels of consciousness. Pittenger accepts Lloyd-Morgan's suggestion that this nisus which

---

[149]WI, 46.

[150]W. Norman Pittenger, Theology and Reality: Essays in Restatement (Greenwich, Ct.: Seabury, 1955), 13, 46-47.

[151]WI, 147.

[152]Ibid, 155. Pittenger repeatedly mentions Whitehead and Hartshorne as representatives of a broader cultural and philosophical movement, which includes Samuel Alexander, Conway Lloyd-Morgan, Jan Smuts, Henri Bergson, and Edouard LeRoy (WI, 146; CR, 17; Theology and Reality, 40-43).

[153]WI, 150.

[154]Ibid., 152.

directs evolution should be interpreted theologically as the Logos.[155] Pittenger argues:

> If it is true that there is a nisus such as Dr Lloyd-Morgan desiderated, that nisus must be the manifestation of a 'supra-natural' Reality (in the sense of a Reality not confined to nor exhausted in the 'natural' order), who is the final explanation of the process, from whom it derives, whose purposes it actualizes, and upon whom it 'depends' for its continuance at every moment of its existence.[156]

Human history must be seen as an integral part of the developing cosmic process. Given this perspective, Pittenger protests vigorously against the neo-orthodox tendency to "dismiss nature as simple recurrence, with no significance for a theism which would find the works of God in the striking and fresh and contingent circumstances of historical change."[157] Since God is always already present in the process of evolving natural forms, the revelation of God in Jesus Christ must be integrated into a total vision of the universe. Jesus "is not cut off from the whole movement of God in and to his world, as if he were a visitor from an entirely different sphere."[158]

Pittenger recalls the patristic discussions of the various forms of the Logos as a way of relating the activity of God in the cosmos to the revelation in Jesus Christ. The Logos endiathetos describes the "Word as an eternal indwelling mode of Godhead; Logos prophorikos, the Word proceeding forth in creative activity."[159] Justin Martyr wrote of the "Logos spermatikos, present and working in men as the implanted and seminal Word."[160] The Council of Nicaea spoke of the "Logos enthropesanta, the Word fully embodied or expressed in fleshly human terms."[161] The pres-

---

[155]Ibid.

[156]Ibid.

[157]Ibid., 154.

[158]Ibid., 164.

[159]Ibid., 166-67. Both these expresssions are used by Theophilus of Antioch, Ad Autolycum, ii.

[160]WI, 167; Justin Martyr, Apologia, i, 46 and ii, 13.

[161]WI, 167; cf. also 216. See also Norman Pittenger, God in Process (London: SCM Press, 1967), 28; and Rethinking the Christian Message, 90-92.

ence of the Logos in different ways in the inner life of the Trinity, in the cosmic order, in all human life, and in Jesus Christ offers Pittenger an analogical clue to interpreting all of reality.

Jesus Christ is the focal self-expression of God's activity in the world, an especially intense and full manifestation of the constant divine activity:

> the diffused activity of deity in and for the human race is concentrated at this point [in Christ] as a burning-glass concentrates the sun's rays and by that intensification renders them immensely more effective and powerful.[162]

The revelation of God as love in the person of Jesus Christ offers a clue to God's purpose throughout all levels of the cosmos.

Wisdom, Pittenger, and Rahner

Pittenger, like Whitehead before him, was aware of the continuities between his own thought and the biblical wisdom tradition. He notes that the background of the Logos of John is the wisdom literature of Hellenistic Judaism.[163] In the development of New Testament Christology Pittenger understands the categories of the wisdom tradition as a necessary supplement to the messianic and prophetic categories and as a stage leading to the Logos Christology of John.[164] Pittenger also notes that the wisdom tradition, especially in the Hellenistic period, had a more speculative tendency than much of the Hebrew Bible: "it ought never be forgotten that the more speculative thought of hellenizing Jews did find its way into the Wisdom Literature and is therefore part of the canon of Scripture."[165] The speculative tendency of the Hellenistic Jewish wisdom literature offers Pittenger a precedent for his own use of Whitehead's speculative philosophy.

We have seen that both Pittenger and Rahner agree in claiming that the life, death, and resurrection of Jesus definitively illumine the constant activity of God in human life. Both thinkers see the salvific will of God as constantly present throughout all human experience, and both see human being as essentially oriented

---

[162]WI, 167.

[163]Rethinking the Christian Message, 89.

[164]WI, 79.

[165]Ibid., 37.

to God. Both claim that the illuminating power of the Christ-event is grounded in Jesus's unique, supreme actualization of the human relationship to God, a relationship which is only potential or only partially actualized in other human lives.

The trajectory of the wisdom tradition offers precedent for the endeavors of Pittenger and Rahner to discern an implicit experience of God throughout human life and to correlate this universal experience with the specific historical revelation in Jesus Christ. The invitation of Lady Wisdom at the city gates (Prov 8) articulates an offer experienced through the universally present ordering power of creation. Pittenger's use of the category "classical instance" is similar to the examples of lives transformed by Lady Wisdom in Ben Sira 44-50 and the Wisdom of Solomon 10-19. For Ben Sira and the Wisdom of Solomon, as for Pittenger, the specific revelatory events of the history of Israel elucidate the experience of all people.

The center of Pittenger's Christology is the Logos Christology of John's Gospel, which he describes as the "culmination" of the biblical interpretation of Jesus.[166] Pittenger repeatedly stresses the relation between the revelation of God in Jesus Christ and the universal general revelation of God in all experience. The interpretations of the prologue of John by Dodd and Lightfoot capture the heart of Pittenger's theological program.[167]

The positive, world-constructive side of the wisdom tradition finds echoes in Pittenger's affirmation of the intelligibility of our experience and the possibility of discerning the presence of God in the ordering power of the universe. The world-questioning side of the wisdom tradition, represented by Job and Qoheleth, finds less of an echo in Pittenger. Pittenger does affirm the dimension of mystery in human experience,[168] but he does not express the unsettling experience of the silence of God amid human suffering found in Job and Qoheleth, or even in Rahner's prayer after World War II.[169]

Pittenger's own answer to the problem of suffering is that God suffers with us and is doing everything possible to mitigate suffering: "God is doing the very best he can to 'handle' evil and

---

[166]WI, 79.

[167]Pittenger himself refers to the work of Dodd and Lightfoot in WI, 80-81, n. 4. See Dodd, 285; Lightfoot, 81.

[168]Divine Triunity, 50-52.

[169]Vorgrimler, Understanding Karl Rahner, 4.

he both calls and wants his human children to join him in this enterprise."[170] Pittenger's language on this issue is often very close to Whitehead's. Like Whitehead, he claims that God is "confronted by material with which he must work."[171] Also like Whitehead, Pittenger looks to the demiurge of the _Timaeus_ as an example of the goodness of God working with the material at hand.[172] For both Whitehead and Pittenger, God is in some way limited by the freedom of other entities.

However, where Whitehead locates the limitation of God metaphysically in the finite nature of God, Pittenger denies that his theology implies a finite God,[173] and suggests that God freely wills to be limited because a world of genuine freedom is better than a fully determined world. Thus Pittenger locates the limitation of God in a free decision of God:

> the non-God world has a radical freedom which God himself must and does accept. That is how things are; and theologically we might phrase it by saying that such is how God wants things to be.[174]

Pittenger defends the actual world process, in which God is limited and other agents can freely choose good or evil, as better than a world "in which goodness is automatic and hence not truly goodness at all."[175] A world with the freedom to choose evil offers the only context for truly choosing goodness.

Rahner, in contrast to Whitehead, would refuse to allow any limitation of God by the world which was not itself freely and gratuitously posited by God. For Rahner the relationship of creator and creature is itself freely created by God. Pittenger describes the world as "organic" to God: God would not really be God "unless there is a world in which his creativity is expressed and which is itself an expression of that creativity."[176] While

---

[170]Norman Pittenger, _Goodness Distorted_ (London: A.R. Mowbray & Co., 1970), 39.

[171]_Ibid._, 32.

[172]_Ibid._, 40.

[173]Norman Pittenger, _Catholic Faith in a Process Perspective_ (Maryknoll, N.Y.: Orbis Books, 1981), 55.

[174]_Goodness Distorted_, 32.

[175]_Old Testament Wisdom_, 111.

[176]_Process-Thought and Christian Faith_, 41.

Pittenger's language often is very close to Whitehead's, his view of God as more basically real than the process implies that God is freely responsible for establishing God's relationship to creation. Thus God would freely choose to create a world organic to Godself. This perspective brings his theology significantly closer to Rahner's than his Whiteheadian language would suggest. Where Whitehead offers a theodicy based on the metaphysical limitation of God by a world of freedom, Pittenger rejects the idea of a finite God and implies that all limitations on God are freely chosen by God; Rahner for his part refuses to set any external limits on God and invokes the at times frightening incomprehensibility of God.[177]

Rahner and Pittenger have rather different conceptions of the role of the Christ-event. For Rahner the Christ-event is constitutive of God's relationship to the world precisely because it is the manifestation, the real symbol of God's universal salvific will. Rahner distinguishes the gratuitous act of creation from the doubly gratuitous bestowal of grace in God's self-communication in Christ. Pittenger, on the other hand, does not describe the Christ-event as gratuitously constitutive of the God-world relationship. Though he does not use the terminology, it seems clear that Pittenger would reject the "double gratuity of grace" defended by Rahner, for Pittenger agrees with Schubert Ogden in seeing Jesus as the re-presentation of "the possibility present in human nature as such."[178] Pittenger follows Whitehead in seeing Jesus as the disclosure in act of what Plato and others had discerned in theory.[179] As we have seen, Rahner would not be able to accept this interpretation as it stands.

Underlying the different perspectives on the significance of the Christ-event are basic differences in theological and philosophical method. Rahner's transcendental method in theology accepts the dogmas defined by the Catholic Church as true and asks

---

[177]Pittenger, Goodness Distorted, 41; Vorgrimler, Understanding Karl Rahner, 4; Karl Rahner, "Why Does God Allow Us to Suffer?" TI, XIX, trans. Edward Quinn (New York: Crossroad, 1983), 194-208.

[178]Lure of Divine Love, 113. This issue is the point of contention between Ogden and Rahner. See Schubert Ogden, "The Reformation that We Want," Anglican Theological Review 54(1972): 268-72. For a comparison and contrast of Rahner and Ogden, see John C. Robertson, Jr., "Rahner and Ogden: Man's Knowledge of God," HTR 63(1970), 377-407; and Hentz, "Rahner's Concept," 171-81.

[179]CR, 152; Lure of Divine Love, 101; Process-Thought and Christian Faith, 71.

about the conditions of possibility for them to be understood. According to Rahner,

> a transcendental investigation examines an issue according to the necessary conditions given by the possibility and action on the part of the subject himself. . . . Therefore, if one wishes to pursue dogmatics as transcendental anthropology, it means that whenever one is confronted with an object of dogma, one inquires as to the conditions necessary for it to be known by the theological subject.[180]

Thus in Christology Rahner assumes the dogma of Chalcedon to be true and develops his ontology of real symbol to illuminate the condition of possibility of the incarnation. Even Rahner's later attempt to develop a Christology "from below" explicitly presupposes (1) that Jesus understood himself as the absolute saviour, (2) that the resurrection confirmed his self-understanding and manifested him as the mediator of salvation, and (3) that the first two presuppositions are what is meant by the church doctrine of the incarnation and the hypostatic union.[181] A Christology "from below" which accepts these presuppositions from the outset appears to be another form of transcendental reflection, a reflection informed by biblical exegesis but still addressing the question of how the dogma of Chalcedon is to be understood.[182]

Pittenger's method, following the example of Whitehead, is "like an aviator who takes off from a well-known place, makes the flight, and then returns to earth where once again he is with things that he knows from his own experience."[183] As Pittenger explains it, process thinkers begin from particular experiences, make generalizations which are more widely applicable, and then refer these generalizations to various areas of experience to see if they are useful interpretative principles. The revelation of God in Jesus Christ is one particular experience which is so important that it is the focal manifestation of the activity of God and the meaning of human life. According to Pittenger, the process conception of God can be understood as "nothing other than a generalization from that event [of Christ], a generalization

---

[180]"Theology and Anthropology," TI, IX, 29.

[181]Foundations, 299.

[182]On Rahner's later work in Christology, see Karl Rahner and Wilhelm Thüsing, Christologie--Systematisch und Exegetisch: Arbeitsgrundlagen für eine interdisziplinäre Vorlesung, Quaestiones Disputatae, No. 55 (Freiburg: Herder, 1972).

[183]Lure of Divine Love, 17.

applied to the rest of experience and to the world where we live."[184]

Language

Whitehead and Pittenger were both aware of the special demands that metaphysical and religious assertions make upon the use of language. This section will begin by discussing Whitehead's understanding of the character of metaphysical language and the role of dogmatic formulations in religion. Then I will examine Pittenger's adaptation of Whitehead's perspective in his interpretation of the dogmatic language of Christology. I will conclude by reflecting on the relation between the use of language by Whitehead and Pittenger and the perspectives of Rahner and the wisdom tradition.

Whitehead: The Language of Metaphysics and Dogma

Whitehead views language as unable in principle to formulate the first principles of metaphysics adequately:

Words and phrases must be stretched toward a generality foreign to their ordinary usage, and however such elements of language be stabilized as technicalities, they remain metaphors mutely appealing for an imaginative leap.[185]

According to Whitehead, the use of language always requires a context, a background against which the meaning can be inter-

---

[184]Ibid., 81; cf. Whitehead, RM, 65.

[185]PR, 4; see also Alfred North Whitehead, Modes of Thought (New York: Free Press, 1968), 12 (hereafter cited as MT); Lyman T. Lundeen, Risk and Rhetoric: Whitehead's Theory of Language and the Discourse of Faith (Philadelphia: Fortress, 1972), 54-87; Wilbur M. Urban, "Whitehead's Philosophy of Language and its Relation to his Metaphysics," in The Philosophy of Alfred North Whitehead, ed. Paul Arthur Schilpp (New York: Tudor Publishing Co., 1951), 304; Stephen Theodore Franklin, "Speaking from the Depths: Metaphysics of Propositions, Symbolism, Perceptions, Language and Religion" (2 vols.; Ph.D. dissertation, University of Chicago, 1976); and Donald A. Crosby, "Whitehead on the Metaphysical Employment of Language," Process Studies 1(1971):38-54.

preted; thus "no language can be anything but elliptical, requiring a leap of the imagination to understand its meaning in its
relevance to immediate experience."[186] Whitehead proclaims his
distrust of language and explicitly repudiates the "trust in language as an adequate expression of propositions."[187]

However, given the overall inadequacy of language for formulating metaphysical categories, Whitehead applies the same metaphysical categories to God and other actual entities. Whitehead's
God does not transcend the categories. "God is not to be treated
as an exception to all metaphysical principles, invoked to save
their collapse. He is their chief exemplification."[188] Whitehead
criticizes monistic philosophies such as Spinoza's or absolute
idealism because in them "the ultimate is illegitimately allowed a
final 'eminent' reality, beyond that ascribed to any of its accidents."[189]

For Rahner, language about God is inadequate because it seeks
to articulate an implicit experience of absolute Being which is
the goal of human transcendence. For Whitehead, metaphysical
language in general is inadequate because it reaches for a sense
of the whole universe and demands the broadest possible application of terms and categories. Language about God shares in the
difficulties of metaphysical language in general.

Most importantly, Whitehead distrusts the subject-predicate
structure of Western languages as a misleading indicator of reality. This suspicion of ordinary linguistic usage expresses a fundamental principle of Whitehead's vision of reality in process.
Whitehead notes that his philosophy differs from Spinoza's "by the
abandonment of the subject-predicate forms of thought, so far as
concerns the presupposition that this form is a direct embodiment
of the most ultimate characterization of fact."[190] This effort
leads to a certain paradox for Whitehead, for by writing in
English he inevitably continues to use a language based on subjects and predicates. It is one of Whitehead's main concerns to
resist the temptation inherent in the structure of the English
language to describe reality in terms of "the 'substance-quality'
concept"; instead he claims that in his philosophy "morphological

---

[186]PR, 13.

[187]Ibid., xiii.

[188]Ibid., 343.

[189]Ibid., 7.

[190]Ibid.

description is replaced by description of dynamic process."[191] Whitehead calls in question "the expression of the facts in current verbal statements."[192] This means that he must use language to make it express his own interpretation of the universe. Whitehead admits that this effort never fully succeeds: "the language of literature breaks down precisely at the task of expressing in explicit form the larger generalities--the very generalities which metaphysics seeks to express."[193]

The subject and object form of language will continue in Whitehead's own very important discussion of propositions. Central to Whitehead's understanding of language is the distinction between a proposition and a verbal statement. A proposition presents a vision of possibilities to a segment of reality; it is "a hybrid between pure potentialities and actualities" which makes relevant certain eternal objects to a particular set of actual entities.[194] Propositions are lures for feeling; they are the way in which novelty enters the world.[195] Any proposition must be interpreted against the background of a vision of the entire universe.

Thus every proposition proposing a fact must, in its complete analysis, propose the general character of the universe required for that fact. There are no self-sustained facts, floating in nonentity.[196]

However, the general character of the universe can never be adequately formulated in language because metaphysical generalizations force us to extend the meanings of words beyond their normal use. The total environment of an actual occasion can never be fully stated, and thus language itself remains indeterminate on a

---

[191]Ibid.

[192]Ibid., 11.

[193]Ibid. Implicit in Whitehead's distrust of the subject-predicate structure of language is a critique of the main course of classical modern philosophy from Descartes to Kant. Whitehead charges that the attempt to describe the world in terms of subject and predicate, substance and quality, particular and universal "always does violence to that immediate experience which we express in our actions, our hopes, our sympathies, our purposes" (p. 49).

[194]Ibid., 185-86; cf. also AI, 243-44.

[195]PR, 187.

[196]Ibid., 11.

certain level because "every occurrence presupposes some systematic type of environment."[197] Because the context of a proposition can never be fully specified, "a verbal statement is never the full expression of a proposition."[198]

Nonetheless, propositions are of the utmost importance for human experience because they incite us "to believe, or to doubt, or to enjoy, or to obey."[199] Through its limited but effective power to express propositions, language plays a central metaphysical role for Whitehead. As visions of what is potential for a given phase of the universe, propositions make possible both progress and error. By opening up new possibilities and exciting our interest, propositions mobilize energies for taking risks and making decisions. Even if a proposition is in error, it still may lure us to new experiences which will result in progress. "Error is the price we pay for progress."[200] Whitehead stresses that the primary function of propositions is not to ground belief but to serve as a lure for feeling.[201] Thus Whitehead claims: "It is more important that a proposition be interesting than that it be true."[202] However, Whitehead also goes on to note that "a true proposition is more apt to be interesting than a false one. Also action in accordance with the emotional lure of a proposition is more apt to be successful if the proposition be true."[203]

Whitehead cautions that propositions, and philosophy in general, should not be left to the logicians. Philosophy is led astray if it seeks means of proof through logical consistency.[204] The goal of philosophical language is not proof but "sheer disclosure."[205] The aim at disclosure brings philosophical language into a close relationship to and a partial dependence upon poetic and religious language. Philosophy can be understood as an at-

---

[197]Ibid., 12; see also MT, 66.

[198]PR, 192.

[199]AI, 243.

[200]PR, 187.

[201]Ibid., 184-86.

[202]AI, 244.

[203]Ibid.

[204]MT, 48-52.

[205]Ibid., 49; cf. also 112.

tempt to re-state in other terminology the insights of the great
poets and religious figures:

> Philosophy is the endeavour to find a conventional phraseolo-
> gy for the vivid suggestiveness of the poet. It is the
> endeavour to reduce Milton's 'Lycidas' to prose; and thereby
> to produce a verbal symbolism manageable for use in other
> connections of thought.[206]

Whitehead turns to the romantic poets, especially Shelley and
Wordsworth, for an inventory of the elements with which philosophy
must deal. The romantic poets are particularly important for
their expression in vivid language of the aesthetic values that
are intrinsic to experience but are methodically excluded from
scientific descriptions of nature.

> Both Shelley and Wordsworth emphatically bear witness that
> nature cannot be divorced from its aesthetic values; and that
> these values arise from the cumulation, in some sense, of the
> brooding presence of the whole on its various parts.[207]

Whitehead finds in romantic poetry the fundamental notions
which his philosophy of organism will seek to relate: "change,
value, eternal objects, endurance, organism, interfusion."[208]
Poetry is a critical source of insight and a test for philosophy.
"I hold that the ultimate appeal is to naive experience and that
is why I lay such stress on the evidence of poetry."[209] Thus
Whitehead warns us that if we want to understand nature, we must
consult not only the scientists but also the poets of the human
race.

In an analogous way Whitehead looks to the expressions of
religious language for data for philosophy. Religious language
bears eloquent witness to humankind's sense of the whole: "The
best rendering of integral experience, expressing its general form
divested of irrelevant details, is often to be found in the utter-
ances of religious aspiration."[210] Whitehead quotes two lines of
a hymn as "an almost perfect expression of the direct intuition
from which the main position of the Platonic philosophy is
derived":

---

[206]Ibid., 50.

[207]SMW, 87-88.

[208]Ibid., 88.

[209]Ibid., 89.

[210]PR, 208.

Abide with me;
Fast falls the eventide.[211]

If philosophers stress the intuition of the first line, they produce philosophies of substance and permanence; if they stress the intuition of the second line, they offer philosophies of change and flux. The concrete reality of experience involves both elements together, and therefore "we find that a wavering balance between the two is a characteristic of the greater number of philosophers."[212] The róle of philosophy is to weave the direct intuitions of poetic and religious language into a relatively coherent and adequate scheme of understanding. This task is in principle never complete. "We can never fully understand. But we can increase our penetration."[213]

According to Whitehead, even religious language is unable to express the fullness of religious insight. Religious expressions arise from an immediate awareness which cannot be adequately put into words. This awareness is not a direct intuition of any particular being but rather a sense of the rightness in the nature of things.[214]

Yet mothers can ponder many things in their hearts which their lips cannot express. These many things, which are thus known, constitute the ultimate religious evidence, beyond which there is no appeal.[215]

On the one hand, metaphysics needs religious expressions as a source of data and a guide to the character of immediate experience; but on the other hand, religious language itself needs metaphysics both to establish the meanings of the words it uses and to purify it and guard it from the excess of emotion. Religious language arises from a particular intuition but it generalizes this insight into a conviction about the nature of things. "This universalization of what is discerned in a particular instance is the appeal to a general character inherent in the nature of things."[216] In order to express this general character religion

---

[211]Ibid., 209.

[212]Ibid.

[213]MT, 51.

[214]RM, 60-65.

[215]Ibid., 65.

[216]Ibid.

must turn to metaphysical language for a description of the whole.
Religion repeatedly uses a multitude of terms which only have
meaning against the background of an interpretation of the entire
universe.

But it is impossible to fix the sense of fundamental terms
except by way of reference to some definite metaphysical way
of conceiving the most penetrating description of the universe.
　　　Thus rational religion must have recourse to metaphysics
for a scrutiny of its terms.[217]

Whitehead notes that there is a particular affinity between
the doctrine of the Logos in the Gospel of John and Platonic philosophy. The Logos of John modifies "the notions of the unequivo-
cal personal unity of the Semitic God" and stresses the immanence
of God as "a factor in the universe."[218] Whitehead points out
that the immanence of God in the universe through the Logos was
explicated in the theology of the early church fathers. "Christian theology was then Platonic; it followed John rather than
Paul."[219]

There is another reason why Whitehead insists that religion
needs metaphysical scrutiny. "Religion is the last refuge of
human savagery."[220] The direct deliverances of religious emotion
have led to a long series of horrors in history: "human sacrifice,
and in particular the slaughter of children, cannibalism, sensual
orgies, abject superstition, hatred as between the races, the
maintenance of degrading customs, hysteria, bigotry."[221] Metaphysical reflection upon religious experience integrates religious
intuitions into an overall perspective of the universe based on
the conviction of the rightness of things. Whitehead's rational
reflection turns to reason to protect religion from its own distortions: "reason is the safeguard of the objectivity of religion;
it secures for it the general coherence denied to hysteria."[222]

Whitehead understands all language as a form of symbolism,
and his interpretation of the role of symbolism and expression is

---

[217]Ibid., 76.

[218]Ibid., 70-71.

[219]Ibid., 72.

[220]Ibid., 36.

[221]Ibid.

[222]Ibid., 63; see also 81.

the basis for his interpretation of dogmatic language. For Whitehead symbolism is an essential factor in all human experience.
"[I]t is inherent in the very texture of human life. Language
itself is symbolism."[223]

Symbolism takes many forms. In any form of symbolism Whitehead finds that "some components of its [the human mind's] experience elicit consciousness, beliefs, emotions, and usages, re-
specting other components of its experience."[224] Whitehead is
particularly interested in the symbolic reference between the two
aspects of experience which he calls causal efficacy and presentational immediacy.[225] The more precise and clear experience in the
mode of presentational immediacy functions as a symbolic reference
to the more vague and primitive experience in the mode of causal
efficacy. The relationship between these two forms of experience
is the origin of all human symbolism. Human symbolism arises from
"the symbolic interplay between two distinct modes of direct perception of the external world."[226]

Whitehead applies his definition of symbolism to language in
a twofold sense, finding in the use of language "a double symbolic
reference--from things to words on the part of the speaker and
from words back to things on the part of the listener."[227] For
example, the word "tree" and the trees themselves can each symbolize the other. Normally we use the word "tree" to symbolize the
trees, but a poet seeking inspiration may well "walk into the
forest in order that the trees may suggest the appropriate
words."[228] In such a case, "the trees are the symbols and the
words are the meaning."[229]

Symbolism in a variety of forms is essential to humankind's
ability to express itself. "Mankind, it seems, has to find a

---

[223]Alfred North Whitehead, Symbolism: Its Meaning and Effect
(New York: Capricorn Books, 1959), 62 (hereafter cited as Sym).

[224]Ibid., 8.

[225]Ibid., 30-59.

[226]Ibid., 30.

[227]Ibid., 12.

[228]Ibid.

[229]Ibid.

symbol in order to express itself. Indeed 'expression' is 'symbolism.'"[230] Through symbolic reference the thing symbolized gains increased significance for experience. "The object of symbolism is the enhancement of the importance of what is symbolized."[231]

Whitehead understands dogmatic language as an example of symbolism, an expression of the relation of an individual experience to the whole. Whitehead maintains that "[i]n human nature there is no such separate function as a special religious sense."[232] We learn religious truths from especially significant experiences of the world, "from knowledge acquired when our ordinary senses and intellectual operations are at their highest pitch of discipline."[233] Religion arises from a particularly important intuition and generalizes this insight. The role of dogma, for Whitehead, is to articulate the relationship between the individual experience and the sense of the whole. "A dogma is the precise enunciation of a general truth, divested so far as possible from particular exemplification."[234]

Any dogma is meaningful only in relation to a particular understanding of the universe. It acquires its specific meaning within a particular context, and the context of religious language is constantly changing. Whitehead cites the example of "The Fatherhood of God," an expression which would carry very different meanings in the early Roman Republic and in modern America.[235] Thus Whitehead warns us that dogmas always require interpretation within a specific frame of reference. "You cannot convey a dogma by merely translating the words; you must also understand the system of thought to which it is relevant."[236]

Because human systems of thought are ever-changing, there is no permanent context which can guarantee the stability of dogmatic language. If we claim that the dogmas of the early Christian Church "express finally and sufficiently the truths concerning the topics about which they deal," then we must also claim that "the

---

[230]Ibid., 62.

[231]Ibid., 63.

[232]RM, 119.

[233]Ibid., 120.

[234]Ibid., 122.

[235]Ibid., 125.

[236]Ibid.

Greek philosophy of that period had developed a system of ideas of equal finality."[237] Dogmas can be more or less adequate in their ability to relate abstract concepts; they can never be final.[238] Dogmas, for Whitehead, remain the same only by changing. They must relate their insight and their claims to other aspects of human experience which are always in flux. Thus religion is "expanded, explained, modified, adapted."[239] However, dogmas must also remain in touch with the situations thay gave them birth; religion "maintains its identity by its recurrence to the inspired simplicity of its origin."[240]

Dogmas must be understood as symbols, expressions of religious intuitions. Dogmas abstract from the original experience "so that a coherent doctrine arises which elucidates the world beyond the locus of the origin of the dogmas in question."[241] Whitehead understands expression in explicitly sacramental terms. Expression "is the outward and visible sign of an inward and spiritual grace."[242] An expressive sign can be interpreted by others because it elicits an intuition in the recipient. There is a creative power in such an expression: "It elicits the intuition which interprets it," and in this sense can be understood to function *ex opere operato*.[243]

The greatest expressions of the human race reinterpret a reality which is in some sense already known, but they do so with an element of originality which can never be captured by a formula. The major expressions of the human race

> deal with what all men know, and they make it new. They do not bring to the world a new formula nor do they discover new facts, but in expressing their apprehensions of the world, they leave behind them an element of novelty--a new expression forever evoking its proper response.[244]

---

[237]Ibid., 126.

[238]Ibid.

[239]Ibid., 133.

[240]Ibid.

[241]Ibid., 139.

[242]Ibid., 127.

[243]Ibid., 128.

[244]Ibid., 131.

Because of their power in expressing and eliciting religious intuitions, dogmas have an authority over those to whom they communicate. Their authority arises from their success in interpreting experience.[245]

> Every true dogma which formulates with some adequacy the facts of a complex religious experience is fundamental for the individual in question and he disregards it at his peril.[246]

Dogma mediates the transition from the private religious experience of the solitary individual to the public community. "Expression, and in particular expression by dogma, is the return from solitariness to society."[247] While arising from the special intuition of a particular moment, dogmas maintain their power through their ability to illumine and interpret experience. Thus Whitehead looks to a pragmatic criterion of verification in experience: "what is known in secret must be enjoyed in common, and must be verified in common."[248]

Pittenger: The Language of
Religion and Christology

On the issue of language about God, Pittenger is strongly influenced by Whitehead's presuppositions, but differs somewhat from him. For Pittenger "it is necessary to recognize frankly that the language of religion is inevitably metaphorical."[249] Pittenger uses a variety of terms to stress the non-literal character of religious discourse; it is akin to "the language of drama, the language of poetry, the language of story."[250]

Pittenger notes that the heart of Christology is found in the narrative account of God's revelation in Jesus Christ. This account involves history; indeed it is "the focal historical reality for the Christian in his understanding of God and God's will for

---

[245]Ibid., 120.

[246]Ibid., 132.

[247]Ibid.

[248]Ibid., 133.

[249]WI, 38; see also W. Norman Pittenger, Reconceptions in Christian Thinking: 1817-1967 (New York: Seabury, 1968), 20.

[250]WI, 33.

174

his world."[251] However, as a story, "it can be told only in language which is poetical and imaginative."[252]

Pittenger stresses that religious language involves a poetic dimension: "We must talk as poets if we are going to talk at all."[253] He cites W.H. Auden's remark that this involves a frontal assault on the common prejudice that poetry is less true than prose: "the only way in which we can ever hope to convert modern men to the Christian religion is by first convincing them that poetry is always _truer_ than prose."[254] Pittenger grounds this claim in theological anthropology, in the "mysterious but very real connection between imagination and the 'image of God' in which man is made."[255]

Pittenger accepts Bultmann's statement of the problem of interpreting biblical language for the contemporary world. He agrees with Bultmann that the use of electricity renders impossible the belief in demonic possession as understood in the Bible.[256] He further agrees with Bultmann "that the whole biblical way of seeing things, above all its way of understanding of God to the world, is basically 'mythological' in nature."[257]

However, Pittenger challenges Bultmann's proposed resolution of the problem. Pittenger charges that Bultmann failed to distinguish between the biblical _weltbild_ ("the quasi-scientific mythology in the Bible") and the biblical _weltanschauung_ ("the over-all biblical view of man's situation and of the relationship of God to man in the world").[258] Pittenger claims that we can abandon the scientific errors and mythological cosmology of the Bible (the _weltbild_) and retain the biblical _weltanschauung_, the description of God as creator, of "history as the sphere of divine action,"

---

[251]_Ibid_.

[252]_Ibid_.

[253]_Ibid_., 34.

[254]_Ibid_.

[255]_Ibid_.

[256]_Ibid_., 35.

[257]_Ibid_.

[258]_Ibid_., 36.

of "nature as made by God and open to him," and of the human person as a creature of God but corrupted by sin.[259] Pittenger also charges that Heidegger's philosophy "is not adequate to the full Christian position, which is not only intent on man and his 'authentic' existence but also on the total picture of reality, both with a lower and an upper case 'R.'"[260]

Moreover, Pittenger maintains that "any statements which are made about religion must always be in the nature of symbol."[261] The symbolic character of religious language does not prevent there being a "metaphysic implicit in the metaphor"; but Pittenger warns that "the attempt to translate the language of metaphor into a metaphysics seems always to result in a reduction of vividness and vitality."[262]

Despite Pittenger's reservations about Bultmann's position, his own position on the interpretation of biblical language shares significant emphases with the work of Bultmann. Bultmann himself had distinguished between the mythical cosmology of the Bible and the understanding of human existence which the Bible communicates.[263] Bultmann expressed his own program schematically: "whereas the older liberals used criticism to eliminate the mythology of the New Testament, our task to-day is to use criticism to interpret it."[264] Pittenger's criticism of Heidegger fails to deal adequately with Heidegger's goal of approaching the question of Sein through the existential analytic of Dasein; Heidegger's intention was never anthropological in a sense that was opposed to being ontological.[265] Pittenger does differ from Bultmann in turning to Whitehead's contemporary cosmology as an interpretative

---

[259]Ibid.

[260]Ibid.

[261]Ibid.

[262]Ibid., 37.

[263]Rudolf Bultmann, "New Testament and Mythology," in Kerygma and Myth: A Theological Debate, ed. Hans Werner Bartsch (New York: Harper & Row, 1966), 1-11; see Norman Perrin, The Promise of Bultmann (Philadelphia: J.B. Lippincott Company, 1969), 74-85.

[264]"New Testament and Mythology," 12.

[265]Martin Heidegger, Being and Time, trans. John Macquarrie and Edward Robinson (New York: Harper & Row, 1962), 21-63. See John Macquarrie, Martin Heidegger (Richmond, Va.: John Knox Press, 1968), 4-50.

framework for retrieving the biblical language and in being willing to make statements about God's triune life.[266] Pittenger also differs markedly from Bultmann on the possibility of salvation apart from an encounter with the preaching of the Christian Gospel.[267]

Pittenger insists that every statement which describes God acting as the subject of a verb must be interpreted as non-literal, and he refers to Thomas Aquinas with approval on the analogical character of language about God.[268] Pittenger argues that non-literal language akin to poetry can express the truth "in a deeper and more evocative fashion" than scientific or philosophical language.[269] He retrieves and accepts the ancient sense of symbol as "participating in and therefore declaring 'as in a mystery' the truth which it symbolizes."[270]

Pittenger applies the term "myth" to accounts of creation and of the end of the world as "ultimate and unique 'events'"; he applies the term in a slightly different sense to the account of the fall of humans in Genesis as a universal or general truth of the human condition.[271] However, he is reluctant to use the term myth in relation to Christology. He distinguishes mythical accounts from interpretations of specific historical events expressed in the stories of the incarnation and the atonement. While Pittenger acknowledges that these stories involve metaphorical or even "mythological" language, he maintains that they "are

---

[266]WI, 37; see also The Divine Triunity, 15-29. Bultmann seeks to interpret the language of the New Testament without the use of metaphysical or trinitarian speculation. According to Bultmann, the theologian can talk about God only by talking about human existence as determined and transformed by God: "It is man . . . that is the object of theology." Rudolf Bultmann, "The Historicity of Man and Faith," in Existence and Faith: Shorter Writings of Rudolf Bultmann, ed. and trans. Schubert M. Ogden (New York: Meridian Books, 1960), 93.

[267]On Bultmann's claim of the impossibility of authentic existence apart from the encounter with the Christian Gospel, see Bultmann, Theology, I, 302; and Perrin, The Promise of Bultmann, 34-36. On Pittenger's position, see WI, 260-61; Lure of Divine Love, 164-65.

[268]WI, 38.

[269]Ibid., 39.

[270]Ibid.

[271]Ibid.

tied up with a specific historical event; they have their grounding in something that actually happened in the course of human history."[272] Thus Pittenger warns that it is misleading to classify the narrative accounts of Jesus Christ in the category of myth:

> [O]n the one hand they are not _outside_ history, and on the other they are not true of _all_ history. They are concerned with what Christians believe was done _in_ history and through the factuality of _particular_ historical happenings.[273]

Pittenger is afraid that the use of the category of myth in Christology might suggest "that the incarnate life of Christ and his redemptive work are nothing more than types or helpful representations of what is universally true of human experience in relationship with God."[274] This caution is especially important as a clarification of Pittenger's own description of the Christ-event as the "classical instance" of God's saving activity and his later acceptance of Ogden's re-presentative Christology.[275]

Pittenger prefers the terms "saga or story" to describe the life of Jesus Christ as "God's supreme and definitive action."[276] Pittenger acknowledges that a large number of the stories of Jesus, including the nativity stories, resurrection stories, and the accounts of the Ascension and Pentecost, are not historical events but are "legends" which express the significance of Jesus Christ for those who encountered him.[277] The narrative accounts of Jesus Christ have the power to awaken a response of faith in hearers. Pittenger locates the revelation of God in the entire complex of events: "the thing which occurs, which is known to us through imaginative re-telling, and the response to it in faith."[278]

While Pittenger is very careful to distinguish the poetic language of the Bible from philosophical language, he nonetheless

---

[272]Ibid.

[273]Ibid.

[274]Ibid., 40.

[275]Lure of Divine Love, 113.

[276]WI, 40.

[277]Ibid., 40-41, 68-69; see also Rethinking the Christian Message, 37-38.

[278]WI, 44.

argues that there are metaphysical and ontological claims being made in the biblical language. He argues against the Ritschlian interpretation of Jesus, maintaining that "an 'evaluation' of him [Christ] demands ontological affirmation as well."[279] The ontological affirmation arises from reflection on the experience of Jesus Christ and the value of this experience for the believer. However, Pittenger claims,

> that is not the same thing as saying that his divinity is a value-judgement. The evaluation refers to a real ontological relationship which is deeper than, although it is the occasion for, the judgement which has been given to his 'value.'[280]

Pittenger argues that the ontological claim which he finds implicit in the biblical accounts of Jesus invites contemporary philosophical articulation. This is Pittenger's justification for using Whiteheadian metaphysical language as an interpretative guide to the meaning of the New Testament. The heart of Pittenger's case is the claim that if the Christian theologian begins with the biblical revelation, "he will then find that of all the available metaphysical points of view, the 'process' approach serves him most satisfactorily."[281] Pittenger takes up the work of Hartshorne as an example of how Whitehead's thought can contribute to a Christian panentheist understanding of God.[282] Pittenger is critical of what he terms the idealist epistemology of Hartshorne's philosophy, but claims that this is not essential to Hartshorne's description of God's involvement in the world; what most interests Pittenger in the thought of Hartshorne is the latter's

> use of the thought of Alfred North Whitehead as a basis not only for a satisfactory metaphysic adequate to the findings of scientific study, but also for a world-view which will be able to accommodate the data of religious experience in its highest Jewish and Christian expression.[283]

Hartshorne questions the traditional Christological formulas and views Jesus instead as

---

[279]Ibid., 120.

[280]Ibid.

[281]WI, 155.

[282]Ibid., 127, 155.

[283]Ibid., 170.

179

the supreme symbol furnished to us by history of the notion
of a God genuinely and literally 'sympathetic (incomparably
more literally than any man ever is), receiving into his own
experience the sufferings as well as the joys of the
world.[284]

Pittenger suggests that a retrieval of the ancient sense of symbol
as "a genuine participant in the reality symbolized" would bring
Hartshorne's perspective very close to the affirmation of classical Christology.[285]

Pittenger also turns to the metaphysics of Whitehead and
Hartshorne to defend the cognitive value of aesthetic and religious language against the charge of meaninglessness. Pittenger
reviews the claims of A.J. Ayer and the Vienna circle that religious, theological, and metaphysical statements cannot specify the
means of their verification and thus are meaningless.[286] In response to the challenge of the verification-falsification debate,
Pittenger follows Whitehead in insisting on the importance of aesthetic and religious values which are in experience but which in
principle escape "a particular sort of mesh which is useful in
physics or chemistry or biology or other scientific areas."[287]
Pittenger further agrees with Whitehead that statements have an
implicit metaphysical context whether this is admitted or not. He
notes that more recently Ayer himself had admitted "that the restriction of truth to such verifiable propositions is itself a
'metaphysical' assumption."[288]

Regarding the general character of the universe which is the
background for our thinking and acting, Pittenger accepts Pascal's
contention that "everybody must gamble."[289] Once again following
Whitehead, Pittenger insists that strict logic is not the ultimate
arbiter of metaphysics. He acknowledges that Whitehead's and
Hartshorne's metaphysics cannot be proved, but claims that it
"helps us to understand empirical data, religious and otherwise"

---

[284]Charles Hartshorne, Reality as Social Process (Boston:
Beacon Press, 1953); quoted by Pittenger, WI, 127.

[285]WI, 128.

[286]Reconceptions, 16-17.

[287]Ibid., 18; see also 34-35, 47.

[288]Ibid., 17.

[289]Ibid., 19.

and that "it can outargue the linguistic thinkers."[290] Pittenger
embraces Whitehead's insistence that "the artist, the poet, the
lover, and the believer have their right to be heard."[291]

For Pittenger, the poetic language of religion and worship
requires the complement of conceptual, metaphysical language whenever religious people relate their faith to other areas of experience. The task of the theologian is to use ideas and concepts,
"to state the meaning of the 'religious encounter' . . . in relationship to the whole of human life and experience."[292] Theological statements refer back to the religious experience of worship,
prayer, and commitment; they find their verification in "the living reality of the Christian life."[293] Philosophical concepts and
analysis neither ground nor disprove religious experience; they do
reflectively articulate the significance of religious experience
for the understanding of the whole. The theologian is responsible
for the meaning of theological claims "not only in and to the specifically religious community, but also in the public domain of
human experience and reflection."[294]

Pittenger, like Rahner, stresses the dimension of mystery in
religious experience and language. He agrees with Thomas Aquinas
that "'everything runs out into, or issues in, mystery' (omnia
abeunt in mysteria)."[295] Mystery is the all-encompassing context
of human life. "We live in the midst of mystery, and we ourselves
are participants in mystery."[296] Pittenger accepts Gabriel Mar-
cel's distinction between a problem and a mystery. Where a problem however difficult can in principle be resolved, a mystery
"presents us with ultimate questions" for which we cannot in principle find answers; "a mystery is recognized for what it is and we

---

[290]Ibid., 21. On this point Pittenger agrees with Whitehead
that a metaphysics cannot be proved. Hartshorne, however, would
disagree and defend the possibility of metaphysical proofs. See
Charles Hartshorne, A Natural Theology for Our Time (LaSalle, Il.:
Open Court, 1965; and idem, Anselm's Discovery: A Re-Examination
of the Ontological Proof of God's Existence (LaSalle, Il.: Open
Court, 1965).

[291]Reconceptions, 19.

[292]Ibid., 20.

[293]Ibid.; see also Divine Triunity, 59.

[294]Reconceptions. 22.

[295]Divine Triunity, 51.

[296]Ibid.

must accept it for what it is."[297] The wide variety of religious forms of experience and expression are to be understood as humankind's "response to the presence of such a mystery."[298]

The indissoluble presence of mystery in human life can only be articulated in non-literal, allusive aesthetic and religious expressions.[299] Pittenger claims that in most cultures there is a pattern of progression of the focal images used to express the mystery. In the earliest expressions mystery appears as "the manifestation of sheer power."[300] In time, mystery comes to be interpreted as "justice and goodness"; eventually it is understood as love, not in the sense of "mild benevolence" or sentimental emotion, but as "strength in giving-and-receiving, mutuality, outgoing of self with courage and forgetfulness of self, and a positive goodness that is intense and entire."[301] According to Pittenger, the words that express the mystery can share in the numinous power of the mystery itself.[302] Pittenger, like Whitehead, finds a clear sense of progress in the essential character of religious development.

The Play of Language:
God and Wisdom in Process

We turn next to the analogies between the uses of language by Whitehead and Pittenger and the wisdom tradition. I will begin by reflecting on the movement of language between the particular and the universal and then will explore the role of negative experience for the sages and the process thinkers. I will also note similarities to and differences from Rahner's perspective.

For Whitehead what forces a non-literal meaning in metaphysical language is not, as for Rahner, the incomprehensibility of God, but rather the necessity of stretching words beyond their accustomed usage to reach for a description of the whole.[303] In

---

[297]Ibid., 51-52.

[298]Ibid., 52.

[299]Ibid., 52-56.

[300]Ibid., 56.

[301]Ibid.

[302]Rethinking the Christian Message, 19.

[303]PR, 4.

Whitehead's metaphysics, the meaning of language is not to be found on either the level of the individual or of the whole but rather in a constant to-and-fro movement between the individual and the whole, a movement of meaning which never comes to rest and which cannot be translated into a static, univocal assertion. In Whitehead's philosophy "it is presupposed that no entity can be conceived in complete abstraction from the system of the universe."[304] We only understand each individual moment of experience in light of an understanding of the whole universe. However, it is impossible to describe the entire processing system of the universe without a metaphorical use of language. We only understand the whole in light of generalizations based upon individual instances, and these generalizations require a non-literal usage of language. Whitehead uses the term symbolic reference to express the movement of meaning from one area of experience to another.[305]

There is an analogous to-and-fro movement between the individual instance and the whole in the wisdom tradition. Proverbs often use a concrete image to offer insight into a more general human situation.

As vinegar to the teeth, smoke to the eyes,
so the sluggard to the one who sends him (Prov 10:26).

No wood, and the fire goes out;
no talebearer, and quarreling dies down (Prov 26:20).

Charcoal for live embers, wood for fire,
for kindling strife a quarrelsome man (Prov 26:21).

The concrete image offers meaning only when it is grasped in relationship to a more general pattern of experience. For the sages and for Whitehead insight into a particular moment of experience implies an awareness of a larger order underlying experience. As von Rad comments, the analogies of the sages "point to an all-embracing order in which both phenomena are linked with each other. . . . They were drawn into a sphere of order."[306] The wisdom tradition never proposed an all-embracing metaphysical scheme, but the sages did offer images of Lady Wisdom which articulate a sense of the order of the universe and its relationship to human experience. Christian has distinguished Whitehead's presystematic, systematic, and postsystematic uses of language. In presystematic language, "Whitehead is evoking and describing the

---

[304]Ibid., 3.

[305]Sym, 7-8.

[306]Wisdom, 120.

concrete experiences he takes as his basic data"; in systematic language he "is constructing and developing the concepts which compose his categorical scheme"; in postsystematic language he "uses these systematic terms to interpret sense experience, the order of nature, art, morality, or religion."[307]

The presystematic language of Whitehead bears a certain similarity to the proverbs which offer analogies between different areas of experience and describe the values encountered in experience. Both the sages and Whitehead describe various experiences with attention to the similarities between diverse areas. Moreover, both Whitehead and the sages are attentive to the values that humans encounter in experience. Whitehead accords particular importance to romantic poetry and to religious expressions as sources of data for philosophy, as inventories of the elements of experience which metaphysics must coordinate.

Whitehead's systematic language, his conceptual metaphysical scheme, is more systematic and self-consciously philosophical than any language of the wisdom tradition, though the central chapters of the Wisdom of Solomon do use terms from Greek philosophy to describe the universal sway of Lady Wisdom. Whitehead's postsystematic language, his interpretation of experience in light of his system brings him at times close to the language and images of the wisdom tradition. When Whitehead seeks to express the significance of the entire processing world order for human experience, his language uses metaphors and images. He describes the relation of God to each actual entity as "the lure for feeling, the eternal urge of desire,"[308] images which recall Lady Wisdom luring humans to herself and promising them rewards of happiness and life (Prov 8). Whitehead speaks of the transformation of an actual occasion in the consequent nature of God and its return to the world as a datum for future occasions as "the judge arising out of the very nature of things, redeemer or goddess of mischief."[309] The Wisdom of Solomon associated Lady Wisdom with "avenging Justice" (1:8) and understood her to be embedded in the very nature of things (7:22-8:1).

Where Whitehead tries to integrate his description of God into the metaphysical categories of his system so that God is not an exception but the "chief exemplification" of the categories, Pittenger stresses far more than Whitehead the dimension of mystery in our experience of God and the necessity of an analogical application of all language to God. While Pittenger does not use

---

[307]Christian, 3.

[308]PR, 344.

[309]Ibid., 351.

the incomprehensibility of God as a hermeneutical principle in as thoroughgoing a manner as Rahner, he does note the "strain" that language undergoes when applied to the religious experience of mystery. Pittenger understands the New Testament authors to be "straining words to affirm a deep and mysterious experience and to point toward the greater surrounding mystery in relationship with which they were living."[310]

In accordance with this perspective Pittenger stresses the need for imagination in interpreting the Bible.[311] Pittenger cites Aquinas with approval on analogy,[312] and accepts Augustine's view that "we do better to speak thus haltingly and humbly about God than to say nothing at all about so great a mystery."[313] Pittenger's emphasis on the mystery of God and on the analogical application of language to God accords with his sense of God as a Reality more real than the process. In this he differs from Whitehead, for whom mystery would not apply specifically and uniquely to God, and he comes close to Rahner's evocation of mystery.

In the work of each of the contemporary thinkers we have studied, there is an attempt to articulate the to-and-fro movement between the particular instance of experience and the whole. Whitehead uses the method of descriptive generalization for metaphysics and sees an analogous process at work in religious dogma. Pittenger uses the category of "classical instance" to express the importance of special revelation for our understanding of the general revelation of God throughout all experience. Rahner uses the ontology of real symbol to express the relationship between particular, categorical moments of revelation in history and the universal salvific will of God which is always operative on the transcendental level of experience. In each of these perspectives there is an analogy to the procedure of the wisdom tradition, which examined individual moments of experience in search of broader patterns and also interpreted the historical experiences of revelation of the people of Israel as examples of the universal activity of Lady Wisdom. The universal activity of Lady Wisdom through ordinary human experience is comparable to Whitehead's sense of a "rightness of things" in the universe as a whole, to Pittenger's general revelation, and to Rahner's transcendental experience of God. In each case there is an implicit religious dimension of experience which may or may not be adverted to but

---

[310]Divine Triunity, 20.

[311]Ibid.

[312]WI, 38.

[313]Divine Triunity, 19.

which is the context for and has an influence upon all human knowing and acting. The to-and-fro movement between the individual experience and the whole also finds analogy in the cosmological role of Christ in 1 Corinthians 8:6, Colossians 1:14-20, and the prologue of John. In these texts the Christ-event is presented as the revelation of the power which orders the universe, and thus the account of the life, death, and resurrection of Jesus Christ is interpreted in light of the whole, and the whole is interpreted in light of the account of Jesus Christ.

For the wisdom tradition there is not only an oscillation of meaning between the particular and the universal but also, in von Rad's words, "the constant oscillation between grasp of meaning and loss of meaning."[314] This oscillation is found on the level of proverbs in the to-and-fro movement between proverbs which affirm a regular pattern in experience and proverbs which express the incomprehensibility and omnipotence of Yahweh. On the level of the larger works in the wisdom tradition there is the to-and-fro movement between the grasp of meaning in the largely, though not exclusively, world-constructive projects of Proverbs, Ben Sira, and the Wisdom of Solomon and the loss of meaning in the unsettling, world-questioning programs of Job and Qoheleth.

In Rahner's theology there is a constant oscillation between the grasp of meaning, grounded in the intelligibility of Being and the loss of meaning resulting from the incomprehensibility of God. The threat of loss of meaning and the role of negative experience is much less prominent in Whitehead's metaphysics than in Rahner's theology. Whitehead is aware of the possibility of loss of meaning; he comments that apart from a religious vision, "human life is a flash of occasional elements lighting up a mess of pain and misery, a bagatelle of transient experience."[315] However, Whitehead's confidence that religious vision "persistently shows an upward trend" encompasses the negative moment of loss of meaning in a fundamentally positive progression.[316] Whitehead's rationalist faith resembles the principle of the intelligibility of Being of Rahner and the sages' trust in the presence of Wisdom in the world order. However, Whitehead's rationalist faith does not receive the sharp, dialectical challenge of Rahner's principle of the incomprehensibility of God or of Job's and Qoheleth's descriptions of the order of the world as hidden from human understanding.

---

[314]Wisdom, 106.

[315]SMW, 192.

[316]Ibid.

Pittenger for his part tries to integrate a Whiteheadian cosmology into a more traditional sense of God as the incomprehensible mystery enveloping human life. While philosophically Pittenger differs considerably from Rahner, his religious sense of mystery brings him close to Rahner.

Critical Reflections on Rahner, Whitehead, and Pittenger

Thus far I have sought to interpret and understand the relationships between the biblical wisdom tradition and the thought of Rahner, Whitehead, and Pittenger. I turn now to several difficulties that these approaches to Christology encounter. There have been a wide range of philosophical and theological criticisms of both Rahner and process thought.[317] I will not survey the entire variety of criticisms but will rather examine a few crucial issues which present challenges to a Wisdom Christology. The first two issues that I will explore are classical dilemmas of Christian theology: (1) the difficulty of relating God to a world in time, and (2) the aporia of suffering in relation to claims of wisdom.

Three specific challenges to the wisdom tradition and contemporary retrievals of it are posed by political and liberation theology, feminism, and pluralism. As a transition to the fourth chapter I will briefly note (3) the criticism from political and liberation theologians that the wisdom tradition and the theologies of Rahner and process thought lack a political dimension, (4) the charge from some feminist writers that Christology is essentially sexist, and (5) the challenge of religious and cultural pluralism and the difficulty of moving from particular experiences to universal claims. The fourth chapter will take up the last three issues and will explore the resources of the trajectory of Wisdom Christology for addressing them.

God and a World in Time

The relation of God to a world of temporal process is one of the traditional difficulties of Christian theology, and it is of particular importance for a wisdom perspective that relates the experience of God to the ordering power of the cosmos. The claims that God is involved in the ongoing process of the universe and

---

[317]On Rahner, see Eicher, van der Heijden, Fabro, and Gaboriau; on Whitehead, see Robert C. Neville, Creativity and God: A Challenge to Process Theology (New York: Seabury, 1980), and Pols; on Pittenger, see David Ray Griffin, "The Process Theology of Norman Pittenger: A Review Article," Process Studies 1(1971): 136-49.

that God is specially revealed in the person of Jesus Christ raise the question of how to understand the relation of God to time. My purpose is not to resolve the question but to note the difficulties encountered by both Rahner's theology and Whiteheadian thought.

The charge has often been repeated by process thinkers that the "classical conception of God" is unable to explain how God can love creatures who come to be and pass away in time. Since God is understood by Aquinas to be eternally a se and as actus purus free of all potentiality, process thinkers charge that Thomas has no means of giving a metaphysical explanation to the biblical image of God as love.[318] Rahner is clearly concerned to describe God as involved in the world process and in human life, and yet he also wants to accept at least one side of Thomas's understanding of God as eternal and unchanging.

Rahner attempts to affirm both the immutability of God and the mutability of God as two "dialectical assertions." On the one hand, he insists that the belief in "an unchangeable and unchanging God in his eternally complete fullness" is not simply a non-biblical philosophical postulate; it is rather "a dogma of faith, as was once again explicitly defined in the First Vatican Council (D.S. 3001), and the substance of this is already present in the scriptures of the Old and New Testaments."[319]

However, Rahner also argues that God can become "subject to change in something else"; because the Logos became human, "our time became the time of the eternal one."[320] Rahner thus proposes to affirm that "in and in spite of his immutability [God] can truly become something; he himself, he in time."[321] Rahner is clearly concerned both to respect the perspective of the Christian tradition that God is eternal and absolute and also to affirm that God is really involved in the world and thus in some way subject to change through the incarnation. Rahner's insistence on applying the language of becoming to God leaves unresolved what it

---

[318]Schubert M. Ogden, The Reality of God and Other Essays (San Francisco: Harper & Row, 1977), 17-18, 49-51; John B. Cobb, Jr. and David Ray Griffin, Process Theology: An Introductory Exposition (Philadelphia: Westminster, 1976), 44-46. For a defense of Thomas on this issue, see Burrell, 78-89; and Catherine M. LaCugna, "The Relational God: Aquinas and Beyond," TS 46(1985): 647-63.

[319]Foundations, 219.

[320]Ibid., 220.

[321]Ibid., 221.

means to continue affirming God's immutability. The question that arises is whether Rahner's application of the category of "dialectical assertions" to the claims of mutability and immutability resolves the problem of God's relation to time or whether it is a way of articulating a problem which is not resolved, and which, given Rahner's own principle of the incomprehensibility of God, perhaps cannot in principle be resolved. We seem to be left with more of a conundrum or an aporia than a solution.

Difficulties arise in the Whiteheadian tradition as well. Despite Ogden's confident claim that "at last" philosophy can relate God and a world in time,[322] perplexing questions also arise in the Whiteheadian approach. Whitehead himself claimed that God is non-temporal,[323] but he also argues that God is constantly prehending every actual entity as it passes into objective immortality. Thus he presents us with the paradox of a non-temporal entity being constantly affected by the passage of time and constantly proposing new initial subjective aims to novel concrescent entities. Whitehead's description of God involves a mini-drama of God prehending a processing world, enjoying the values therein, and transforming these values so that they pass back into subsequent moments of process. Yet this entire drama takes place in a non-temporal entity. It should be noted that the paradox of time also appears on the level of each actual entity. In each concrescence there is a little drama outside of time. There is a progression from the initial stages of prehending the objectified universe and the initial subjective aim through the decision which actualizes certain values to the perishing and passing into objective immortality. This entire emplotment takes place outside of time.

The permanence or everlastingness of God is an issue that defies the categories of becoming. Where Rahner presents us with an immutable God who becomes subject to change in time, Whitehead presents us with a non-temporal God who constantly affects and is affected by temporal process. In Whitehead as in Rahner we seem to find more an articulation of a problem than a resolution.

Hartshorne and Pittenger have both sensed the difficulty in Whitehead's formulation and propose to treat God as a series of actual entities in time. Pittenger writes that "in technical process terms, it might be better to say (with Hartshorne) that [God] is the 'serially-ordered routing of actual entities' which establishes him as self-identical."[324]

---

[322]Reality of God, 62, 64, 68.

[323]PR, 7.

[324]Alfred North Whitehead, 34.

However, Hartshorne's and Pittenger's effort at a resolution runs into difficulties with modern relativity theory, the very theory that provided Whitehead with a stimulus for his own reflections. As Whitehead himself was well aware, in a post-Einsteinian universe the concept of simultaneity has no meaning on a cosmic scale. In Whitehead's formulation, an actual occasion can be contemporary with two other actual occasions without those actual occasions being contemporary with each other.[325] If God is a series of actual entities in time, and if after Einstein there is no meaning to simultaneity on a universal scale, we confront the problem of how one divine actual entity can be related to the entire universe at the same instant in time. As Frederic F. Fost charges:

> Since Hartshorne's dipolar theism was systematically developed within a framework which affirmed both contemporary relations and absolute simultaneity, it is hardly surprising that his subsequent denial of the former and his apparent reconsideration of the latter should introduce incoherence into his system.[326]

Moreover, Whitehead's own argument for God suffers considerable strain if God is conceived of as a route of occasions. Whitehead argued that the order that makes possible a route of occasions requires a permanent, primordial Orderer as the basis of steady relevance and of appropriate initial subjective aims. God makes possible a route of occaions. It would seem that God cannot illustrate a route of occasions without requiring a further God as Orderer.

Neither Rahner nor Whitehead offer a coherent resolution of the question of the relation of God and a world in time; both offer formulations that involve a paradoxical coincidence of temporal and non-temporal statements about God. Hartshorne and Pittenger, attempting to present a more thoroughgoing temporal conception of God encounter difficulties from the very theory of relativity that inspired much of Whitehead's creative endeavor.

---

[325]PR, 319-20; AI, 196.

[326]Frederic F. Fost, "Relativity Theory and Hartshorne's Dipolar Theism," in Two Process Philosophers: Hartshorne's Encounter with Whitehead, American Academy of Religion Studies in Religion, No. 5 (Tallahassee, Fla.: American Academy of Religion, 1973), 91-92; see also John Wilcox, "A Question from Physics for Certain Theists," JR 40(1961):293-300; and Lewis S. Ford, "Is Process Theism Compatible with Relativity Theory?" JR 48(1968): 124-35.

It seems that Ricoeur's comment about time in fiction is applicable to the relation of God and time: "Time is a mystery precisely in that the observations that are to be made regarding it cannot be unified. (This is exactly what, for me, constitutes an unsurpassable enigma. . . .)"[327]

God and Suffering

The relation of God to human suffering again raises difficulties for theology in general and for the claims of the wisdom tradition in particular. The wisdom tradition affirms, in Whitehead's phrase, a basic "rightness of things," a sense of order and justice underlying the flow of experience. Already in antiquity this assertion was questioned by Job and Qoheleth. The massive sufferings of the twentieth century have forced this question to the forefront of contemporary consciousness as well. Again, my goal is not to resolve a classical dilemma but to note the difficulties that this question raises for Rahner and process thought.

Rahner poses the question: "Why does God allow us to suffer?"[328] He reviews and rejects as inadequate a number of traditional theistic answers: (1) "Suffering as a Natural Side Effect in an Evolving World"; (2) "Suffering as an Effect of Creaturely Sinful Freedom"; (3) "Suffering as a Situation of Trial and Maturing"; (4) "Suffering as a Pointer to Another, Eternal Life."[329] Rahner refuses to accept the traditional distinction between God's "permitting" and "causing" suffering:

> For what does 'permitting' mean when we are talking about a God who is purely and simply the ground and cause of all reality, who, moreover, in the absolute sovereignty of his freedom and power, in no way restricted by anyone or anything, encompasses all creaturely freedom and does not come up against any limit there?[330]

The absolute freedom of God renders unsatisfactory each of the proposed explanations. Since the evolving world process and creaturely freedom are themselves created by the freedom of God, they in no way resolve the question of why God allows suffering.

---

[327]*Time and Narrative*, II, 125.

[328]Karl Rahner, "Why Does God Allow Us to Suffer?" *TI*, XIX, 194-208.

[329]*Ibid.*, 197-205.

[330]*Ibid.*, 195.

The explanation of suffering as a trial and a process of maturing, already proposed by Ben Sira (2:1-5; 4:11-18; 6:18-29), flounders on the

> infinitely diverse, terrible suffering in the history of humanity (including the uncertain lot of children dying in infancy and old people in senile decline) which cannot be integrated into a process of maturing and personal probation.[331]

The eschatological resolution of suffering in eternal life offers no explanation either, since eternal life could be conceived without the horrors of suffering in this world. Eternal life "can be seen as a conquest of suffering but not as an authorization of the latter."[332]

Having rejected as inadequate the traditional answers, Rahner invokes the incomprehensibility of God. Even the answer of the angel at the final judgement "must still be only the incomprehensibility of God in his freedom and nothing else."[333] While Rahner's answer is consistent with his doctrine of God, we may wonder whether his doctrine of God itself is not here on the brink of collapse. It appears that an all-powerful God wills in absolute freedom the multitude of horrors of human history and that all the good that is achieved through suffering could have been achieved in some other fashion.[334] Before the question of suffering Rahner's principle of the intelligibility of Being appears to offer little intelligibility and only the consolation of a trusting plunge into the abyss of God's incomprehensible freedom.

Whitehead's God has neither the absolute freedom nor the frightening responsibility of Rahner's God. Whitehead's God is doing the best that is possible amid often refractory circumstances. God is "the great companion--the fellow-sufferer who understands."[335] By accepting actual accasions into God's consequent nature, God enables each actual occasion to function both as a means and as an end, as an "individual self-attainment" but also

---

[331]Ibid., 204.

[332]Ibid., 205.

[333]Ibid., 208.

[334]Ibid., 206.

[335]PR, 351.

with a "sense of worth beyond itself."[336] Whitehead claims that this process transforms "the immediacy of sorrow and pain" into

> an element of triumph. This is the notion of redemption through suffering which haunts the world. It is the generalization of its very minor exemplification as the aesthetic value of discords in art.[337]

After the terrors of history, the massive and long-lasting oppressions and executions of millions of people in the twentieth century, it is dangerous to speak of transforming "the immediacy of sorrow and pain" into "an element of triumph." The analogy with discords in art becomes even more dangerous insofar as it suggests an aesthetic integration of massive suffering as a positive contribution into a larger, harmonious whole. The transformation of pain into triumph and the aesthetic resolution of suffering into harmony run the risk of appearing to accept the horrors of history. While Whitehead does speak of the consequent nature of God as a judgement, "[i]t is the judgement of a tenderness which loses nothing that can be saved. It is also the judgement of a wisdom which uses what in the temporal world is mere wreckage."[338]

The heart of religious experience for Whitehead is the conviction of "the rightness of things."[339] While the problem of massive suffering in history does not itself disprove this conviction, it does force a more frightening and paradoxical turn to the claim than Whitehead seems to acknowledge. If there is indeed a rightness or a wisdom in the nature of things, its affirmation demands the simultaneous recognition of the frightening incomprehensibility and hiddenness of the world order.

Moreover, in Whitehead's system there remains the question of the source of novel evil possibilities. Novel forms appear that are morally negative, and so the question arises: Where did those possibilities come from? Whitehead, like the classical Christian tradition, clearly does not want to make God responsible for evil; but the there still remains the question of the relationship of God as lure to the appearance of novel evil possibilities. It would seem that to make God a lure rather than a creator does not in the end resolve the problem of theodicy.

---

[336]Ibid., 350.

[337]Ibid.

[338]Ibid., 346.

[339]RM, 60-65.

Pittenger's attempt at a theodicy also faces difficulties. For Pittenger in Goodness Distorted the limitations on God's power by the freedom of creatures effectively bracket the question of the responsibility of God for suffering.[340] However, in Catholic Faith in a Process Perspective, Pittenger denies that his theology implies a "finite God," thus implying that any limitations on God are freely accepted by God and not imposed metaphysically on God.[341] Pittenger argues that God is omnipotent, but he proposes to redefine the meaning of omnipotence to mean "that God has all the power necessary to accomplish his will, not in spite of, but rather through, the decisions of his creation."[342] In a similar manner, Pittenger continues:

> God's infinitude or transcendence is not to be seen as absolute power to do anything, but rather in his capacity to work inexhaustibly towards the accomplishment of his purpose, with resources which are adequate to meet and overcome in the long run (and sometimes the run may be very long! but God has all time to work in) everything that would distort and obstruct the end which he has in view.[343]

However, a problem still arises regarding the relation of God's power to "the long run." God may have all time but humans do not, and the eventual triumph of God's plan in some indefinitely postponed future offers little consolation or explanation to those afflicted in the meantime. To affirm that God can accomplish the divine will through creaturely decisions brings us back to Rahner's dilemma. If, as traditional Catholic doctrines of grace have affirmed, God can efficaciously persuade individuals to do the good without abrogating human freedom, then why does God not efficaciously lure and persuade humans to do the good in the short run? It would appear that Pittenger must either acknowledge real metaphysical limitations on God (as Whitehead would acknowledge) or confront the frightening dimension of the incomprehensibility of God suggested by Rahner and evoked by Job and Qoheleth.

While Pittenger acknowledges that suffering is evil and that everything possible should be done to eliminate it, he goes on to acknowledge four constructive contributions that suffering makes to human experience:

---

[340]Goodness Distorted, 39-41.

[341]Catholic Faith in a Process Perspective, 55.

[342]Ibid.

[343]Ibid.

1. Suffering can deepen our understanding of life in this world. 2. Suffering can purify our motives and desires. 3. Suffering can enrich our relationships with others, both through greater sensitivity to their inner experience and through providing us with opportunity to assist them. 4. Suffering can enable us to grasp more profoundly the nature of God as 'cosmic Lover' who shares in suffering because he identifies himself with his creation.[344]

While each of Pittenger's points expresses a truth of human experience, the danger of his perspective, like Whitehead's, is that it appears to integrate suffering too easily into a larger harmony without adequately noting the crisis suffering creates for a doctrine of God.

Political and Liberation Theology

If the questions of God in relation to time and suffering lead us into aporias which defy comprehension, the necessity of action in an ambiguous and even incomprehensible world raises questions about the political dimension of the trajectory of Wisdom Christology and its contemporary representatives. One major criticism of the wisdom tradition and of Rahner and process thought has been that these approaches lack a political dimension which can contribute to the contemporary struggle for liberation. By recognizing Lady Wisdom or the Logos or God's revelation everywhere, these perspectives may appear to legitimate the status quo. The case of Eusebius proclaiming Constantine as the friend and representative on earth of the Logos is a classic example of this danger.[345]

Johann Baptist Metz warns us that "Christology without an apocalyptic vision becomes no more than an ideology of conquest and triumph."[346] In The Crucified God Jürgen Moltmann casts suspicion upon any theology which correlates the revelation of God in Jesus Christ with a universal presence of God in the world and in other religions:

---

[344]Ibid., 61.

[345]Eusebius, The Life of Constantine, excerpts in The Medieval World: 300-1300, ed. Norman F. Cantor (2nd ed.: New York: Macmillan Col., 1968), 6-8.

[346]Johann Baptist Metz, Faith in History and Society: Toward a Practical Fundamental Theology, trans. David Smith (New York: Seabury, 1980), 176.

For the Christian there is no gradation between the crucified Jesus and the gods, as though God were less evident in the world, world history and world politics, and more evident in Christ. This notion of a gradation between a natural theology and a Christian theology can easily be unmasked as the ideology of a state church.[347]

Juan Luis Segundo has directly questioned the usefulness of the wisdom tradition for liberation theology:

> Moreover, it is a well known fact that from the time of the Babylonian exile on, the sapiential literature became more individualistic, inner-directed, and apolitical.[348]

> . . . can one really maintain that the authentic import of the Exodus event is more clearly spelled out in the more spiritualistic and subjective intepretation of the sapiential books?[349]

In response to the questions and suspicions of political and liberation theologians, I will explore the potential of the trajectory of Wisdom Christology for developing a critical political stance in the first section of the fourth chapter.

Feminist Theology

Feminist scholars have challenged the predominantly masculine language used of God in the Christian tradition.[350] The prologue of John uses the masculine ho logos instead of the feminine he sophia, and this usage has dominated most of the Christian tradition, including the language of Rahner and Pittenger. This usage invites the accusation that Christology is essentially sexist

---

[347]Jürgen Moltmann, The Crucified God: The Cross of Christ as the Foundation and Criticism of Christian Theology, trans. R.A. Wilson and John Bowden (New York: Harper & Row, 1974), 196.

[348]Juan Luis Segundo, The Liberation of Theology, trans. John Drury (Makryknoll, N.Y.: Orbis, 1982), 111.

[349]Ibid., 115.

[350]See Rosemary Radford Ruether, Sexism and God-Talk: Toward a Feminist Theology (Boston: Beacon Press, 1983).

because it suppresses the feminine element in the divine and presents a male redeemer who reveals a male God.[351] Feminist writers have raised the question: "Can a male saviour save women?"[352] In response to the questions and suspicions of feminist writers, the second section of the fourth chapter will examine the possibility of a retrieval of the figure of Lady Wisdom as an articulation of our experience of God and of the presence of God in Jesus Christ.

Religious Pluralism

The challenge of religious and cultural pluralism is one of the most perplexing issues of our age. The awareness of pluralism raises questions about the assertion of any universal claim based upon particular historical experiences and particular cultural and philosophical traditions.[353] If the reality that Christians name God is actively present throughout human experience in a wide variety of religious traditions, then in what way is it meaningful and true to claim that Jesus Christ is the definitive, normative revelation of God? To what degree are contemporary theological claims about Jesus Christ imposing a European or North American world view on a very diverse range of human cultures? The encounter with other religious traditions of great depth and vitality challenges the universal claims of the trajectory of Wisdom Christology. The last section of the fourth chapter will look to the biblical wisdom tradition and to Rahner and Pittenger not for a resolution to this question but rather for a path for approaching it.

---

[351]Mary Daly, Beyond God the Father: Toward a Philosophy of Women's Liberation (Boston: Beacon Press, 1985), 69-97.

[352]Rosemary Radford Ruether, To Change the World: Christology and Cultural Criticism (New York: Crossroad, 1983), 45-56.

[353]For a survey of contemporary perspectives, see Paul F. Knitter, No Other Name? A Critical Survey of Christian Attitudes Toward the World Religions, American Society of Missiology Series, No. 7 (Maryknoll, N.Y.: Orbis, 1985); and Lucien Richard, What Are They Saying About Christ And World Religions? (New York: Paulist Press, 1981).

CHAPTER IV

WISDOM CHRISTOLOGY AND CONTEMPORARY THEOLOGY

The trajectory of Wisdom or Logos Christology, including its
contemporary representatives appears open to suspicion from three
angles: political and liberation theology, feminist theology, and
the awareness of pluralism in the encounter with other world religions. We turn now to the challenges that these perspectives pose
and to the resources of the trajectory of Wisdom Christology for
addressing each of these issues.

The Political Dimension of Wisdom Christology

Political and liberation theologians have looked to the historical, prophetic, and apocalyptic traditions of the Bible for
theological insight and scriptural precedent for the contemporary
struggle for liberation.[1] The political resources of the wisdom
tradition, by contrast, have been somewhat neglected,[2] and at
times viewed with outright suspicion.[3]

However, the biography of one important forerunner of liberation theology suggests a more critical political and social dimension to the wisdom tradition of Israel, specifically in its later
stages. In the first generation of Christians in Latin America, a
slave owner named Bartolomeo de Las Casas was to deliver a sermon
based upon a text from the book of Ben Sira. The passage condemned those who lived unjustly from the labors of others. The
words of the ancient sage so profoundly disturbed Las Casas that

---

[1]For example, see Gustavo Gutiérrez, A Theology of Libera-
tion: History, Politics and Salvation, trans. and ed. Caridad Inda
and John Eagleson (Maryknoll, N.Y.: Orbis, 1984), 155-68, 190-203;
Gustavo Gutiérrez, The Power of the Poor in History, trans. Robert
R. Barr (Maryknoll, N.Y.: Orbis, 1984), 5-22; Jürgen Moltmann,
Theology of Hope: On the Ground and Implications of a Christian
Eschatology, trans. James W. Leitch (New York: Harper & Row,
1975), 102-229; Metz, 169-79.

[2]However, Gutiérrez does occasionally refer to the wisdom
literature. See Theology of Liberation, 292, and Power of the
Poor, 8.

[3]E.g. Segundo, 111, 115.

he changed his life, becoming one of the foremost defenders of the rights of Indians.[4]

The historical anecdote suggests that the wisdom tradition may offer resources of its own to contemporary political and liberation theology. This section will explore the political dimension of the trajectory of Wisdom Christology as a resource for contemporary political and liberation theology. I will begin by examining the historical and sociological basis for suspecting the sages' political stance and will respond by investigating the potential for political criticism in the wisdom books of the Hebrew Bible and the Deuterocanonical corpus. Then I will turn to the political dimension of the association of Jesus and the wisdom tradition in the New Testament. In the third section I will examine the dangers of various biblical approaches to political action and will propose the perspective of the wisdom tradition as a complement and corrective to other biblical trajectories as a resource for political action. The concluding section will examine the challenge that political and liberation theology poses to the Christologies of Rahner and Pittenger and the contributions that their theologies can make to political and liberation theology.

Politics and Wisdom in Israel

Justice in society was a central concern of the wisdom tradition of ancient Israel.[5] The association of the wisdom teachers with the royal court in Jerusalem and with the upper classes in general has led some scholars to interpret the tradition as fundamentally conservative. Gordis has argued:

Wisdom Literature, which reached its apogee during the earlier centuries of the Second Temple, roughly between the fifth and first half of the second centuries, B.C.E., was fundamentally the product of the upper classes in society, who lived principally in the capital, Jerusalem. . . . As is to be expected, the upper classes were conservative in their outlook, basically satisfied with the status quo and opposed to change.[6]

[4]Martin E. Marty, The Public Church: Mainline-Evangelical-Catholic (New York: Crossroad, 1981), 149.

[5]Israel inherited this concern as part of the common heritage of the ancient Near East. See F. Charles Fensham, "Widow, Orphan and the Poor in Ancient Near Eastern Legal and Wisdom Literature," Journal of Near Eastern Studies 21(1962):129-39.

[6]Robert Gordis, "The Social Background of Wisdom Literature," Hebrew Union College Annual 18(1943):81-82.

Gordis sets the "conservative political ideas of Wisdom" in "the sharpest possible contrast with the rest of the Bible,"[7] and cites Proverbs 24:21 as "the most conservative passage in the Bible, unparallelled elsewhere":

My son, fear the Lord and the king
And do not become involved with those who seek change.[8]

In a similar vein, Crenshaw stresses the "emphasis upon moderation" of the professional class of sages:

The sages did not want anyone to rock the boat. Accordingly, they encouraged any means that would mollify anger, and they refused to become involved in efforts at social reform. Powerless themselves, the sages quickly learned their place in the social world, and recognized the usefulness of bribes, obsequiousness, and general 'yesmanship.'[9]

There are two sides to Gordis's interpretation: (1) that the wisdom literature was "fundamentally the product of the upper classes in society," and (2) that it was basically conservative. It should be noted that there is no necessary connection between the two claims. The question of the sociological origin of the wisdom tradition does not necessarily determine the question of its political function and usage, for it is possible for the upper classes to offer a criticism of the wealthy and the powerful from within their own class.[10] Both sides of Gordis's interpretation bear examination.

Wisdom literature most certainly did function in the royal court and the upper classes of Israel as counsel to the powerful and formation to the young. However, recent scholarship has questioned the supposition that wisdom literature was "fundamentally the product of the upper classes in society," and has stressed the

---

[7]Ibid., 115.

[8]Ibid., 116; translation by Gordis.

[9]Old Testament Wisdom, 20; see also 28-31.

[10]For example, see Breasted's interpretation of the emergence of a sense of social justice in Egypt among the members of the ruling class: "The high ideal of justice to the poor and oppressed set forth in this tale [of the Eloquent Peasant] is but a breath of that wholesome moral atmosphere which pervades the social thinking of the official class." James Henry Breasted, Development of Religion and Thought in Ancient Egypt (Philadelphia: University of Pennsylvania Press, 1972), 226.

broader and less affluent origins of the wisdom tradition in fami-
lies, clans, and local communities.[11] Scott suggests that the
wisdom tradition should not be understood as the product of any
one social group:

> Wisdom was rather the fine fruit of a tradition originally
> rooted in the mores of the family and tribe and local commu-
> nity, and hence to a degree as old as society itself.[12]

The wisdom books often present themselves as a royal literary
genre, usually claiming authorship by Solomon[13]; however, the

---

[11]Whybray in particular has argued against the assumption
that wisdom literature was produced by a professional class of
sages paid by the wealthy. For Whybray, wisdom was not the product or prerogative of any one class but formed part of the common
cultural stock of Israel. Wisdom referred to "simply a natural
endowment which some persons possess in greater measure than others." As such it was not a static possession or set content to be
learned but rather a natural shrewdness and ability to cope with
life. R.N. Whybray, The Intellectual Tradition in the Old Testament (Berlin: Walter de Gruyter, 1974), 6.
The studies of Berend Gemser, J.P. Audet, and Erhard Gersten-
berger have found a strong association between proverbial wisdom
and the ancient legal forms of the family and local community,
suggesting the origins of wisdom are to be found in the early family circles. See Berend Gemser, "Motive Clauses in Old Testament
Law," Vetus Testamentum Supplement, I(1953):50-66; J.P. Audet,
"Origines comparées de la double tradition de la loi et de la
sagesse dans la proche-orient ancient," Acten Internationalen
Orientalen-Kongresses, 1(Moscow, 1962):352-57; Erhard Gerstenber-
ger, Wesen und Herkunft des apodiktischen Rechts, Wissenschafliche
Monographie zum Alten und Neuen Testament, 20 (Neukirchen-Vluyn:
Neukirchener, 1966).

[12]Way of Wisdom, 3. James Crenshaw, who accepts the view
that a specific class of professional sages existed in Israel,
notes that most proverbs do not presuppose the setting of the
royal court or special houses of learning but rather the setting
of the family and the clan: "It seems likely, therefore, that most
biblical proverbs arose in this family setting" (Old Testament
Wisdom, 56). See also Donn F. Morgan, Wisdom in the Old Testament
Traditions (Atlanta: John Knox Press, 1981), 30-44.

[13]E.g., Prov 1:1; 10:1; 25:1; 31:1; Qoh 1:1. See McKane,
262. While the Wisdom of Solomon does not mention Solomon by
name, it is clear that the author identifies with him. See
Winston, 5, 139. On the relation of wisdom to ancient monarchies
in Israel and the Near East, see Leonidas Kalugila, The Wise King:
Studies in Royal Wisdom as Divine Revelation in the Old Testament
and Its Environment, Coniectanea Biblica, Old Testament Series 15
(Lund, Sweden: CWK Gleerup, 1980).

smaller genres contained in the wisdom books, such as the proverb (mashal), the parable (melisah), the words of the wise (dibre hakamim), and the riddles (hidoth) mentioned in Proverbs 1:6, are essentially open to all human beings.[14] Proverbs enshrine an insight or counsel that is accessible through ordinary human experience and transcends class distinctions. As Scott comments, wisdom sayings "would be at home on all levels of society, for they embody the shrewd observations and counsels of folk wisdom."[15] While wisdom literature did find a home in the royal court and the upper classes of Israel, these circles were drawing upon a tradition that had existed on every level of society from the earliest times in Israel.

Gordis's "sharpest possible contrast" between "conservative" wisdom and "the rest of the Bible" also needs to be modified in light of more recent studies which have found substantial parallels between wisdom and prophetic or historical literature.[16] Indeed, instead of finding a sharp contrast, recent scholarship has risked going to the opposite extreme of finding wisdom influence everywhere in the Bible.[17]

---

[14]On these forms, see Scott, Way of Wisdom, 53-55; Crenshaw, Old Testament Wisdom, 32-39; and McKane, 22-23, 267.

[15]Way of Wisdom, 51.

[16]Fichtner, who essentially accepted Gordis's thesis, had to admit that Isaiah bears a clear relationship to the wisdom tradition. Johannes Fichtner, "Isaiah Among the Wise," in Studies in Ancient Israelite Wisdom, 429-38. Terrien outlined eight points of correspondence between Amos and the wisdom tradition. Samuel Terrien, "Amos and Wisdom," in Studies in Ancient Israelite Wisdom, 448-55. Wolff argues that both Micah and Amos were influenced by wisdom literature. Hans Wolff, Amos the Prophet (Philadelphia: Fortress, 1973). Weinfeld relates the Deuteronomic school to the sages of Hezekiah and Josiah. Moshe Weinfeld, Deuteronomy and the Deuteronomic School (Oxford: Clarendon Press, 1972). Whedbee finds wisdom influence on Isaiah. J. Whedbee, Isaiah and Wisdom (Nashville: Abingdon, 1971). See also Morgan, 63-93.

[17]On this question, see James L. Crenshaw, "Method in Determining Wisdom Influence upon 'Historical' Literature," JBL 88 (1969):129-42. As Collins notes, even the prophets' attacks on wisdom (e.g. Jer 9:23; Is 44:25) find parallels in the wisdom sayings which express the limits of all human wisdom (e.g. Prov 3:7; 21:30; 26:12; 28:26). See Collins, "Proverbial Wisdom and the Yahwist Vision," 1-17.

In regard to the second side of Gordis's interpretation, we find that the concern for justice and the warning of punishment for injustice appear again and again in the pages of wisdom literature. The sages expressed a lively sense of God's partisan concern for the poor and the powerless and stressed the obligation of the wise to share that concern:

Because a man is poor, do not therefore cheat him,
     nor, at the city gate, oppress anybody in affliction;
for Yahweh takes up their cause,
     and extorts the life of their extortioners (Prov 22:22-23).

Do not displace the ancient landmark
     or encroach on orphans' lands,
For he who avenges them is strong
     and will take up their cause upon you (Prov 23:10-11).

To oppress the poor is to insult his creator,
     to be kind to the needy is to honour him (Prov 14:31).

The virtuous man is concerned for the rights of the poor,
     the wicked shows no such concern (Prov 29:7).

Whoever gives to the poor shall never want,
     whoever closes his eyes to them will bear many a curse
     (Prov 28:27).

Whoever shuts his ear to the poor man's cry
     shall himself plead and not be heard (Prov 21:13).

These proverbs could well have had their origin within the upper classes of Israel, but they represent a sharp awareness of the claims of the poor and a criticism of the abuses of power by the wealthy. The verse that Gordis cites as "the most conservative passage in the Bible" (Prov 24:21) is probably less a statement of political philosophy than a prudent caution against the selfish schemes of ambitious aristocrats. "Those who seek change" most likely refers to intriguing nobles who seek not a just reordering of society but rather their own political advantage.[18]

If the prophet and the sage share a common concern for justice and a common conviction that injustice will be punished, they do differ nonetheless in basing their appeals on different kinds

---

[18]McKane, 406. There are textual problems with the verse that render any reading less than certain. Scott amends the Masoretic text in accordance with the Septuagint reading and translates: "Reverence the Lord, my son, and also the king, And do not be rebellious against either" (Proverbs. Ecclesiastes, 146-47).

of experience. Where the prophet appeals to the extraordinary experience of being specially called by God,[19] the sage makes no claim of special experience but appeals to experience accessible to all and to the listener's own understanding and desire for well-being.[20] The sage associates the stability of justice and the punishment of injustice with the constant working of the primordial world order which is experienced by all people.

The wisdom tradition does have its own articulation of an experience of revelation in the descriptions of Lady Wisdom, who offers life and truth to all people. Lady Wisdom explicitly associates herself with justice and prosperity (Prov 8:20-21), and she warns those who reject her that they are harming themselves (Prov 8:36). Elsewhere, Lady Wisdom demands justice and threatens sudden disaster on those who refuse her call (Prov 1:10-33). It is noteworthy that the punishment of the wicked is not the result of a special supernatural intervention by God but is the natural result of unjust action in a justice-loving world-order.[21]

This perspective clearly possesses the potential for developing a political criticism of unjust practices and powers in society, a potential that would be developed later by the Wisdom of Solomon. While the ancient sages themselves probably had no conception of changing the social and political structures of Israelite society, they did reiterate the basic principle of justice upon which such a change could be based. Injustice is inherently unstable and leads to its own destruction. Justice brings fulfillment and lasting prosperity because it is demanded by the very structure of the world in which we live.

As we have noted, Segundo sees the post-exilic wisdom tradition as becoming "more individualistic, inner-directed, and apolitical," and he questions the wisdom tradition's "more spiritualistic and subjective interpretation of the Exodus event."[22]

---

[19]E.g. Is 6; Jer 1; Ezek 1; Hos 1; Amos 1; 7:14-16; Joel 1. Prophetic literature typically presents itself as a special oracle or vision from God. On the social location and function of this claim, see Robert R. Wilson, Prophecy and Society in Ancient Israel (Philadelphia: Fortress, 1980); and Thomas W. Overholt, "Commanding the Prophets: Amos and the Problem of Prophetic Authority," CBQ 41(1979):517-32. See also J. Lindblom, Prophecy in Ancient Israel (Philadelphia: Fortress, 1976), 105-219.

[20]See the repeated appeals in Proverbs 1-7 that wisdom and virtue bring a full and happy life. Cf. Collins, "Biblical Precedent," 42-46.

[21]See von Rad, Wisdom in Israel, 124-37.

[22]Segundo, 111, 115.

While Segundo's charge of becoming individualistic and apolitical may apply to Qoheleth, Qoheleth does not offer an interpretation of the Exodus event. The two works of the later wisdom tradition that do discuss the Exodus event are Ben Sira and the Wisdom of Solomon. In response to Segundo's suspicions, we now turn to the social and political concerns of Ben Sira and the Wisdom of Solomon and to their interpretations of the Exodus event.

It is true that Ben Sira offers us much advice on matters of personal and family life, even suggesting that we advance our position in life by pleasing princes (20:27-28). However, Ben Sira also knows the demand for justice, the threat of judgement upon economic injustice, and God's special preference for the poor:

> Panic and violence make havoc of palaces,
>> similarly, desolation overtakes the houses of the proud.
> A plea from a poor man's mouth goes straight to the ear of God,
>> whose judgement comes without delay (21:4-5).

> To build your house on other people's money
>> is like collecting stones for your own tomb (21:8).

> Save the oppressed from the hand of the oppressor,
>> and do not be mean-spirited in your judgements (4:9).

Ben Sira has an acute sense of the dilemma of business ethics; the desire for wealth leads to sinful business practices, which in turn brings inevitable destruction:

> It is difficult for a merchant to avoid doing wrong
>> and for a salesman not to incur sin.
> Many have sinned for the sake of profit,
>> he who hopes to be rich must be ruthless.
> A peg will stick in the joint between two stones,
>> and sin will wedge itself between selling and buying.
> If a man does not earnestly hold to the fear of the Lord,
>> his House will soon be overthrown (26:29-27:3).

> The man who loves gold will not be reckoned virtuous,
>> the man who chases after profit will be caught out by it.
> Many have gone to their ruin for the sake of gold,
>> though destruction stared them in the face (31:5-6).

These passages contain the principles for a thoroughgoing critique of capitalist economic systems of later centuries.[23]

With regard to the Exodus event, Ben Sira describes Moses and Aaron as "illustrious men" who merit praise and imitation. They stand as models who show clearly to all nations the benefits of Lady Wisdom (45:1-22).[24] However, for Ben Sira the revelatory experience of the Exodus is neither individualistic nor subjective but rather cosmological. As we have seen, Ben Sira understands the revelation of the Torah as the dwelling of Lady Wisdom in Israel (24:13). The commandments of Moses reveal the ordering principle of creation and allow the wise to live in harmony with the order of the universe. As the dwelling of Lady Wisdom in Israel, the Torah articulates the demand for justice which is built into creation itself. This correlation of Lady Wisdom and the Torah allows for a genuine knowledge of God throughout the earth, for Lady Wisdom is everywhere (24:6); it also gives a cosmological grounding to "the Law which Moses enjoined on us" (24:23).

The Wisdom of Solomon differs in many respects from the older wisdom literature. What is significant for this aspect of this investigation is its development of the potential we discovered in the earlier tradition for a political critique of injustice. Lady Wisdom is closely associated with "avenging Justice" who spares no one who "gives voice to injustice" (Wis 1:8).[25] The Wisdom of Solomon presents itself as an explicitly political document, a message from King Solomon to the other rulers on earth, probably with the Roman Emperor in mind (1:1; 6:1).[26] The opening line proclaims its central call: "Love justice, you who rule on earth" (1:1). The author urgently warns the other monarchs:

> If, as administrators of his kingdom, you have not governed
> justly

---

[23]See also additional examples from Ben Sira cited by Martin Hengel, _Property and Riches in the Early Church: Aspects of a Social History of Early Christianity_, trans. John Bowden (Philadelphia: Fortress, 1980), 16-17.

[24]See von Rad, _Wisdom in Israel_, 257-58.

[25]Winston notes that the perspective of Wisdom 1:12 on injustice bringing its own destruction is already found in Proverbs 8 (p. 106).

[26]See Winston, 3-25.

nor observed the law,
nor behaved as God would have you behave,
he will fall on you swiftly and terribly.
Ruthless judgement is reserved for the high and mighty;
the lowly will be compassionately pardoned,
the mighty will be mightily punished (6:4-6).

Lest there be any lingering doubt about the intended audience, the author reiterates:

Yes despots, my words are for you,
that you may learn what wisdom is and not transgress (6:9).

The Wisdom of Solomon develops the potential of the older wisdom tradition for political criticism in the portait of the virtuous man (chs. 2-5). The wise man is not the smooth-tongued courtier who pleases princes to win favor, but rather is a troublesome critic of the powerful who practice injustice. The mighty in society are portrayed as godless cynics who fear no judgement and make a pact with Death (1:16). The wise man opposes their way of life and reproaches them for their breaches of the law (2:12). Rather than conforming to the status quo, the just man holds aloof from the doings of the wicked as though from filth (2:16). "The paths he treads are unfamiliar" (2:15). Because of his criticism of injustice, the virtuous man is tortured and condemned to a shameful death, seemingly abandoned by God (2:19-20).

The wicked are confounded, in turn, as they are brought to judgement and are confronted with their crimes. In fulfillment of Lady Wisdom's age-old warning (Prov 1:26), the Lord laughs at the godless (Wis 4:18) as they "shake with cowards' fear" before the sight of the virtuous man (5:2).[27] The example of the just man who is tortured, executed, and vindicated by God is presented as an illustration of the working of God through creation to avenge injustice (5:17). The moral of the story is clear:

So lawlessness will bring the whole earth to ruin
and evil-doing bring the thrones of the mighty down (5:23).

It is noteworthy that the problem of injustice in this world is here resolved by means of an apocalyptic vision of a judgement after death.[28] The confidence of the older wisdom tradition in Proverbs that justice would be done in this world appears to be under some strain, for the Wisdom of Solomon must look beyond the grave for a vindication of the just and wise. Nonetheless, the account of the history of Israel in chapers 10-19 does look to

---

[27]Ibid., 146-50.

[28]On the similarities to apocalyptic literature, see Winston, 32-33, 146-49; and Nickelsberg, 88-89.

historical events as confirmation of the power of justice to avenge oppression in this world.

The Wisdom of Solmon understands the Exodus event as a type, a paradigmatic example of the constant working of Lady Wisdom or of God in the world:[29]

A holy people and a blameless race,
this she [Lady Wisdom] delivered from a nation of oppressors (10:15).

Neither the Israelites nor the Egyptians are named, for the interest of the account is not in their unique historical identities but in their character as examples of the pattern of Lady Wisdom's activity. Lady Wisdom appears as the avenger of oppression and the saviour of the oppressed (10:15-21). The miracles of the Exodus event punish injustice not by disrupting the cosmic order but by a "retuning or refashioning of nature."[30]

The interpretation of the Exodus by the Wisdom of Solomon is neither individualistic nor subjective nor spiritualistic nor apolitical. Rather, it incorporates the historical memory of the Exodus into a cosmology which is the basis for just government. The disaster which fell upon Pharoah and the Egyptians is a harsh warning of the avenging justice which threatens the rulers of every society.

This investigation thus far has suggested that the wisdom tradition does offer resources for a critical political stance in society. Although the wisdom tradition could function among the upper classes as a guide to success, it could also offer a sharp criticism of the wealthy classes from within their own ranks. Moreover, the wisdom tradition was never limited to the upper classes; its origins and its appeal were rooted in the folk wisdom of the people and are essentially universal in scope. While the sages did not envision the transformation of the political and economic structures of their society, their repeated demands for justice contained principles for the criticism of political structures of society.

---

[29]The description of the Exodus event begins by attributing the liberation of the Israelites to Lady Wisdom (10:15-21), but in 11:4 the author abruptly shifts to "you" addressed to God. With the exception of 14:2, 5, there is no further mention of Wisdom in the book. The shift reveals the close association between God and Lady Wisdom.

[30]Goodrick, 367.

The wisdom trajectory in the New Testament continues many of
the themes of the Hebrew and Jewish wisdom tradition. We have
noted the presence of numerous wisdom sayings on the lips of Jesus
in the Synoptic tradition. Much of this strand of the Synoptic
tradition shares the perspective of the earlier wisdom tradition
on justice working through the order of the world. Commenting on
the logia of Jesus as the teacher of wisdom, Bultmann notes that
"the spirit of such a piety is that of the popular belief in God,
which--alongside a recognition of God's sovereign sway--sees a
retributive righteousness in world events."[31]

Among the wisdom sayings of Jesus we find traditional warning
on the use of wealth and counsels on giving to the poor. Thus,
following Bultmann,[32] we may compare:

(1) Mt 5:42: "Give to him who begs from you,
       and do not refuse him who would borrow from you,"

and Prov 28:27: "He who gives to the poor will not want,
       but he who hides his eyes will get many a curse,"

and Sir 4:4: "Do not reject an afflicted suppliant,
       nor turn your face from the poor";

(2) Mt 6:19-20: "Do not lay up for yourselves treasures on
       earth where moth and rust will consume and where thieves
       break in and steal, but lay up for yourselves treasures
       in heaven,"

and Prov 11:4: "Riches do not profit in the day of wrath,
       but righteousness delivers from death,"

and Baba Bathra 11a: "Treasures gained by wickedness do not
       profit, but righteousness delivers from death."

Betz notes the similarity of much of the Sermon on the Mount
to Jewish wisdom material, and sees its ethics as grounded in a
theology of creation, in particular in "God's creatio continua,
his creational activities in the present."[33] Betz further notes

---

[31]History, 104.

[32]Ibid., 106-07.

[33]"Cosmogony and Ethics in the Sermon on the Mount," 159-60.

that the political perspective of the Sermon on the Mount is expressed "only in oblique form or through metaphors."[34] Betz suggests that the community of the Sermon on the Mount saw itself as "an embattled minority" and viewed the Roman Empire "in mostly negative terms"; nonetheless, the members of the community "were convinced that, despite their situation as a suppressed and even a persecuted minority, they had a grip on history (cf. Matthew 5:13-18)."[35] In light of the suspicions of the political and liberation theologians, it is significant that in the Sermon on the Mount Jewish wisdom material and a theology of continuous creation and providence do not serve to justify the present political powers but rather strengthen the identity of a small minority which is in opposition to the dominant political powers.

Other wisdom materials in the Synoptic tradition offer a critical perspective on the use of wealth. The parable of the rich fool (Lk 12:16-20) is an expansion and development of Ben Sira 11:18-19.[36] As Luise Schottroff and Wolfgang Stegemann comment, the security that the wealthy farmer seeks is not simply a private matter of an individual's peace of mind; rather

> he has taken part in an economic crime that is of major importance in the economy of antiquity . . . he has harmed society by holding back his harvests. That is what drives up the price of grain.[37]

It is interesting to note the similarity to Proverbs 11:26: "The people's curse is on the man who hoards the wheat, a blessing on him who sells it."

Many of the sayings of Jesus confront the hearer with unsettling and disorienting reversals of expectation. The unsettling, defamiliarizing perspectives of many sayings of Jesus are not directly translatable into concrete political conclusions. Such sayings function not as a concrete formula for specific action but as an imaginative shock that makes possible but does not prescribe different forms of action. Tannehill notes that the jarring saying does not give any direct conclusion for action. He comments on the function of Matthew 5:39b-42:

---

[34]Ibid., 161.

[35]Ibid.

[36]Bultmann, History, 97.

[37]Luise Schottroff and Wolfgang Stegemann, Jesus and the Hope of the Poor, trans. Matthew J. O'Connell (Maryknoll, N.Y.: Orbis, 1986), 97.

The focal instance does not leave the decision maker without help. It helps not by deciding for him what he is to do but by throwing a strong light on his situation from one direction, forcefully calling to his attention one factor in the situation.[38]

The articulation of the limits of all human claims to wisdom undermines the self-understanding of any established political order, but it also undermines the claim of any utopia to be an adequate vision of and program for the just society willed by God. This jolt to the imagination confronts the listener with the necessity of making decisions in a world where no one human perspective is adequate to the complexity and mystery of human life.

The picture of Jesus as a teacher of wisdom raises also the question of the relation of Jesus to Lady Wisdom. Luke presents Jesus as an envoy of Lady Wisdom, the culmination of a long series of messengers sent by Lady Wisdom who have been persecuted and killed:

And that is why the Wisdom of God said, 'I will send them prophets and apostles; some they will slaughter and persecute, so that this generation will have to answer for every prophet's blood that has been shed since the foundation of the world, from the blood of Abel to the blood of Zechariah, who was murdered between the altar and the sanctuary' (Lk 11:49-51).

What is significant for this investigation is the dangerous and controversial character of Lady Wisdom's envoys. They are always in conflict with the powers of their time and are rejected and put to death. Lady Wisdom evidently is not confirming the status quo but is attempting to criticize and change it. Thus her messengers, like the wise man of the Wisdom of Solomon, suffer persecution and death.

As we have seen, New Testament hymns such as John 1:1-14 and Colossians 1:14-20 interpret Jesus as Wisdom incarnate. The Wisdom Christology of John and Colossians is an interpretation of the universal and cosmological significance of the life, death, and resurrection of Jesus. We have seen that Dodd and Lightfoot both argue that the key to understanding the Gospel of John lies precisely in the identification of Jesus and the Logos (or Wisdom). From this perspective, the conflict of Jesus with the Jewish and Roman authorities of his time reveals the relation of Wisdom (or the Logos) to the ruling powers of every human society. The fate of Jesus, like that of the wise man of the Wisdom of Solomon, is a critical judgement upon the powerful of every age who ignore the

---

[38]Tannehill, 74.

212

call of Lady Wisdom to practice justice. The critical political potential of this angle of vision is evident.

The Bible as a Resource for Political and Liberation Theology

Thus far this investigation has suggested that there is a potential for a critical political stance in the wisdom trajectory of the Bible. The use of any biblical tradition as a resource for contemporary political action plunges us into the problem of hermeneutics and forces us to recognize the danger of political action in the name of religion. The wisdom tradition offers relatively abstract principles, such as justice and concern for the poor and the proper use of wealth, and challenges its hearers to use their own discernment to apply these principles in practice. The historical, prophetic, and apocalyptical traditions which have inspired political and liberation theologians often tend to be more concrete than the wisdom tradition, but problems arise in the application of each of these traditions. The problem is that often the Bible is all too precisely concrete, material, and political; and twentieth-century believers have difficulty accepting many of the concrete political and social proposals of the Bible as revelatory of the will of God. What the Bible understands justice in society to be is often in stark contrast to twentieth-century understandings, and contemporary theologians often must argue directly against the concrete political theologies of the Bible. Gutiérrez seeks to interpret the Bible's political perspectives concretely and cites the promises of God to Abraham in Genesis as an example of God's liberating intention for humanity.[39] The concrete political message of the text, however, is that it is the will of God for one people (the descendants of Abraham) to conquer and rule over a multitude of other peoples:

> To your descendants I give this land, from the wadi of Egypt to the Great River, the river Euphrates, the Kenites, Kenizzites, the Kadmonites, the Hittites, the Perizzites, the Rephaim, the Amorites, the Canaanites, the Girgashites, and the Jebushites (Gen 15:18-21).

Von Rad notes that "the size of the Promised Land corresponds to the extent of Solomon's kingdom at the period of its greatest extent (I Kings 4.21)."[40] The author of the passage was most likely a theologian at the court of Solomon, writing to legitimate the conquests of the Israelite Empire. To read history "from the

[39]Theology of Liberation, 160; Power of the Poor, 10.

[40]Gerhard von Rad, Genesis: A Commentary, Old Testament Library (Philadelphia: Westminster Press, 1972), 188.

underside," as Gutiérrez suggests,[41] requires us to be suspicious of the imperialistic writing of a court theologian and to ask about the concerns of those oppressed and forgotten by history, the Kenites, Kenizzites, and others. The argument that God wills the social, political, and economic liberation of all peoples is an argument to be made directly against the concrete political meaning of the text of Genesis 15.

The Exodus event has served as a central paradigm of God's action in history for liberation theologians. As Gutiérrez understands it, "[t]he Exodus is the long march towards the promised land in which Israel can establish a society free from misery and alienation."[42] The liberating God of the Exodus does have a very concrete program for organizing the structures of society in the Promised Land (Ex 20-23). Unfortunately, this program gives explicit divine legitimation to the buying and selling of slaves (21:1-11). A male Hebrew slave can be sold for six years (21:2); however, a man may sell his daughter and "she shall not regain her liberty like the male slaves" (21:7). Again, the argument that God wills the social and political liberation of all people is to be made directly against some of the concrete political theology of the book of Exodus.

The prophets and apocalyptic writings have also served as an important biblical precedent for political and liberation theology.[43] The prophets and apocalyptic writers most certainly do bear eloquent witness to the desire of God for justice; however, their concrete proposals often differ rather starkly from the agenda of contemporary theologians. The aging prophet Samuel rages at Saul because the young monarch did not immediately execute the captured enemy king, Agog (1 Sam 15:10-23). Samuel, as prophet, demands blind obedience to his version of the will of God and accuses Saul of rebellion and presumption (1 Sam 15:22-23). The will of God, as understood by the theology of the holy war, is that all members of the enemy group (as well as their animals) be killed (1 Sam 15:3).[44] The prophetic demand for blind obedience, the ideology of the holy war, and the denial of any grounds for

---

[41]Power of the Poor, 169-214.

[42]Theology of Liberation, 157.

[43]Ibid., 162-64; 195-96; Metz, 169-79.

[44]On the holy war, see R. Smend, Yahweh War and Tribal Confederation (Nashville: Abingdon Press, 1970); and P.D. Miller, The Divine Warrior in Early Israel (Cambridge, Mass.: Harvard University Press, 1973). On the conflict between Samuel and Saul, see P. Kyle McCarter, Jr. I Samuel, Anchor Bible, vol. 8 (Garden City, N.Y.: Doubleday & Co., 1980), 260-71.

discussion regarding the will of God are dangerous precedents for political action by a religious group.

Lindblom suggests that the social ideals of the pre-exilic prophets in general were not so much revolutionary as reactionary:

There is a conspicuous reactionary tendency in the preaching of these prophets. For them the best of times were times long past. . . . The prophets embodied the good old customs in their admonitory preaching and gave them divine sanction. . . . In the prophetic preaching we do not find any rational motivation of moral demands.[45]

Metz's retrieval of apocalyptic eschatology presupposes that action in history can make a difference; that presupposition contrasts sharply with the view of the Book of Daniel. Collins comments that for the author of Daniel "[t]here is no question of averting that which is to be. The apocalypses can only mediate a knowledge and understanding of the inevitable. They cannot change it."[46] The maskilim of Daniel are not called to change the world but only to interpret it so that fellow believers can remain faithful and be rewarded at the end of this age. In the New Testament the Book of Revelation offers a powerful condemnation of Roman rule but responds with a call to withdraw into a separate group that awaits its own reward. Adela Yarbro Collins comments:

The response to the perceived crisis elicited by the book [of Revelation] involves the establishment of Christian independence and identity by withdrawing from Greco-Roman society into an exclusive group with rigorous rules and an intense expectation of imminent judgement against their enemies and of their own salvation.[47]

The above observations do not deny the very real and valuable resources for political theology to be found in the Bible. They do argue that no biblical political theology can be directly translated into a concrete program of political action for the twentieth century. When the Bible is most concrete about the ordering of society, it is very often the most problematic. While claiming to be more concrete in their reading of the Bible, political and liberation theologians are often much more comfortable with more abstract biblical principles, such as justice or God's

[45]Lindblom, 344-46.

[46]John J. Collins, The Apocalyptic Vision of the Book of Daniel (Missoula, Mont.: Scholars Press, 1977), 87.

[47]Adela Yarbro Collins, Crisis and Catharsis: The Power of the Apocalypse (Philadelphia: Westminster Press, 1984), 137.

concern for the poor, which can then be filled with concrete contents that differ radically from the concrete biblical applications.

The wisdom tradition can offer a helpful perspective on the hermeneutical question of the responsible application of a religious tradition. It is here that its particular value as a complement and corrective to other biblical traditions may be found. While much of the wisdom tradition is concerned with constructing a world-view and passing this on to the next generation, the sages do not ask blind obedience to a supernatural message but grant their students the right, and indeed impose on them the duty, to listen critically and to apply the wisdom of the received tradition in accordance with their own experience and insight. While the sages do claim an experience of revelation in their descriptions of Lady Wisdom, this revelation is not limited to a chosen few but is accessible to all humans through the ordinary experience of life.

The sages challenge their students to discern the times. There is a proper time for action and waiting, for speech and silence; but no one else can tell us what the time is. We must discern it for ourselves. One proverb may be more fruitful for practical action or non-action at one time, and another contradictory proverb may be more fruitful at another time.

The wisdom tradition turns back critically upon itself in the books of Job and Qoheleth. When Bildad of Shuah advises Job to be guided by the tradition of his ancestors (Job 8:8), Job rejects his advice in the name of his own ability to reflect on his experience:

> I can reflect as deeply as ever you can,
> I am in no way inferior to you.
> And who, for that matter, has not observed as much (Job 12:3)?

As Crenshaw notes, "[a]bove all, Job insisted that personal experience possessed the power to call dogma into question."[48] Job accuses the traditional orthodoxy of his friends of being dishonest to God when applied to his own situation:

> Will you plead God's defense with prevarication,
> his case in terms that ring false?
> Will you be partial in his favour
> and act as his advocate (Job 13:7-8)?

Though Job himself is reminded of the limits of his understanding (chs. 38-41), in the epilogue of the book God prefers the honest

---

[48]Old Testament Wisdom, 115.

but agonizing questions of Job to the uncritical repetition of the received tradition by his friends (42:7-9).

Qoheleth also challenges the confidence of the wisdom tradition on the basis of his own experience. He asks with biting irony, "What advantage has the wise man over the fool (6:7)?" As Murphy notes, Qoheleth continues the experiential approach of the wisdom tradition even while challenging its teachings.[49] Scott comments that "Qoheleth was an intellectual who searched for wisdom in his own way, and failed to find that the traditional claims made for it were true for him."[50] One of Qoheleth's principal lessons, Scott suggests, is that "his pupils must learn to think for themselves. . . . Common or inherited beliefs which will not stand up under examination must be abandoned as untrue."[51]

Job and Qoheleth stand as biblical examples of how to use a tradition that claims to reveal God. Both figures raise extremely uncomfortable questions about the truth of the tradition of Israel for their own experience; both put the received tradition to a critical test in light of their own experience. By presupposing that the offer of Lady Wisdom is extended to all people through the ordinary experience of life, the more constructive books of the wisdom tradition (Proverbs, Ben Sira, the Wisdom of Solomon) offer a counterpole to the claims of supernaturally revealed knowledge of prophets and apocalyptic writers. The understanding of God and of justice which is available through reflection upon our own experience offers a criterion for assessing concrete political claims, such as the promise of Empire in Genesis 15, the rules for slaves in Exodus 21, or the demand for an execution in 1 Samuel 15, which invoke the authority of God.

The sages demand that we discern the time in which we live in order to decide whether the claims of the tradition are helpful and true. This perspective can ground not only the critical questions of Job and Qoheleth but also the critical questions of contemporary believers who search the Scriptures for insight. While Segundo is very critical of the later stages of the wisdom tradition, his own hermeneutical model of "learning to learn" has a very sapiential character.[52] The goal of instruction in wisdom is not primarily the imparting of a certain body of knowledge but rather the developing of one's natural ability to discern the proper time for the proper action.

---

[49]"Wisdom and Creation," 7.

[50]Way of Wisdom, 140.

[51]Ibid., 185.

[52]Segundo, 118-21.

The wisdom tradition also offers precedent for the hermeneutics of "discernment in the Spirit" of Jose Miguez Bonino.[53] Bonino rejects interpretations which seek "a direct historical correspondence, either in the form of law . . . or as precedent"; as an examples he cautions, "the attempts to derive political conclusions (either revolutionary or pacifist) from the ambivalent relation of Jesus to the Zealots, seems to me a dangerous short cut."[54] Instead, Miguez Bonino looks to the Bible for "mediating concepts," such as "liberation, righteousness, shalom, the poor, love," which indicate general directions; he also looks to the analysis of the present situation through rational and social scientific studies; the correlation between the historical concepts from the Bible and contemporary social analysis "can offer us, not certainly a foolproof key to Christian obedience, but a significant framework for it."[55]

The wisdom tradition was very concerned with justice and with practical action in society, but realized the impossibility of prescribing specific courses of action for all times. The proverbs and wisdom sayings of Israelite sages or of Jesus do not claim to make our concrete political decisions for us but offer us resources, the expressions of others' insights and experiences, which help form our judgement and shape the perspective in which we decide our actions.

Politics, Rahner, and Process Thought

Rahner and process thought have also been accused of lacking a political dimension and thus implicitly accepting the status quo of an unjust social and political order. My purpose in this section is not to develop a Rahnerian or a process political theology but to reflect briefly on Rahner and Pittenger's work in light of

[53]Jose Miguez Bonino, Doing Theology in a Revolutionary Situation (Philadelphia: Fortress, 1975), 86-104.

[54]Ibid., 103.

[55]Ibid., 103-04. Another ethical model of discernment which finds precedent in the wisdom tradition is the theocentric ethics of Gustafson. Gustafson quite rightly claims that his ethics has "a strong biblical base in the creation narratives, in some of the Psalms, in the Wisdom literature, and in some aspects of the New Testament." James G. Gustafson, Ethics from a Theocentric Perspective, (2 vols.; Chicago: University of Chicago Press, 1981, 1984), II, 86. Like the ancient sages, Gustafson seeks to discern the meaning of God from critical reflection on the ordering power experienced in creation (I, 327-42).

this issue, with attention to the political resources of their thought.

It is true that neither Rahner nor Pittenger have devoted major efforts to political and social questions. Rahner himself admitted in response to Johann Baptist Metz that "Metz's critique of my theology . . . is the only criticism which I take very seriously."[56] He went on to add that

> I believe that my theology and that of Metz are not necessarily contradictory. However, I gladly recognize that a concrete mystagogy must, to use Metz's language, be at the same time 'mystical and political.'[57]

Rahner's own failure to develop a political theology does not mean that his thought does not offer resources for articulating a political or liberation theology.[58] Jon Sobrino has developed some implications of Rahner's thought for liberation theology. Sobrino seeks to honor Rahner by reflecting on the Rahnerian theme of God as mystery with attention to its implications for the experience of the church of the poor.[59] Sobrino integrates Rahner's understanding of the relation of humankind to the mystery of God into his own thought in part for an avowedly polemical purpose, to answer the charge that liberation theology's "Church of the Poor" is "a reductive horizontalism."[60]

Sobrino begins with Rahner's insistence that the experience of God "is always a historical experience, that is it can be experienced only through an experience of that which is categorically historical."[61] The categorical, historical nature of the experience of God demands some "concrete and historically specific channel," and Sobrino turns specifically to the channel of the Church of the poor as a privileged place for experiencing and reflecting

---

[56]Karl Rahner, "Introduction" to Bacik, ix.

[57]Ibid., x.

[58]Rahner has addressed some of the concerns of political theology. See Karl Rahner, "The Function of the Church as a Critic of Society," TI, XII, trans. David Bourke, (New York: Seabury, 1974), 229-49; idem, "On the Theology of Revolution," TI, XIV, trans. David Bourke (New York: Seabury, 1976), 314-30.

[59]Jon Sobrino, The True Church and the Poor, trans. Matthew J. O'Connell (Maryknoll, N.Y.: Orbis, 1984), 125-59.

[60]Ibid., 351.

[61]Ibid., 125.

upon the mystery of God.[62] Sobrino gives a sociological reading to Rahner's interpretation of the obediential capacity of the human person for God:

The poor are accepted as constituting the primary recipients of the Good News and, therefore, as having an inherent capacity to understand it 'better' than anyone else. The obediential capacity of the human being to become a hearer of the word is thereby made concrete as the obediential capacity of the poor and the impoverished to hear that word as the Good News and thus as a word of grace.[63]

Sobrino further accepts and reaffirms Rahner's dialectic of the presence and hiddenness of God in human experience.[64]

It is evident that for Sobrino the relationship between liberation theology and Rahner is mutually corrective and mutually complementary. Rahner's reflections on God as mystery, on the transcendental and categorical nature of experience offer Sobrino resources for rebutting the charge of reductive horizontalism; and Sobrino, in turn, develops a potential for political and social critique that Rahner had left undeveloped in his own writings.

Bonino notes the influence of Rahner's thought upon the work of Segundo, observing that Segundo

starts from Karl Rahner's anthropology, which attempts to overcome the dichotomy of nature and grace by conceiving man (humanity) in his very creaturehood as open to God.[65]

Segundo roots his own reflections on the theological notions of concupiscence and liberty in Rahner's anthropology,[66] and he embraces Rahner's perspective on the role of Christological dogmas and dogmatic formulas.[67] While Segundo finds much that is helpful in Rahner's transcendental anthropology, he charges that Rahner's anthropology is too abstract to provide a solid bridge to the historical Jesus: Rahner's transcendental anthropology "helps

---

[62]Ibid., 126.

[63]Ibid., 140.

[64]Ibid., 141.

[65]Bonino, 62-63.

[66]Juan Luis Segundo, Grace and the Human Condition, trans. John Drury (Maryknoll, N.Y.: Orbis, 1973), 23-25, 32.

[67]Juan Luis Segundo, The Historical Jesus of the Synoptics, trans. John Drury (Maryknoll, N.Y.: Orbis, 1985), 12.

us to do away with misunderstandings and naive clichés. But it does not thereby lose the emptiness of its abstractness."[68] In defense of Rahner, we may note the necessity of clarifying the factors in our experience that allow us to understand and respond to the accounts of Jesus. As Richard R. Niebuhr put it:

> All of the dogmatic labors a theologian may devote to the definition of Christ, all of the research that a historian may expend in the search for the historical Jesus . . . will fail to create clarity in the figure of Jesus--until we understand what it is in our world/age that endows our experience with resonance to the world of Jesus and that enables us to recognize his conduct and his method of taking hold of the known and paying deference to the unknown as authoritative, augmenting, and attractive to us in our enigmatic world.[69]

It is precisely this concern that Rahner's transcendental anthropology and searching Christology address. Attention to the historical Jesus or engagement in the political challenges and crises of the contemporary world do not by themselves lessen or answer the need for a necessarily abstract articulation of the aspects of experience that make possible a concrete experience of revelation in history.

Pittenger, like Rahner, has not developed the political implications of his theology in a major way and thus his Christology, like Rahner's, is open to the charge of lacking a political dimension. Nonetheless, Pittenger does stress repeatedly the social character of human existence and the centrality of relationships on both a personal and societal level.[70] While Pittenger himself has not developed the political dimension of process thought, other process thinkers have increasingly begun to explore its potential for social and political criticism.[71] As

---

[68]Ibid., 37.

[69]Richard R. Niebuhr, Experiential Religion (New York: Harper & Row, 1972), quoted by Gustafson, I, 277.

[70]Norman Pittenger, The Meaning of Being Human (New York: Pilgrim Press, 1982), 120-33; idem, Loving Says It All (New York: Pilgrim Press, 1978), 104-09; Catholic Faith in a Process Perspective, 110-18.

[71]See John B. Cobb, Jr. Process Theology as Political Theology (Philadelphia: Westminster Press, 1982); Delwin Brown, To Set at Liberty: Christian Faith and Human Freedom (Maryknoll, N.Y.: Orbis, 1981); John B. Cobb, Jr. and W. Widick Schroeder, eds. Process Philosophy and Social Thought (Chicago: Center for the Scientific Study of Religion, 1981); Schubert M. Ogden, Faith and Freedom: Toward a Theology of Liberation (Nashville, Tenn.: Abingdon, 1979).

in the case of Rahner, Pittenger's Christology offers us not a developed political theology but rather a general orientation which can offer resources to political theology. Jürgen Moltmann himself has accepted Whitehead's criticism of the images of God as "the ruling Caesar, or the ruthless moralist, or the unmoved mover."[72] Moltmann proposes to "follow Whitehead in describing theism in moral, political, and philosophical respects as idolatry."[73] While Moltmann's own constructive proposal on the doctrine of God differs radically from Whitehead's God, it is noteworthy that he finds resources for political theology in a process perspective.

Feminism and Wisdom Christology

The feminist suspicion of any form of Christology has been expressed clearly and forcefully by Naomi Goldenberg:

> Jesus Christ cannot symbolize the liberation of women. A culture that maintains a masculine image for its highest divinity cannot allow its women to experience themselves as the equals of its men. In order to develop a theology of women's liberation, feminists have to leave Christ and the Bible behind them. Women have to stop denying the sexism that lies at the root of the Jewish and Christian traditions.[74]

Similarly, Daly charges, "The idea of a unique male savior may be seen as one more legitimation of male superiority."[75] She notes that defenders of Christology argue that "the symbol [of Jesus as the Christ] 'can be used oppressively' or that it 'has been used oppressively' but insist that it need not function in this way."[76] However, Daly argues that the oppressive "use" of a symbol indicates "some inherent deficiency in the symbol itself."[77] For Daly, the image of a God-Male savior "is one sided, as far as sexual identity is concerned, and it is precisely on the

---

[72]Crucified God, 250.

[73]Ibid.

[74]Naomi Goldenburg, Changing of the Gods: Feminism and the End of Traditional Religions (Boston: Beacon Press, 1979), 22.

[75]Daly, 71.

[76]Ibid., 72.

[77]Ibid.

wrong side, since it fails to counter sexism and functions to glorify maleness."[78]

Despite the criticisms of Goldenberg and Daly, other feminist thinkers continue to look to the Bible and to Jesus Christ as a positive resources for the struggle for the liberation of all humans. Granted that the biblical traditions are androcentric expressions of patriarchal cultures, nonetheless Elisabeth Schüssler Fiorenza argues that contemporary feminists can

reclaim our biblical heritage. This heritage is misrepresented when it is understood solely as a history of patriarchal oppression; it must also be reconstituted as a history of liberation and religious agency.[79]

Fiorenza calls for a shift from viewing the Bible as a "mythical archetype" with unquestioned authority to accepting the Bible as a "historical prototype or as a formative root-model of biblical faith and life."[80] She proposes contemporary feminist experience as the authoritative criterion for accepting or rejecting biblical claims:

Faithfulness to the struggle of women for liberation requires a theological judgement and an insistence that oppressive patriarchal texts and sexist traditions cannot claim the authority of divine revelation.[81]

Ruether criticizes the patriarchal development of traditional Christology but nonetheless sees positive resources in the Bible and in the history of Christology for feminist concerns.[82] Susan Cady, Marian Ronan, and Hal Taussig turn to the figure of Sophia and the wisdom tradition for resources for contemporary feminist spirituality.[83]

---

[78]Ibid.

[79]Elisabeth Schüssler Fiorenza, Bread Not Stone: The Challenge of Feminist Biblical Interpretation (Boston: Beacon Press, 1984), 20.

[80]Ibid., 14.

[81]Ibid., 18.

[82]Sexism and God-Talk, 135.

[83]Susan Cady, Marian Ronan, and Hal Taussig, Sophia: The Future of Feminist Spirituality (San Francisco: Harper & Row, 1986). See also Letty M. Russell, ed., Feminist Interpretation of the Bible (Philadelphia: Westminster, 1985); Patricia Wilson-Kastner, Faith, Feminism, and Christ (Philadelphia: Fortress, 1983); and E.A. Johnson, "Jesus, The Wisdom of God: A Biblical

The Bible in general and the wisdom tradition in particular appear to be profoundly ambiguous for feminist reflection. This section will begin by exploring the perspectives of the wisdom tradition in the Hebrew Bible and Septuagint in light of feminist suspicions and concerns. Then I will examine the implications for feminism of the relation between Jesus and the wisdom tradition in the New Testament and the early development of Christology. I will conclude by reflecting upon the problems and possibilities of Rahner's and Pittenger's thought for feminism.

The Wisdom Tradition

The wisdom tradition in the Hebrew Bible and the Septuagint had a pronounced distrust of women. Students of wisdom are repeatedly warned against the seductive snares of alluring, adulterous women:

Take no notice of a loose-living woman,
for the lips of this alien drip with honey,
    her words are smoother than oil,
but their bitter outcome is bitter as wormwood,
    sharp as a two-edged sword.
her feet go down to death,
    her steps lead down to Sheol;
far from following the path of life,
    her ways are undirected, irresponsible (Prov 5:2-6).

[A] harlot is a deep pit,
    a narrow well, the woman who is a stranger.
Yes, like a robber she is on the watch
    and many are the men she dupes (Prov 23:27-28).

Women are viewed as a source of temptation and destruction (Prov 2:16-19; 5:20-23; 6:23-35; 22:14; Sir 9:1-9; 23:16-27; 25:21). The "alien woman" is described as going out into the streets and looking for a senseless young man, whom she invites to share her bed while her husband is away (Prov 7:6-20).

With her persistent coaxing she entices him,
    draws him on with her seductive patter.
Bemused, he follows her
    like an ox being led to the slaughter,
like a stag caught in a noose (Prov 7:21-22).

The sages place primary responsibility upon the woman and present the young man as a naive victim. Ben Sira interprets Genesis 3:1-6 in a misogynist sense:

Basis for Non-Androcentric Christology," _Ephemerides Theologicae Lovanienses_ 61(1985):261-94.

Sin began with a woman
   and thanks to her we all must die (25:24).

Moreover, Ben Sira sees women's sins as worse than men's:

No wickedness comes anywhere near the wickedness of a woman,
   may a sinner's lot be hers (25:19)!

Crenshaw comments:

A definite bias against women permeates biblical wisdom.
Women are responsible for perverting a good creation, and
they 'drink from any available fountain or open their quiver
for every arrow,' to paraphrase Sirach.[84]

When the sages praise women, it is usually because of their
relationships to their husbands and children:

A perfect wife is the joy of her husband,
   he will live out the years of his life in peace.
A good wife is the best of portions,
   reserved for those who fear the Lord (Sir 25:2-3).

The perfect wife of Proverbs 31:10-31 is exceedingly indus-
trious and capable at home, but her diligence and competence allow
her husband to participate in civic affairs at the city gates
(31:23).[85]

The Hebrew wisdom tradition shared and supported the patriarchal bias of its culture and tended to view women as either dangerous temptresses to male virtue or as helpful assistants to
their husbands. Despite the patriarchal orientation of the sages,
two elements of the wisdom tradition offer positive resources for
contemporary feminist reflection: (1) the role of experience as a
critical challenge to tradition and (2) the figure of Lady Wisdom. While the sages present a sexist, patriarchal view of male-
female relationships, they also present their students with the
principle of the authority of experience as a criterion for assessing their claims. The wisdom teachers did not demand blind
obedience to the received tradition but challenged their students
to think critically, to discern the proper time for the proper
decision, and to test advice against their own experience. Job
and Qoheleth both used the insights of their own experience to put
in question the teaching of the received tradition.
   The wisdom tradition's use of experience as a critical principle of evaluation offers precedent for contemporary critical

---

[84]Old Testament Wisdom, 23.

[85]See McKane, 669.

225

feminist reflection upon the Bible. Fiorenza argues that the criterion for feminist biblical interpretation "is not a revealed principle or a special canon of texts that can claim divine authority. Rather it is the experience of women struggling for liberation and wholeness."[86] Fiorenza's use of experience as a critical counterbalance to the received tradition finds precedent in the sages, but the sages themselves would probably not acknowledge a sharp dichotomy between reflection on experience and claims of revelation, for it was precisely in and through reflection on experience that the sages received the revelation of Lady Wisdom. Moreover, the later wisdom tradition did acknowledge a genuine divine revelation in the events of the history of Israel.

Moreover, the search for wisdom was open to women as well as men in the ancient world. The mother of Lemuel, king of Massa, is reported to have taught him the sayings in Proverbs 31:1-9. The Queen of Sheba was evidently quite expert at the testing and discerning of wisdom (1 Kgs 10:1-13). She puts Solomon to the test and acclaims his sagacity according to her criteria.[87]

The figure of Lady Wisdom is of considerable importance for feminist reflection because she is one of the most prominent feminine figures in the Bible. While Lady Wisdom has sometimes been acclaimed as a feminine image of God,[88] Ruether cautions that Lady Wisdom "in Hebrew thought . . . has become a dependent attribute or expression of the transcendent male God rather than an autonomous, female manifestation of the divine."[89] Ruether sees Lady Wisdom as "a secondary persona of God, mediating the work and will of God to creation"; in Proverbs she is "an offspring of God," while in the Wisdom of Solomon she "is the manifestation of God through whom God mediates the work of creation, providential guidance, and revelation."[90]

As we have seen, the Hebrew wisdom tradition does not identify God and Lady Wisdom, but the Hebrew texts of Proverbs 8 and Job

---

[86]Fiorenza, xvi.

[87]See John Gray, I & II Kings: A Commentary (Philadelphia: Westminster, 1976), 257-62; Kalugila, 120.

[88]Virginia Ramey Mollenkott, The Divine Feminine: The Biblical Imagery of God as Female (New York: Crossroad, 1983), 97-104; Leonard Swidler, Biblical Affirmations of Woman (Philadelphia: Westminster, 1979), 37-49.

[89]Sexism and God-Talk, 57.

[90]Ibid.

28 do appear to present Yahweh and Wisdom as equiprimordial.[91]
In these passages Yahweh does not create Wisdom but rather discov-
ers her, and she allows Yahweh to do the ordering work of creation. There seems to be an interplay between masculine and feminine figures in the origin of the cosmos without any clear subordination of one to the other.

Ruether's interpretation is more accurate for the later history of Lady Wisdom. The Septuagint translation of Proverbs 8:22
presents Lady Wisdom as a creation of the Lord and thereby does
subordinate Lady Wisdom to God. Similarly, Ben Sira describes
Lady Wisdom as a creature of God (24:8-9) who comes forth from the
mouth of the Most High (24:3) and receives instructions from her
creator (24:8-9).

The Wisdom of Solomon comes close to presenting Lady Wisdom
as the presence of God in the world, as Deus quoad nos. Larcher
suggests that in this work Lady Wisdom can be viewed as "une
représentation symbolique de l'activité de Dieu dans le monde,"
provided that one recalls that this symbol "n'addresse pas à une
réalité distincte: la Sagesse personnifie une influence divine qui
reste en contact essentiel avec sa source et rend Dieu présent à
divers degrés."[92]

The Wisdom of Solomon describes Lady Wisdom as sitting on the
throne beside God (9:4). She is close to God (8:3); God has no
secrets from her, and she is the chooser and artificer of God's
works (8:4). Lady Wisdom does not appear to perform actions un-
worthy of God, for the same activites of creating (7:21), and
ordering (8:1), and leading the people of Israel (chs 10-19) are
variously attributed to Lady Wisdom or to God with little change
in meaning. Lady Wisdom does appear to be the way in which humans
experience God's creative and providential power, but the Wisdom
of Solomon nonetheless retains a certain distinction between Lady
Wisdom and God, for she is never completely identified with God.
Fiorenza comments on the Wisdom of Solomon: "One can sense here
how much the language struggles to describe Sophia as divine
(without falling prey to ditheism)."[93] Fiorenza stresses the
positive implications for feminism of the relationship between God
and Lady Wisdom: "Divine Sophia is Israel's God in the language
and Gestalt of the goddess."[94]

---

[91]Supra, 12-15.

[92]Larcher, 410.

[93]Elisabeth Schüssler Fiorenza, In Memory of Her: A Feminist
Theological Reconstruction of Christian Origins (New York: Crossroad, 1984), 133.

[94]Ibid., 133.

However, Ruether expresses reservations about embracing Lady Wisdom as the "feminine side" of God:

We should guard against concepts of divine androgyny that simply ratify on the divine level the patriarchal split of the masculine and the feminine. In such a concept, the feminine side of God, as a secondary or mediating principle, would act in the same subordinate and limited roles in which females are allowed to act in the patriarchal order.[95]

Joan Chamberlain Engelsman uses a psychoanalytic model of repression to interpret the relation between God and Lady Wisdom. She sees Lady Wisdom as an archetypal figure, "a bearer of notions from the collective unconscious" who was parallel to, though not necessarily historically derived from, Isis and Maat and Semitic goddesses.[96] Engelsman claims that there was growing attention to Lady Wisdom in Hellenistic Judaism and suggests that "there must have been a growing tension in Judaism between Yahweh and Sophia."[97] Engelsman sees this tension being resolved in two ways: (1) by the splitting of the archetypal feminine into opposing positive and negative figures, Lady Wisdom and Lady Folly, and (2) by the repression of Lady Wisdom. "Splitting her attributes between two competing figures helped Israel limit the power of Sophia. That, in turn, helped assure the restriction of Sophia to a hypostasis."[98]

Engelsman discerns a negative side of Lady Wisdom herself in passages which describe Lady Wisdom as disciplining or judging humans (Prov 1:20-32; 8:35-36; 9:12; Sir 4:17-19; 6:20-22), and sees Lady Folly as "a negative hypostasis of God."[99]

Engelsman sees the Wisdom of Solomon and Enoch 91:10-92:1 as "the apex of Sophia's power and her development as a hypostasis of

---

[95]Sexism and God-Talk, 61.

[96]Joan Chamberlain Engelsman, The Feminine Dimension of the Divine (Philadelphia: Westminster, 1979), 75. On the historical difficulties involved in the attempt to derive Lady Wisdom from Isis, see Robert M. Grant, Gods and the One God, Library of Early Christianity, vol. 1 (Philadelphia: Westminster, 1986), 100-04.

[97]Engelsman, 75.

[98]Ibid., 76.

[99]Ibid., 86.

God."[100] However, she sees Lady Wisdom's power as being challenged and repressed by the masculine figure of the Logos in the
thought of Philo. Engelsman notes that Philo uses the two figures
interchangeably, but she claims that for Philo

> Logos is in the process of usurping the role and function of
> the older and established Sophia, and . . . any synonymous
> usage of the two terms is meant to reinforce the right of
> Logos to replace Sophia.[101]

Philo, according to Engelsman, reduces Sophia to "a pale and
sickly copy of her sister Isis," a weak figure who flees from the
earth to avoid evil:

> Philo's repression of the goddess led him to create a 'dain-
> ty' Sophia who could only survive in the rarefied air of
> heaven and who needed to be protected from the contamination
> of the flesh.[102]

Engelsman sees the repression of the feminine in Philo as the
context for the repression of Sophia in the New Testament.
Engelsman's psychoanalytic interpretation rests, in part, upon
psychological theory whose consideration exceeds the scope of this
essay. However, it is noteworthy that the usefulness of Jungian
thought for feminist reflection is itself a matter of debate. Ann
Belford Ulanov, like Engelsman, proposes a Jungian approach to
"the feminine."[103] However, Ruether warns against the use of
Jungian thought: "This way of defining androgyny is typical of
Jungianism; it makes Jungianism seductive for women who fail to
perceive its fundamentally androcentric and antifeminist
bias."[104]

Lady Wisdom, like the wisdom tradition in general, appears to
be of ambiguous value for feminist reflection. She originally
appears as the discovery, not the creation, of Yahweh, and thus
does not appear to be subordinate to Yahweh. The philological
argument of Vawter on Proverbs 8 and Job 28 deserves attention in

---

[100]Ibid., 93.

[101]Ibid., 98.

[102]Ibid., 102.

[103]Ann Belford Ulanov, The Feminine in Jungian Psychology and
in Christian Theology (Evanston, Il.: Northwestern University
Press, 1971).

[104]Sexism and God-Talk, 273, n. 9.

feminist reflection.[105] However, the Septuagint translation of Proverbs 8:22 presents her as clearly a creature of God, and in Ben Sira she receives orders from God. The Wisdom of Solomon attributes divine activities to Lady Wisdom without completely identifying her with God. Ruether's reservations are necessary cautions in a feminist retrieval of Lady Wisdom. Nonetheless, it remains true that the wisdom tradition expressed the activity of God upon the cosmos in general and upon human life in particular in feminine imagery. Terrien comments: "The sapiential circles detected in the cosmos a certain quality of order, harmony, equilibrium, charm, and even playfulness which suggested to them the realities of the feminine principle."[106]

Feminism, Jesus and Lady Wisdom

The portrait of Jesus as a teacher of wisdom in the Synoptic tradition differs radically from the earlier wisdom tradition on the attitude toward women. It is striking that the wisdom sayings of Jesus in the Synoptic tradition do not include any of the traditional sapiential warnings against women. Carlston comments on this silence:

> I know of no way of accounting for this phenomenon except on the grounds that Jesus was perfectly at ease in the company of women and that for him the equality between the sexes was not so much a distant legislative goal as a rather self-evident fact.[107]

To what degree one can reconstruct the emotions and relationships of the historical Jesus himself from the sayings of the Synoptic tradition is a most problematic question, but Carlston is certainly correct in his assessment of the significance of the portrait of Jesus as a teacher of wisdom in the Synoptic Gospels.

We have seen that the relation between Jesus and Lady Wisdom in the Synoptic tradition is complex and diverse. In Luke (and presumably in Q) Jesus appears to be a messenger or child of Lady Wisdom, and so it would seem that he is subordinate to her and acts in her place as her representative. It is certainly noteworthy for feminist reflection that in one of the earliest Christo-

---

[105]"Prov 8:22: Wisdom and Creation," 205-16.

[106]Samuel Terrien, "Toward a Biblical Theology of Womanhood," Religion in Life 42(1973):329.

[107]Carlston, 96-97.

logies of the Christian community Jesus is sent by the feminine figure of Lady Wisdom.[108]

Matthew substitutes Jesus in place of Lady Wisdom, but the significance of the substitution appears ambiguous: is Jesus to be understood as the incarnation of Lady Wisdom herself and thus as the revelation of a feminine figure, or is Jesus replacing Lady Wisdom and thereby eliminating the feminine figure of Lady Wisdom from Christian awareness? On this question the exegetes differ: Suggs's reading of Matthew supports the first alternative while Marshall Johnson's and Russell Pregeant's readings would argue for the latter.[109] Pregeant poses the question of the ambiguity of the substitution:

> Does this mean that Jesus is Wisdom incarnate, or does it mean simply that Matthew is reluctant to work with the somewhat suspect figure of Wisdom? Does Jesus speak as Wisdom, or has the category been largely supplanted?[110]

The identification of Wisdom and Christ in the Pauline trajectory, especially in 1 Corinthians and Colossians, is more explicit and more developed cosmologically than in the Synoptic tradition. However, the Pauline trajectory itself is decidedly ambiguous on the place of women in the Christian community. Paul's proclamation of Christ as the "Wisdom of God" (1 Cor 1:24) presents Jesus as the revelation of a feminine figure, and Galatians 3:28 provides a charter of Christian feminism. As Fiorenza comments: "Feminist critical theology is driven by the impetus to make the vision of Gal 3:28 real within the Christian community."[111] However, Paul himself was reluctant to draw out concrete implications of equality from this principle (e.g. 1 Cor 11:2-16),[112] and the later deutero-Pauline literature proposes a patriarchal model of the family which demands the subordination of wives to their husbands.[113]

---

[108]See Fiorenza, In Memory of Her, 134-35.

[109]Supra, 30-32; and Russell Pregeant, Christology beyond Dogma: Matthew's Christ in Process Hermeneutic (Philadelphia: Fortress, 1978), 93. Fiorenza accepts Suggs's reading of Matthew without responding to the questions and objections of Johnson (In Memory of Her, 132 and 158, n.77).

[110]Pregeant, 93.

[111]Elisabeth Schüssler Fiorenza, "Feminist Theology as a Critical Theology of Liberation," TS 36(1975):619.

[112]See Fiorenza, In Memory of Her, 208-36.

[113]Ibid., 251-79.

In the Gospel of John there does not appear to be any subordination of women to men. Raymond E. Brown concludes his study of the "Roles of Women in the Fourth Gospel" by saying:

> In researching the evidence of the fourth Gospel, one is still surprised to see to what extent in the Johannine community women and men were already on an equal level in the fold of the Good Shepherd.[114]

Brown sees the Johannine community as realizing the principle of Galatians 3:28 better than the Pauline communities themselves did.[115]

In the Gospel of John the relation of Jesus to Lady Wisdom is never mentioned explicitly, but it is nonetheless a dominant influence in the interpretation of Jesus Christ. The silence of John on Lady Wisdom is ambiguous. Engelsman interprets the replacement of Lady Wisdom by Christ and the Logos in John as an act of repression which led to her disappearance from early Christianity: "Ultimately, Sophia's powers were so totally preempted by Christ that she herself completely disappeared from the Christian religion at that time."[116] Engelsman raises the question of whether Sophia was replaced by the Logos precisely because she was feminine, and argues:

> Whatever the reason, it is nevertheless apparent that Sophia reached her pinnacle and was then abruptly replaced by a masculine figure. As a result of this transference of attributes, overt access to the feminine dimension of the divine in the Judeo-Christian tradition was cut off or repressed.[117]

Engelsman interprets later Christian appearance of Lady Wisdom in early Church discussions as "the return of the repressed," which led to a second, definitive "re-repression" in the fourth century.[118]

---

[114]Raymond E. Brown, "Roles of Women in the Fourth Gospel," TS 36(1975):699.

[115]Ibid.

[116]Engelsman, 120.

[117]Ibid.

[118]Ibid., 139-48.

Without using the psychoanalytic theory of repression, Ruether also notes the unfortunate consequences of replacing Lady Wisdom by Logos:

The figure of divine wisdom in Proverbs 8 and in the Wisdom of Solomon is theologically identical to what the New Testament describes as the Logos, or 'Son' of God. Because Christianity chooses the male symbol for this idea, however, the unwarranted idea develops that there is a necessary ontological connection between the maleness of Jesus' historical person and the maleness of Logos as the male offspring and disclosure of a male God. The female figure of divine wisdom is displaced from the orthodox Trinity . . . [119]

Adela Yarbro Collins, however, notes that the association of Jesus Christ and Sophia was not simply negative but rather ambiguous from a feminist perspective. Noting the difficulty of speculating about the author's intention in linking Jesus and Wisdom, Collins comments:

It may well have been that he was attempting to show Jesus's superiority to and fulfillment of wisdom's role. In that case, he would have been making an attempt to masculinize the wisdom tradition.[120]

However, the relationship has another, more positive significance as well: "The evangelist may not have intended to do so, but the prologue and the portrayal of Christ as Sophia imply that there is a feminine dimension of divine reality."[121]

Whatever the subjective intentions of the author (and possible redactors) of the Gospel of John may have been,[122] the language of the Prologue has kept the masculine Logos in the forefront of Christological discussion for centuries and dominates the

---

[119]Sexism and God-Talk, 117.

[120]Adela Yarbro Collins, "New Testament Perspectives: The Gospel of John," Journal for the Study of the Old Testament 22 (1982):51.

[121]Ibid.

[122]Speculation on this question is probably irresolvable historically and not ultimately of decisive significance for the post-romantic hermenutical positions of Gadamer and Ricoeur. See Paul Ricoeur, "The Hermeneutical Function of Distanciation," Philosophy Today 17(1973):129-41. Schnackenburg, for his part, speculates that the choice of Logos over Sophia was "to link up with the term familiar to Hellenistic tradition, to give the Gospel message resonance and appeal" (p. 125).

usage of Rahner and Pittenger. However, the associations of Jesus and Lady Wisdom were not eliminated by the dominant use of Logos instead of Sophia. Early church discussions of the Trinity repeatedly turned to Lady Wisdom and the descriptions of her in Proverbs 8 and the Wisdom of Solomon. It is not historically accurate to make the absolute claim, as Ruether does, that "[t]he female figure of divine wisdom is displaced from the orthodox Trinity."[123] Engelsman herself, after claiming that Sophia "completely disappeared form the Christian religion of that time," goes on to discuss later appearances of Lady Wisdom but interprets these appearances as "the return of the repressed."[124]

The interplay of the feminine Sophia and the masculine Logos has other implications which are more supportive of feminine imagery for God. It would appear that it was through the identification of Jesus Christ with Lady Wisdom that Wisdom herself came to be viewed as fully divine by the early Church. The identification of Lady Wisdom and the Logos influenced many of the early Church writers, leading them to quote Proverbs 8 and the Wisdom of Solomon in Christological and trinitarian speculation. The result was that feminine imagery was used of God. Together the masculine Logos and the feminine Sophia name the divine in Christ, the divine activity in ordering the world, and the divine trinitarian relationships. This interplay undermines the one-sided attribution of masculine names to God.

Lady Wisdom did not disappear from Christian reflection on God but had a decisive impact on the reflections of the early Church. This is not to claim that early Christian writers were feminist in the modern sense of the term, or even that they were supportive of equality for women in the Christian community. It is to note that Lady Wisdom did not disappear from the orthodox Christian tradition but played a role that is hard to overestimate.

1 Clement 57:3-7 quotes sayings of Lady Wisdom (Prov 1:23-33) in urging the Corinthians to resolve their differences. Irenaeus identifies Wisdom with the Spirit: "God tells us, through the mouth of Solomon, that Wisdom is the Spirit."[125] However, the dominant interpretation was to identify Logos and Sophia.

---

[123]Sexism and God-Talk, 117.

[124]Engelsman, 120, 139-48.

[125]Irenaeus, Adversus Haereses, IV, xx, 3; in The Early Christian Fathers: A Selection from the Writings of the Fathers from St. Clement of Rome to St. Athanasius, trans. and ed. Henry Bettenson (London: Oxford University Press, 1969), 85.

In the late second century Theophilus of Antioch describes Logos and Sophia together as forms of God's activity in the world: "holy Logos leads, Wisdom teaches, Life controls, God reigns."[126] As Grant comments: "For his [Theophilus's] theology the most important correlation is that of Logos with Wisdom. At creation the Wisdom of God was in him and the holy Logos was with him."[127]

Origen writes that Christ "is called Wisdom," and goes on to specify that this means that "the only begotten Son of God is God's wisdom hypostatically existing."[128] Moreover, Lady Wisdom is the key to all knowledge and understanding:

> For wisdom opens to all other beings, that is, to the whole creation, the meaning of the mysteries and secrets which are contained within the wisdom of God, and so she is called the Word, because she is as it were an interpreter of the mind's secrets.[129]

It is through Lady Wisdom that we come to know God:

> when wisdom outlines first in herself the things which she wishes to reveal to others, by means of which they are to know and understand God, then she herself may be called the express image of God's substance.[130]

Lady Wisdom, and especially the description of her in Wisdom 7:25-26, is central to Origen's interpretation of our knowledge of God, of Christology, and creation.[131]

Engelsman notes the crucial role of Proverbs 8:22 and Colossians 1:15 in the Arian controversy and further argues that we should view

> the Arian controversies as Sophia's revenge. The theft of her attributes, powers, and functions now contaminated Christology by casting Jesus in the same relationship with

---

[126]Theophilus, Ad Autolycum III, 15; see Grant, After the New Testament, 60.

[127]After the New Testament, 63.

[128]Origen, De Principiis, I, 2, 1-2, trans. G.W. Butterworth, Origen, On First Principles (Gloucester, Mass.: Peter Smith, 1973), 15.

[129]Ibid., I, 2, 3; p. 16.

[130]Ibid., I, 2, 7; p. 21.

[131]Grant, After the New Testament, 74-77.

God the Father that she had been confined to by the scrupulous monotheism of the Jews.[132]

The defeat of the Arian position, according to Engelsman, involved a rejection of the identification of Sophia and Christ: "What was lost in this process was direct access to the feminine dimension of God which had struggled so long for recognition in the guise of Sophia."[133]

However, one of the first major thinkers to develop a post-Nicene trinitarian theology, Marius Victorinus, accorded a major role to Wisdom and explicitly stressed the feminine dimension of the divine, though he did not identify the feminine dimension of God with Wisdom, but rather with life. Victorinus describes an interplay of masculine and feminine elements in the activity of God in creation and redemption, seeing the downward movement of life as feminine and the upward movement of wisdom returning to God as masculine:

> Therefore this existence of all existents is life, and insofar as life is movement, it received a kind of feminine power, because it desired to vivify. But since, as has been shown, this movement, since it is one, is both life and wisdom, life converted to wisdom and, what is more, to the paternal existence, better still, by a movement of return toward the paternal power, and having been fortified by that, life, returning to the Father, has been made male. For life is descent; wisdom is ascent.[134]

Victorinus can also claim: "He who understood the Holy Spirit to be the mother of Jesus was not therefore mistaken,"[135] and he sees the Logos as being "both male and female."[136]

The ambiguity in the relationship between Jesus Christ and Lady Wisdom need not lead to a rejection of the relationship but rather invites a critical appropriation of the theme of Jesus as Wisdom incarnate from a feminist perspective. As Adela Yarbro Collins proposes: "The gospel of John thus provides Christian

---

[132]Engelsman, 147.

[133]Ibid., 148.

[134]Marius Victorinus, Adversus Arium 1B, 51; trans. Mary T. Clark, Marius Victorinus, Theological Treatises on the Trinity (Washington, D.C.: Catholic University of America Press, 1981), 174-75.

[135]Ibid., 1B, 56; p. 184.

[136]Ibid., 1B, 64; p. 193.

theologians today the opportunity to affirm a feminine aspect of the divine and to recover for Christians the richness of the wisdom literature."[137]

Similarly, Patricia Wilson-Kastner responds to the criticisms of Engelsman by stressing the positive significance of Wisdom and Logos Christology for feminism:

Engelsman contends that the figure of the divine Word usurped the role of the feminine in the personification of the divine. One can also, I would suggest, judge this mixing of feminine and masculine elements in the Logos as positive because it permitted the introduction of feminine imagery in the portrayal of God active in the Logos.[138]

While acknowledging and rejecting the patriarchal elements in the wisdom tradition and in the relationship of Jesus and Lady Wisdom, a contemporary Wisdom Christology can retrieve the figure of Lady Wisdom as an articulation of our experience of God and of the presence of God in Jesus Christ.

Rahner, Whitehead, and Pittenger

Rahner did not address feminist concerns in his central Christological works, and his use of the masculine term Logos without the balancing of the feminine Sophia continues the tradition of using predominantly or exclusively masculine language about God. However, Rahner did express support for the full equality and liberation of women. He insisted upon the principle: "In her own personal life too the Church must recognise without reserve the fact that women have equal value and equal rights with men."[139] Rahner stressed above all the necessity for women themselves to determine their role in society and in the Church:

In the new situation in history of the world and of society woman is presented with fresh problems to solve for the world. These are such as can be solved by woman herself and in her own way, and not, in any direct or adequate sense, by

[137]"Gospel of John," 51; see also Elizabeth A. Johnson, "The Incomprehensibility of God and the Image of God Male and Female," TS 45(1984):447-51, 462-63; and idem, "Jesus the Wisdom of God," 291-92.

[138]Faith, Feminism, and Christ, 95.

[139]Karl Rahner, "The Position of Woman in the New Situation in which the Church Finds Herself," TI, VIII, trans. David Bourke (New York: Herder & Herder, 1971), 81.

directives issued by the authorities of the Church and in their preaching.[140]

Rahner argues that "the Church of women themselves" must accept the task of discerning constructive patterns of life for Christian women today. He reiterates his basic principle: "This task belongs inalienably and exclusively to woman. It cannot be taken away from her by the official authorities."[141]

Rahner was very critical of the "Declaration on the Question of the Admission of Women to the Ministerial Priesthood" from the Sacred Congregation for the Doctrine of the Faith in 1976, and he expressed his support for the sociological emancipation of women in theory and practice and its consequences in the life of the Church.[142]

Rahner also stressed the wide variety of situations of women in the Church and the world today and the consequent difficulty of making concrete assertions or recommendations about all women: "There is very little that can validly be asserted of the woman as a single and entirely homogenous type with a definite concrete position in the Church capable of being investigated."[143] Consistent with his own insistence that women themselves must develop liberating patterns of life which will be faithful to the Gospel and fruitful in the contemporary world, Rahner refrained from giving advice on how this project should proceed.

Whitehead did not address feminist concerns in his work, but a number of feminist thinkers have found Whitehead's philosophy a valuable resource in developing their own thought and in overcoming oppressive dualisms. Marilyn Thie suggests that the themes of Whitehead's theory of symbolic reference "converge to provide a philosophical analysis that supports and encourages feminist criticism of the operative cultural symbols."[144] Above all, Thie suggests, what unites Whitehead and feminist thought is "the emphasis in both on experience as a process of becoming in which entities are engaged in self-creation."[145] Thie uses Whitehead's

---

[140]Ibid., 86.

[141]Ibid., 88.

[142]Karl Rahner, "Women and the Priesthood," TI, XX, trans. Edward Quinn (New York: Crossroad, 1981), 35-47.

[143]"Position of Woman," TI, VIII, 75.

[144]Marilyn Thie, "Feminist Concerns and Whitehead's Theory of Perception," Process Studies 8(1978):187.

[145]Ibid., 186.

theory of symbolic reference to analyze the way in which the assumptions of a culture are embedded in language and the way in which changes in language can shape what is interpreted as important in experience.[146]

Sheila Greeve Davaney stresses the similarities between Whitehead's and feminism's critiques of traditional understandings of self, world, and God:

The vision of reality developed by Alfred North Whitehead and proponents of the process school of thought offers a metaphysical system based upon an understanding of the self consistent with women's emerging reflection upon our experience.[147]

Valerie C. Saiving uses Whitehead's description of reality to develop a feminist model of androgynous life which integrates both individuality and relatedness in human being.[148] Marjorie Suchocki stresses the themes of mutuality and openness which unite Whitehead and feminist thinkers, and develops these themes in relation to God and concrete social action.[149] Penelope Washbourn argues for a natural kinship between feminism and process thought because "the forces which influenced the development of process thought . . . were the same that produced the feminist critique of society."[150] Washbourn lists as concerns common to feminists and process thinkers:

[a] dedication to process rather than stasis, to egalitarian structures of social order rather than monarchial ones, an openness to the future, a critique of concepts of absolute power and authority, a new view of interrelationships.[151]

---

[146]Ibid., 187-88.

[147]Sheila Greeve Davaney, ed., Feminism and Process Thought: The Harvard Divinity School/Claremont Center for Process Studies Symposium Papers (New York: Edward Mellen Press, 1981), 3.

[148]Valerie C. Saiving, "Androgynous Life: A Feminist Appropriation of Process Thought," in Feminism and Process Thought, 22-26.

[149]Marjorie Suchocki, "Openness and Mutuality in Process Thought and Feminist Action," in Feminism and Process Thought, 63-81.

[150]Penelope Washbourn, "The Dynamics of Female Experience: Process Models and Human Values," in Feminism and Process Thought, 87.

[151]Ibid.

Burton Cooper has argued that Whitehead's metaphysics can provide a helpful framework for developing a feminist Christology.[152]

Though not himself a feminist, Pittenger has used process thought to develop a holistic approach to human sexuality.[153] Pittenger opposes any dualistic opposition between mind and body:

> [B]ecause we are not souls who have bodies but animated bodies with mental and spiritual capacity, the business of becoming a lover includes our embodied, psychosomatic, and socially conditioned nature. This tells us that our human development in loving has for its basis the fact of our being physiologically and psychologically sexual creatures.[154]

Pittenger sees sexuality as "the all-pervasive erotic aspect of human existence that is present in all we say and think and do, in every relationship with others and also in our relationship with God."[155] In line with his understanding of general and special revelation, Pittenger finds two bases for a Christian interpretation of human sexuality:

> [O]ne is the revelation of God in Christ, the other is the result of our attempt reasonably to understand ourselves and our brethren in light of such knowledge as we possess apart from that 'special' revelation.[156]

Pittenger draws upon both sources in developing a sacramental understanding of human experience and expression.[157]

While neither Rahner nor Pittenger themselves developed a feminist Christology, it appears that their theologies, in combination with the figure of Lady Wisdom, offer resources for the

---

[152]Burton Cooper, "Metaphysics, Christology and Sexism: An Essay in Philosophical Theology," Religious Studies 16(1980):179-93.

[153]Norman Pittenger, Making Sexuality Human (New York: Pilgrim Press, 1970; idem, Love and Control in Sexuality (New York: Pilgrim Press, 1979); idem, A Time for Consent (London: SCM Press, 1967); Lure of Divine Love, 63-73; The Meaning of Being Human, 60-74.

[154]Lure of Divine Love, 65.

[155]Ibid., 67.

[156]Christian Understanding of Human Nature, 74.

[157]Ibid, 75-92.

development of a contemporary feminist interpretation of Jesus Christ.

Wisdom in a Pluralistic World

The challenge of religious pluralism is one of the most per-plexing issues of our age. The encounter with other world reli-gions has radically challenged Christianity's self-understanding and has raised questions about traditional Christian claims of revelation. If the reality that Christians name God is actively present throughout human experience in a wide variety of religious traditions, then how are Christians to understand the revelation of God experienced in Jesus Christ? The tradition of Logos Christology is one of the oldest and most frequently used Chris-tian approaches to this question. As we have seen, behind the Logos Christology of John lies the wisdom tradition of Israel. The biblical wisdom tradition offers not a resolution of the ques-tions raised by the encounter with other religions but rather suggests perspectives for approaching the encounter.

Wisdom in Israel and
the Ancient Near East

As we have seen, the trajectory of the wisdom tradition of-fers solid precedent for acknowledging a general activity of God throughout human experience and for correlating the universal activity of God with specific historical events of revelation. The sages of Israel recognized a genuine knowledge of God and a real grasp of wisdom in non-Israelite traditions, and they were very open to learning and borrowing from other Near Eastern tradi-tions.[158] As Gordis comments, the Hebrew wisdom tradition "is the

---

[158]On the relation of wisdom in Israel to the wisdom tradi-tions of Egypt and Mesopotamia, see H. Duesberg and I. Fransen, Les Scribes Inspirés (Belgium: Editions de Maredsous, 1966), 15-95; O.S. Rankin, Israel's Wisdom Literature: Its Bearing on The-ology and the History of Religion (Edinburgh: T. & T. Clark, 1964), 35-39; Whybray, Wisdom in Proverbs, 53-71; Ernst Wurthwein, "Egyptian Wisdom and the Old Testament, in Studies in Ancient Israelite Wisdom, 113-31; R.B.Y. Scott, "Solomon and the Begin-nings of Wisdom in Israel," in Studies in Ancient Israelite Wis-dom, 84-101; Gerhard von Rad, "Job XXXVIII and Ancient Egyptian Wisdom," in Studies in Ancient Israelite Wisdom, 267-77; Crenshaw, Old Testament Wisdom, 212-35; John Gray, "The Book of Job in the Context of Near Eastern Literature," Zeitschrift für die Alt-testamentliche Wissenschaft 82(1970):251-69. For an extensive review of Egyptian, Babylonian, and Assyrian proverbs as an intro-duction to the biblical book of Proverbs, see McKane, 51-208.

least national and the most broadly universal element in the cultural heritage of ancient Israel."[159] In particular, biblical scholars have concluded that Proverbs 22:17-24:22 is based upon the Egyptian work Amen-em-ope.[160] Job is a non-Israelite, and the book of Proverbs includes sayings of non-Israelite sages such as Lemuel, king of Massa (31:1-9) and Agur ben Jakeh (30:1). Jon D. Levenson comments on the perspective that made this borrowing possible:

> In all likelihood the Wisdom teachers considered the gods of the gentiles, or at least of the sagacious and ethical gentiles, as not different in kind from YHWH, the God of Israel. Perhaps they thought the different gods were really only different names for the one all-pervasive reality, which can be intuited in general human experience.[161]

Levenson also notes that the international scope of the search for wisdom made possible the dialogue between Solomon and the Queen of Sheba. "There is no hint that she is regarded as 'pagan' in the pejorative usage, and her religion does not seem to interfere with her appreciation of Solomon's perspicacity."[162]

The sapiential themes of trust in general human experience and the awareness of the limits of all human understanding combine to encourage dialogue and mutual exchange between different traditions. Since the sages base their claims on experience that is open to all humans, it is possible for representatives of different sapiential traditions to find a common ground for discussion. Since Lady Wisdom's activity is universal, it is possible for non-Israelites to respond to her invitation and receive her gift of insight and understanding. Thus representatives of various sapiential traditions can acknowledge one another's genuine insights into the meaning of experience.

On the other hand, the sages' insistence on the limits of all human claims of wisdom undercuts any claim to have understood adequately the meaning of experience or the patterns of God. The

---

[159]Book of God and Man, 54.

[160]McKane, 369-401; Scott, Proverbs. Ecclesiastes, 20-21. Couroyer has interpreted Ben Sira 4:11 against the background of Egyptian wisdom literature. B. Couroyer, "Un Egyptianisme dans Ben Sira IV, 11," Revue Biblique 82(1975):206-17.

[161]Jon D. Levenson, The Universal Horizon of Jewish Particularism (New York: The American Jewish Committee, 1985), 6.

[162]Ibid.

sages, like Rahner, knew well that God is incomprehensible mystery. The necessity of discerning the time for the application of any particular proverb implies an awareness that any human perspective is limited and any insight is partial and time-bound. Thus in approaching dialogue with other traditions, representatives of the biblical wisdom tradition need not, indeed cannot claim either to have definitively understood the mystery of God or to have a perspective with absolute and universal validity. This is not to deny the sages' belief in revelation. As we have seen, the trust in experience and the recognition of human limits did not eliminate the sages' acknowledgement of the revelation offered by Lady Wisdom. It was in ordinary human experience that Lady Wisdom made her call, and it was in the limits of human understanding and control that the sages gained a sense of the power and incomprehensibility of Yahweh.

Moreover, as we have seen, the wisdom tradition itself includes a variety of competing perspectives. Not only does the wisdom tradition represent a distinct form within the religion of Israel, it includes a pluralism within its own development. Job and Qoheleth challenge the basic presuppositions of the accessibility of wisdom, the intelligibility of the patterns of experience, and the graciousness of God. The examples of Job and Qoheleth are biblical witnesses to the necessity of critically testing the claims of the biblical tradition itself. The acceptance of Job and Qoheleth within the wisdom tradition and within the biblical canon constitutes a jarring counterpoint to the themes of God's love and care for humans and calls into question any over-arching description of God and human experience. Job and Qoheleth suggest that the sages were able to live with a pluralism of directly conflicting views of God and human life without any theoretical resolution.

The wisdom tradition of Israel reaches for descriptions of universal human experience, but it repeatedly undercuts any particular claim adequately to have understood God or to have articulated universal human experience. By juxtaposing perspectives which are sometimes directly contradictory, the sages challenged their students to recognize the complexity and ambiguity of human experience and to discern for themselves what stance is more helpful at any given time.

The wisdom tradition in general and the figure of Lady Wisdom in particular offer intriguing possibilities for discussion in the encounter with other religions. Almost every culture has a tradition analogous to the biblical wisdom tradition.[163] Crenshaw notes similarities between Chinese and African and biblical prov-

---

[163]John Mark Thompson, 20-21.

erbs and claims: "The urge to secure human existence through the use of reason is universal."[164]

The image of Lady Wisdom as the ordering power of the universe bears analogies to such widely separated concepts as the Logos in Greece, rta in India,[165] dharma in Hinduism and Buddhism,[166] and the Tao in China.[167] These concepts clearly are not to be identified, but they do offer analogous ranges of meaning that can provide an entry-point into inter-religious dialogue. Merton suggests:

> If we want to understand the position of writers like these ancient Chinese philosophers, we must compare them not only with Plato or Parmenides but also with the Hebrew scribes, the transmitters of the wisdom tradition in the so-called sapiential books of the Old Testament.[168]

Wisdom and Pluralism
in the New Testament

The interpretation of Jesus as the incarnation of Lady Wisdom in the New Testament served to universalize the claims of Christianity. By presenting Jesus Christ as the Wisdom of God, the logos through whom all things were made, the New Testament writers were claiming that the religious dimension implicit in all human experience has been revealed in a definitive and unsurpassable way

---

[164]Old Testament Wisdom, 12-13.

[165]Eliade describes rta as "an order that is at once cosmic, liturgical, and moral. . . . rta rules both the cosmic rhythms and moral conduct." Mircea Eliade, A History of Religious Ideas, vol. 1: From the Stone Age to the Eleusinian Mysteries, trans. Willard R. Trask (Chicago: University of Chicago Press, 1978), 201.

[166]Fenton notes: "Eventually, the theory developted into the belief that all things fit within an all-encompassing cause-and-effect structure (dharma)." John Y. Fenton, "Introduction," in John Y. Fenton, Norvin Hein, Frank E. Reynolds, Alan L. Miller, Niels C. Nielsen, Jr., Religions of Asia (New York: St. Martin's Press, 1983), 29.

[167]Merton notes that John C.H. Wu translated the beginning of the Gospel of John into Chinese as: "In the beginning was Tao, and Tao was with God, and Tao was God". Thomas Merton, Mystics and Zen Masters (New York: Delta, 1967), 72.

[168]Ibid., 72.

244

in the life, death, and resurrection of Jesus Christ. This interpretation makes possible a recognition of a universal knowledge of God in all religious traditions through the presence of Wisdom,[169] but it also claims a definitive and normative superiority for the revelation of God experienced in Jesus Christ. It is precisely this claim that raises problems for inter-religious dialogue. It is not my purpose to attempt to resolve this issue but rather to call attention to the interplay between the themes of intelligibility and incomprehensibility in the relation of Jesus and Wisdom and the implications of this interplay for a pluralistic situation.

On the one hand, the claim that there is Wisdom or Logos at the heart of creation holding all things together implies a fundamental intelligibility to reality and human experience. The claim that Lady Wisdom or the Logos has been revealed in Jesus Christ implies that the ordering power of creation can be interpreted and understood in light of the account of Jesus Christ. On the other hand, the world-questioning sayings of Jesus, Paul's paradoxical claim that Wisdom is revealed in the folly of the cross, and the multitude of competing Christologies within the New Testament itself all caution us against any simple and direct claim to have understood the meaning of the revelation in Christ. The New Testament claims universal significance for Jesus Christ but offers a pluralism of interpretations of exactly what this significance is.

Not least among the paradoxical aspects of the New Testament's presentations of Jesus are the sayings of Jesus himself. The claim that Lady Wisdom is incarnate in Jesus directs us to scrutinize the sayings of Jesus remembered in the early church tradition for a clue to the nature of human life. William A. Beardslee has traced the history of modern interpretations of the proverbs and parables of Jesus and notes the shift from an earlier emphasis on the ordering power of God in the continuities of life to the more recent stress on the "creative disruptions" of Jesus' sayings.[170] Beardslee suggests that the shift in interpretation reflects (1) a major cultural change in modern Western consciousness and (2) a dual emphasis in the sayings themselves.[171] While appreciative of Crossan's reading of Jesus against the background of Borges, Beardslee agrees with Amos Wilder that "Jesus' mythos

---

[169]See the debate between Dodd and Bultmann on the Gospel of John, supra, 48-51; and Pregeant, 146-47.

[170]William A. Beardslee, "Parable, Proverb, and Koan," Semeia 12(1978):151-59.

[171]Ibid., 157-59, 167-72.

of the Kingdom of God has more content to it than this kind of ontological reversal."[172]

Both aspects of the parables and proverbs of Jesus offer an opening to dialogue with other traditions. The ordering power of God in the continuities of experience is rooted in the older wisdom tradition and participates in a search for understanding that transcends religious boundaries. As Carlston has noted, there are numerous parallels between the wisdom sayings of Jesus and the wisdom of the Hellenistic world.[173]

The creative disruptions of the language of Jesus confront the hearer with discontinuities and reversals of expectation and undermine any stable patterns of order. Beardslee compares this side of the sayings and parables of Jesus to the Apophthegmata of the desert fathers in Egypt and to Zen koans which provoke "a realization of creative nothingness."[174] Beardslee suggests that recent interpretations of proverbs and parables see in them a function similar to that of the Zen koan. In a manner not unlike the sayings of the Zen masters, Jesus' words

> serve to open the hearer to an experience of the creative Nothing, the transcendent creativity which escapes all conceptualization and is known, as Crossan puts it . . . only in moments when structure is broken.[175]

By presenting Jesus as the incarnation of Lady Wisdom, the New Testament implies that both sides of the sayings and parables of Jesus are revelatory of the cosmological power of creation. Commenting on the conflict in aspects of Jesus' language, Beardslee notes that "the experience of mystery, of the transcendent, is indeed a complex one. It is wise to assume that this complexity has real ontological roots."[176] The New Testament, like the earlier wisdom tradition, makes universal claims about the ordering power of creation, but the world-questioning sayings of Jesus himself put in jeopardy any claim to have grasped a universal pattern of order.

The paradoxical intertwining of the themes of intelligibility and incomprehensibility in Wisdom Christology offer principles for a possible approach to inter-religious dialogue. The reality that

---

[172]Ibid., 159.

[173]Carlston, 99-103.

[174]"Parable, Proverb, and Koan," 159-68.

[175]Ibid., 168.

[176]Ibid., 169.

Christians name God is a universal reality who cannot be confined to the limits of any area or period of the history of humankind or the cosmos. If Jesus Christ is indeed the revelation of God, then this revelation possesses significance for all of human history, indeed for the entire cosmos. However, the world-questioning sayings of Jesus himself put in doubt any overall scheme that pretends to explain God and the cosmos; these sayings set up an unresolved tension at the heart of Wisdom Christology itself and can open their hearers to the widely different experiences of other religious traditions.

Rahner, Pittenger, and the Encounter with Other Religions

Rahner was very concerned with the implications of the revelation of God in Jesus Christ for non-Christians. He developed his concept of the "anonymous Christian" to address the relationship between the Christ-event and people outside of Christianity.[177] Rahner intended this term not for use in inter-religious dialogue but rather for internal Christian reflection on the meaning of the Christ-event.[178] The earlier discussion of Rahner's Christology has already examined the heart of Rahner's argument: the Christ-event is not the exclusive limitation of the saving grace of God but rather the real-symbolic expression of a universal salvific will which has always already influenced all of human history without exception.[179] Rahner's perspective is a retrieval of the classical tradition of Logos Christology and finds biblical precedent in Dodd's and Lightfoot's readings of John's Gospel.

Rahner insists that other religious traditions are not simply to be rejected as erroneous; they serve as positive mediations of the grace of God.[180] Indeed, Rahner claims that non-Christian religions are positively willed by God as the proper way for their adherents to encounter grace:

---

[177]Karl Rahner, "Anonymous Christians," TI, VI, 390-98; "Atheism and Implicit Christianity," TI, IX, 145-64. On this topic, see Nikolaus Schwerdtfeger, Gnade und Welt: Zum Grundgefüge von Karl Rahners Theorie der "anonymen Christen", (Freiburg: Herder, 1982); and Anita Röper, The Anonymous Christian, trans. Joseph Donceel (New York: Sheed & Ward, 1966).

[178]Knitter, 128.

[179]Supra, 85-94.

[180]"Christianity and the Non-Christian Religions," TI, V, 125, 129.

That which God has intended as salvation for [an individual] has reached him, in accordance with God's will and by his permission (no longer adequately separated in practice), in the concrete religion of his actual realm of existence and historical condition.[181]

However, Rahner also defends the uniquely definitive and normative character of the revelation of God in Jesus Christ and refuses to acknowledge any other religion on an equal basis: "Christianity understands itself as the absolute religion, intended for all men, which cannot recognize any other religion beside itself as of equal right."[182] Rahner seeks to preserve the universal claim of Christianity while also acknowledging a positive divine revelation in other religious traditions. However, it is not clear what Rahner means by Christianity's being intended for all people, given his insistence cited above that what God intends as salvation for all people reaches them through their own various religions. Rahner's God is in the rather paradoxical position of willing all people to be saved through Christ but of also willing most humans in their concrete historical setting to be saved through non-Christian religious traditions.

In a pluralistic situation Rahner's method of transcendental reflection appears at first sight to offer little direct guidance because it assumes what is in question, viz. that Christianity is the absolute religion, and then asks about the conditions of possibility for this assertion to be understood. However, Rahner's double affirmation of the absoluteness of Christianity and the concrete will of God operative in other religious traditions raises an interesting question for transcendental reflection: What is the condition of possibility for God to reveal Godself definitively and irrevocably in Jesus Christ and yet to use non-Christian traditions as the divinely willed means of grace for the majority of humankind? Moreover, Rahner's own principle of the incomprehensibility of God functions as a hermeneutical guide to the universal claims of Christianity. For Rahner, the truth of Christianity's absoluteness, like every other truth, is true only in "the process in which the truth becomes a question which remains unanswered because it is asking about God and his incomprehensibility."[183]

Whitehead did not himself directly address the question of the encounter of various world religions. He viewed Christianity

---

[181]Ibid., 129.

[182]Ibid., 118.

[183]"Thomas Aquinas on the Incomprehensibility of God," S125.

and Buddhism as the "two main rational religions," "the two Catholic religions of civilization," but he saw them both as being in decay in modern civilization.[184] Whitehead's general perspective inclines to viewing different religious perspectives as partial perspectives on experience. In informal discussion with Lucien Price about the latter's earlier study of and attraction to Buddhism, Whitehead advised:

> Never swallow anything whole. . . . We live perforce by half-truths and get along fairly well as long as we do not mistake them for whole-truths, but when we do so mistake them, they raise the devil with us.[185]

From Whitehead's perspective the clash between different religious traditions can be viewed as an invitation and an opportunity for a wider sampling of experience which awaits adequate systematic reflection and organization. Whitehead's rationalist faith presupposes that there is an ordering principle behind even the most disparate phenomena of our experience. Neville comments on the encounter between Christianity and Buddhism that a natural model

> for a Whiteheadian . . . is to conceive contemporary people as seeking to weave a position for themselves from and within the wider environment of unintegrated resources. The diverse histories of the different traditional resources in our world make them mutually incompatible in many respects as they stand. But so are the givens for any occasion of existence, in the Whiteheadian sense.[186]

For Whitehead, however, the metaphysician stands as arbiter among the conflicting religious traditions. Religious emotions are too strong to be trusted and thus require the "dispassionate criticism" of the philosopher:

> Religion requires a metaphysical backing; for its authority is endangered by the intensity of the emotions which it generates. Such emotions are evidence of some vivid experience; but they are a very poor guarantee for its correct interpretation.[187]

---

[184]RM, 42-43.

[185]Lucien Price, Dialogues of Alfred North Whitehead (Boston: Little, Brown, & Co., 1954), 302.

[186]Neville, 119-20.

[187]RM, 81.

Thus the discernment of what is of value in the various religious traditions becomes the task of the metaphysician who transforms the raw data of religious experience into rational religion.

Whitehead's perspective offers helpful resources for approaching other religions, but it does not resolve the problem. Any metaphysics, including Whitehead's, is based upon a particular cultural tradition and thus is partial and limited just as any religious tradition. Whitehead's claim to arbitrate among religions assumes that Western culture and the philosophy arising from it can perform a universal role over against religious traditions. In a pluralistic situation that assumption is just as much in question as any religious claim of universality and superiority.

Pittenger adopts much of Whitehead's perspective but retains a more strictly religious and theological perspective, refusing to allow the metaphysician the final judgement. For Pittenger it is the authority of Christian experience and the Christian tradition that determines the use of metaphysics, not vice versa. Pittenger, following Whitehead's method of empirical generalization, approaches the question of the encounter with other religions pragmatically. In Pittenger's view the meaning of the claim that Jesus Christ is the definitive revelation of God is to be ascertained by examining the role of Jesus Christ in shaping our experience. The truth of the claim is to be verified in its ability to illumine and enrich our experience: "in at least one sense we can only employ a pragmatic test for the universality of Christ."[188] In his earlier work (1959) Pittenger was confident that the pragmatic test would prove Christianity to be "the supreme religion."[189] He quotes an unnamed Hindu in India as saying: "There is no one else who is seriously bidding for the heart of the world except Jesus Christ. There is no one else in the field."[190]

In his more recent work (1979), however, Pittenger has accepted the suggestion of Knitter that we "recognize the possibility that other 'saviours' have carried out . . . for other people" the redemption which Christians experience through Christ.[191] Pittenger agrees with Knitter in arguing that "this does not imply simplistically to water down the content of the Christ-event and proclaim that all religions are 'talking about the same

---

[188]WI, 257.

[189]Ibid., 265.

[190]WI, 260.

[191]Lure of Divine Love, 164-65; Pittenger is quoting Paul F. Knitter, "World Religions and the Finality of Christ," Horizons 5(1978):153.

thing.'"[192] As to the claim of finality for Christianity in this perspective, Pittenger follows his earlier Christological interpretation and argues that

Christianity does not claim finality for itself. Rather, it stresses the decisiveness of Jesus Christ as the one who is 'important' and (in Professor W.E. Hocking's fine word) 'unlosable,' because in him there is the 'representation,' in vivid and compelling fashion, of what God is always up to in the world.[193]

Rahner and Pittenger agree in acknowledging a universal salvific activity of God throughout a wide variety of religious traditions. Both acknowledge that Christians can learn from non-Christian traditions. While their respective positions do not resolve the problems posed by the encounter with other religions, they offer helpful resources for approaching dialogue.

---

[192]*Lure of Divine Love*, 165; quoting Knitter, "World Religions and the Finality of Christ," 153.

[193]*Lure of Divine Love*, 165.

CONCLUSION

This investigation has examined the relationships between the biblical trajectory of Wisdom Christology and the theologies of Rahner and Pittenger and has offered some proposals for the contribution that the wisdom trajectory can make to contemporary theological reflection. While neither Rahner nor Pittenger explicitly drew upon the wisdom tradition in a major way, this investigation has argued that strong biblical precedent for their approaches to theology can be found in the perspectives of the wisdom tradition.

While using differing philosophical approaches, Rahner and Pittenger both develop a Logos Christology which seeks to correlate the universal presence of God in human experience with the historical revelation of God in Jesus Christ. This project finds biblical grounding in the endeavors of the ancient wisdom tradition to articulate the experience of God in ordinary experience and in the identification of Jesus Christ as the incarnation of Lady Wisdom in the New Testament. Like the ancient sages, Rahner and Pittenger acknowledge both the intelligibility and the incomprehensibility of God and of human experience, though Rahner develops the theme of incomprehensibility in a more radical manner than Pittenger. The philosophy of Whitehead, which Pittenger uses, bears it own similarities to the ancient sages, as it undertakes the project of explicating the wisdom in the nature of things.

Given the importance of the wisdom tradition for the origins of Logos Christology, the absence of explicit reflection on the perspectives of the ancient sages in the theologies of Rahner and Pittenger is a striking lacuna. While participating in the history of effects of the wisdom tradition, Rahner and Pittenger do not reflect explicitly on the original biblical roots of the tradition in which they stand.

The trajectory of Wisdom Christology offers a number of invitations for contemporary theological reflection. The wisdom tradition accords a high value to reflection on human experience, while also acknowledging the limits of all human understanding and the necessity of receiving wisdom as a gift from God. The wisdom tradition of Israel shows a remarkable openness to learning and borrowing from other sapiential traditions; it also has an openness to philosophical and cosmological reflection, an openness which is developed in the Wisdom of Solomon and which invites further dialogue with the philosophical and cosmological perspectives of later ages. The interpretation of Jesus Christ as the incarnation of Lady Wisdom claims a cosmic dimension for Christology and opens the way for reflection on the relation of

Christ to the order of creation and the world-process. The sages also showed a remarkable ability to criticize their own presuppositions and to acknowledge the challenge that human suffering poses to claims of wisdom.

The tradition of Wisdom Christology is not without its difficulties. Political and liberation theologians, feminist thinkers, and other religious traditions all pose serious challenges and questions to the claims of Wisdom Christology, and to the Christologies of Rahner and Pittenger. These critical questions can stimulate a fruitful re-reading of the wisdom trajectory in light of current theological concerns. The wisdom tradition does have a political dimension of its own and can offer valuable resources to political and liberation theology. The fact that Lady Wisdom is a feminine figure was historically an important basis for using feminine imagery to describe God and invites further reflection in dialogue with contemporary feminist perspectives. The openness of the sages to other religious and sapiential traditions offers encouragement and biblical precedent for contemporary efforts at dialogue with other religious traditions.

The playful figure of Lady Wisdom herself is one of the most evocative images of the Bible. Both hidden and revealed, both inviting and threatening, she articulates the human experience of the cosmos and of God. While her role in the New Testament is often more implicit than explicit, she was of decisive importance for the early Church's interpretation of Jesus Christ, and has had a lasting impact upon the history of Christian reflection and offers resources for the future.

SELECTED BIBLIOGRAPHY

Aletti, Jean Noël. Colossiens 1,15-20: Genre et exégèse du texte: Fonction de la thématique sapientielle. Rome: Biblical Institute Press, 1981.

Bacik, James J. Apologetics and the Eclipse of Mystery: Mystagogy according to Karl Rahner. Notre Dame, Ind.: University of Notre Dame Press, 1980.

Beardslee, William A. "Parable Proverb, and Koan," Semeia 12 (1978):151-73.

_____. "Uses of the Proverb in the Synoptic Gospels." Interpretation 24(1970):61-73.

Bergant, Dianne. What Are They Saying About Wisdom Literature? New York: Paulist Press, 1984.

Betz, Hans Dieter. "Cosmogony and Ethics in the Sermon on the Mount." In Cosmogony and Ethical Order. Eds. Robin W. Lovin and Frank E. Reynolds. Chicago: University of Chicago Press, 1985.

Bonino, Jose Miguez. Doing Theology in a Revolutionary Situation. Philadelphia: Fortress, 1975.

Branick, Vincent P. An Ontology of Understanding: Karl Rahner's Metaphysics of Knowledge in the Context of Modern German Hermeneutics. St. Louis, Mo.: Marianist Communications Center, 1974.

Brown, Raymond E. The Gospel according to John. Anchor Bible, vols. 29-29A. Garden City, N.Y.: Doubleday & Co., 1966, 1970.

Brueggemann, Walter. "Scripture and an Ecumenical Life-Style." Interpretation 24(1970):3-19.

Buckley, James J. "On Being a Symbol: An Appraisal of Karl Rahner." Theological Studies 40(1979):453-73.

Bultmann, Rudolf. The Gospel of John: A Commentary. Trans. G.R. Beasley-Murray. Eds. R.W.N. Hoare and J.K. Riches. Oxford: Basil Blackwell, 1971.

_____. The History of the Synoptic Tradition. Trans. John Marsh. Rev. ed. New York: Harper & Row, 1976.

Cady, Susan; Ronan, Marian; and Taussig, Hal. Sophia: The Future of Feminist Spirituality. San Francisco: Harper & Row, 1986.

Carlston, Charles E. "Proverbs, Maxims, and the Historical Jesus." Journal of Biblical Literature 99(1980):87-105.

Carr, Anne. The Theological Method of Karl Rahner. American Academy of Religion Dissertation Series 19. Missoula, Mont.: Scholars Press, 1977.

_____. "Theology and Experience in the Thought of Karl Rahner." The Journal of Religion 53 (1973):369-76.

Christ, Felix. Jesus Sophia: Die Sophia-Christologie bei den Synoptikern. Zürich: Zwingli Verlag, 1970.

Christian, William. An Interpretation of Whitehead's Metaphysics. New Haven, Ct.: Yale University Press, 1967.

Collins, Adela Yarbro. "New Testament Perspectives: The Gospel of John." Journal for the Study of the Old Testament 33(1982): 47-53.

Collins, John J. "The Biblical Precedent for Natural Theology." Journal of the American Academy of Religion 45 Supplement (1977):35-67.

_____. "Cosmos and Salvation: Jewish Wisdom and Apocalyptic in the Hellenistic Age." History of Religions 17(1977):121-142.

_____. "Proverbial Wisdom and the Yahwist Vision." Semeia 17 (1980):1-17.

_____. "The Root of Immortality: Death in the Context of Jewish Wisdom." Harvard Theological Review 71(1978):177-192.

Conzelmann, Hans. "The Mother of Wisdom." In The Future of Our Religious Past: Essays in Honour of Rudolf Bultmann. Ed. James Robinson. Trans. Charles Carlston and James Robinson. New York: Harper & Row, 1971.

Cooper, Burton. "Metaphysics, Christology and Sexism: An Essay in Philosophical Theology." Religious Studies 16(1980):179-93.

Crenshaw, James. Old Testament Wisdom: An Introduction. Atlanta: John Knox Press, 1981.

_____, ed. Studies in Ancient Israelite Wisdom. New York: KTAV Publishing House, 1976.

Crenshaw, James, ed. Theodicy in the Old Testament. Philadelphia: Fortress, 1983.

_____. A Whirlpool of Torment: Israelite Traditions of God as an Oppressive Presence. Philadelphia: Fortress, 1984.

Daly, Mary. Beyond God the Father: Toward a Philosophy of Women's Liberation. Boston: Beacon Press, 1985.

Davaney, Sheila Greeve, ed. Feminism and Process Thought: The Harvard Divinity School/Claremont Center for Process Studies Symposium Papers. New York: Edward Mellen Press, 1981.

Dey, L.K.K. The Intermediary World and Patterns of Perfection in Philo and Hebrews. Society of Biblical Literature Dissertation Series 25. Missoula, Mont.: Scholars Press, 1975.

Dhorme, E. A Commentary on the Book of Job. Trans. Harold Knight. London: Thomas Nelson & Sons, Ltd., 1967.

Dodd, C.H. The Interpretation of the Fourth Gospel. Cambridge: Cambridge University Press, 1965.

Doud, Robert Eugene. Rahner's Christology: A Whiteheadian Critique. Ann Arbor, Mich.: University Microfilms, 1977.

_____. "Rahner's Christology: A Whiteheadian Critique." The Journal of Religion 57(1977):144-55.

Duesberg, H. and Fransen, I. Les Scribes Inspirés. Belgium: Editions de Maredsous, 1966.

Eicher, Peter. Die anthropologische Wende: Karl Rahners philosophischer Weg vom Wesen des Menschen zur personalen Existenz. Dokimion 1. Freiburg, Switzerland: Universitätsverlag, 1970.

Emmet, Dorothy M. Whitehead's Philosophy of Organism. London: Macmillan, 1932.

Engelsman, Joan Chamberlain. The Feminine Dimension of the Divine. Philadelphia: Westminster, 1979.

Fabro, Cornelio. La svolta antropologica di Karl Rahner. Milan: Rusconi Editore, 1974.

Fensham, F. Charles. "Widow, Orphan and the Poor in Ancient Near Eastern Legal and Wisdom Literature." Journal of Near Eastern Studies 21(1962):129-39.

Fiorenza, Elisabeth Schüssler. <u>Bread Not Stone: The Challenge of</u>
<u>Feminist Biblical Interpretation</u>. Boston: Beacon Press,
1984.

_____. "Feminist Theology as a Critical Theology of Libera-
tion." <u>Theological Studies</u> 36(1975):605-26.

_____. <u>In Memory of Her: A Feminist Theological Reconstruction</u>
<u>of Christian Origins</u>. New York: Crossroad, 1984.

Fischer, James A. "Ethics and Wisdom." <u>Catholic Biblical Quarterly</u>
40(1978):293-310.

Fischer, Klaus P. <u>Der Mensch als Geheimnis: Die Anthropologie Karl</u>
<u>Rahners</u>. Okumenische Forschungen 6. Freiburg: Herder, 1974.

Ford, Lewis S. <u>The Emergence of Whitehead's Metaphysics: 1925-</u>
<u>1929</u>. Albany, N.Y.: State University of New York Press,
1984.

_____. "Is Process Theism Compatible with Relativity Theory?"
<u>The Journal of Religion</u> 48(1968):124-35.

_____. <u>The Lure of God: A Biblical Background for Process The-</u>
<u>ism</u>. Philadelphia: Fortress, 1978.

Fost, Frederic F. "Relativity Theory and Hartshorne's Dipolar
Theism." In <u>Two Process Philosophers: Hartshorne's Encounter</u>
<u>with Whitehead</u>. American Academy of Religion Studies in Reli-
gion, 5. Tallahassee, Fla.: American Academy of Religion,
1973.

Franklin, Stephen Theodore. "Speaking from the Depths: Metaphysics
of Propositions, Symbolism, Perceptions, Language, and Religion." 2 vols. Ph.D. dissertation, University of Chicago,
1976.

Gaboriau, Florent. <u>Le tournant théologique aujourd'hui selon K.</u>
<u>Rahner</u>. Paris: Desclée, 1968.

Gadamer, Hans-Georg. <u>Truth and Method</u>. Trans. and ed. Garrett
Barden and John Cumming. New York: Crossroad, 1982.

Gammie, John G. et al., eds. <u>Israelite Wisdom: Theological and</u>
<u>Literary Essays in Honor of Samuel Terrien</u>. Missoula, Mont.:
Scholars Press, 1978.

Gilbert, M., ed. <u>La Sagesse de l'Ancien Testament</u>. Gembloux, Belgium: Editions J. Duculot, S.A., 1978.

Glatzer, Nahum N., ed. The Dimensions of Job: A Study and Selected Readings. New York: Schocken Books, 1977.

Goldenburg, Naomi. Changing of the Gods: Feminism and the End of Traditional Religions. Boston: Beacon Press, 1979.

Goodrick, A.T.S. The Book of Wisdom. London: Rivingtons, 1913.

Gordis, Robert. The Book of God and Man: A Study of Job. Chicago: University of Chicago Press, 1978.

_____. Koheleth--The Man and his World: A Study of Ecclesiastes. 3rd ed. New York: Schocken Books, 1968.

_____. "The Social Background of Wisdom Literature." Hebrew Union College Annual 18(1943):77-18.

Grant, Robert M. After the New Testament. Philadelphia: Fortress, 1967.

_____. The Early Christian Doctrine of God. Charlottesville, Va.: University Press of Virginia, 1966.

_____. Gods and the One God. Library of Early Christianity, vol. 1. Philadelphia: Westminster, 1986.

Gustavson, John Arthur. Christian Theology in Process Perspective: A Study of Charles Hartsorne's Dipolar Theism and Norman Pittenger's Process Christology. Ann Arbor, Mich.: University Microfilms, 1969.

Gutiérrez, Gustavo. A Theology of Liberation: History, Politics, and Salvation. Trans. and ed. Caridad Inda and John Eagleson. Maryknoll, N.Y.: Orbis, 1984.

_____. The Power of the Poor in History. Trans. Robert R. Barr. Maryknoll, N.Y.: Orbis, 1984.

Hamerton-Kelly, R.G. Pre-Existence, Wisdom, and the Son of Man: A Study of the Idea of Pre-Existence in the New Testament. Cambridge: Cambridge University Press, 1973.

Hartshorne, Charles, and Peden, Creighton. Whitehead's View of Reality. New York: Pilgrim Press, 1981.

Hartshorne, Charles. Reality as Social Process. Boston: Beacon Press, 1953.

_____. Whitehead's Philosophy: Selected Essays: 1935-1970. Lincoln, Nb.: University of Nebraska Press, 1978.

Heijden, Bert van der. Karl Rahner: Darstellung und Kritik seiner Grundposition. Einsiedeln: Johannes Verlag, 1973.

Hengel, Martin. Property and Riches in the Early Church: Aspects of a Social History of Early Christianity. Trans. John Bowden. Philadelphia: Fortress, 1980.

_____. The Son of God: The Origin of Christology and the History of Jewish-Hellenistic Religion. Trans. John Bowden. Philadelphia: Fortress, 1976.

Hentz, Otto. "Karl Rahner's Concept of the Christ-Event as the Act of God in History." Ph.D. dissertation, University of Chicago, 1977.

Johnson, E.A. "Jesus, The Wisdom of God: A Biblical Basis for a Non-Androcentric Christology." Ephemerides Theologicae Lovanienses 61(1985):261-94.

Johnson, Elizabeth A. "The Incomprehensibility of God and the Image of God Male and Female." Theological Studies 45(1984): 441-65.

Johnson, Marshall D. "Reflections on a Wisdom Approach to Matthew's Christology." Catholic Biblical Quarterly 36(1974): 44-64.

Jordan, Martin. New Shapes of Reality: Aspects of A.N. Whitehead's Philosophy. London: George Allen and Unwin, 1968.

Kayatz, Christa. Studien zu Proverbien 1-9: Eine Form- und Motivgeschichtliche Untersuchung unter Einbeziehung Agyptischen Vergleichnismaterials. Neukirchen-Vluyn: Neukirchener Verlag, 1966.

Knitter, Paul F. No Other Name? A Critical Survey of Christian Attitudes Toward the World Religions. American Society of Missiology Series, no. 7. Maryknoll, N.Y.: Orbis, 1985.

Kraeling, Emil G. The Book of the Ways of God. New York: Charles Scribner's Sons, 1939.

Lang, Bernhard. Die weisheitliche Lehrrede: Eine Untersuchung von Sprüche 1-7. Stuttgart: KBW Verlag, 1972.

_____. Wisdom and the Book of Proverbs: A Hebrew Goddess Redefined. New York: Pilgrim Press, 1986.

Laporte, Jean. "Philo in the Tradition of Biblical Wisdom Literature." In Aspects of Wisdom in Judaism and Early Christianity. Ed. Robert Wilken. Notre Dame, Ind.: University of Notre Dame Press, 1975.

Larcher, C. Etudes sur le Livre de la Sagesse. Paris: Librairie
Lecoffre, 1969.

Levenson, Jon D. The Universal Horizon of Jewish Particularism.
New York: The American Jewish Committee, 1985.

Lightfoot, R.H. St. John's Gospel: A Commentary. Oxford: Oxford
University Press, 1966.

Loader, J.A. Polar Structures in the Book of Qohelet. Berlin:
Walter de Gruyter, 1979.

Lowe, Victor. Understanding Whitehead. Baltimore: Johns Hopkins
Press, 1966.

Lundeen, Lyman. Risk and Rhetoric: Whitehead's Theory of Language
and the Discourse of Faith. Philadelphia: Fortress, 1972.

McCool, Gerald A., ed. A Rahner Reader. New York: Seabury, 1975.

Mack, Burton Lee. Logos und Sophia: Untersuchungen zur Weisheitstheologie im hellenistischen Judentum. Göttingen: Vandenhoeck and Ruprecht, 1973.

Mack, Burton L. Wisdom and the Hebrew Epic: Ben Sira's Hymn in
Praise of the Fathers. Chicago: The University of Chicago
Press, 1985.

McKane, William. Proverbs: A New Approach. Philadelphia: Westminster, 1977.

McKenzie, John L. "Reflections on Wisdom." Journal of Biblical
Literature 86(1967):1-9.

Masson, Robert Louis. Language, Thinking and God in Karl Rahner's
Theology of the Word: A Critical Evaluation of Rahner's Per-
spective on the Problem of Religious Language. Ann Arbor,
Mich.: University Microfilms, 1978.

Metz, Johann Baptist. Faith in History and Society: Toward a
Practical Fundamental Theology. Trans. David Smith. New York:
Seabury, 1980.

Minter, David Curtis. Christology in the Thought of Nels F.S.
Ferre, W. Norman Pittenger and Paul Tillich. Ann Arbor,
Mich.: University Microfilms, 1968.

Moltmann, Jürgen. The Crucified God: The Cross of Christ as the
Foundation and Criticism of Christian Theology. Trans. R.A.
Wilson and John Bowden. New York: Harper & Row, 1974.

Morgan, Donn F. <u>Wisdom in the Old Testament Traditions</u>. Atlanta: John Knox Press, 1981.

Motzko, Elizabeth. <u>Karl Rahner's Theology: A Theology of the Symbol</u>. Ann Arbor, Mich.: University Microfilms, 1976.

Muck, Otto. <u>The Transcendental Method</u>. Trans. William D. Seidensticker. New York: Herder & Herder, 1968.

Murphy, Roland E. "The Interpretation of Old Testament Wisdom Literature." <u>Interpretation</u> 23(1969):289-301.

_____. "Wisdom and Creation." <u>Journal of Biblical Literature</u> 104(1985):3-11.

Nel, Philip Johannes. <u>The Structure and Ethos of the Wisdom Admonitions in Proverbs</u>. Berlin: Walter de Gruyter, 1982.

Neville, Robert. <u>Creativity and God: A Challenge to Process Theology</u>. New York: Seabury, 1980.

Nobo, Jorge Luis. <u>Whitehead's Metaphysics of Extension and Solidarity</u>. Albany, N.Y.: State University of New York Press, 1986.

Noth, M. and Thomas, D. Winton, eds. <u>Wisdom in Israel and in the Ancient Near East</u>. Leiden: E.J. Brill, 1960.

O'Donovan, Leo J., ed. <u>A World of Grace: An Introduction to the Themes and Foundations of Karl Rahner's Theology</u>. New York: Crossroad, 1984.

Parmentier, Alix. <u>La Philosophie de Whitehead et le Problème de Dieu</u>. Paris: Beauchesne, 1968.

Pittenger, Norman. <u>Alfred North Whitehead</u>. Richmond, Va.: John Knox Press, 1969.

_____. <u>Catholic Faith in a Process Perspective</u>. Mary-knoll, N.Y.: Orbis Books, 1981.

_____. <u>The Christian Understanding of Human Nature</u>. Philadelphia: Westminster Press, 1964.

_____. <u>Christology Reconsidered</u>. London: SCM Press, 1970.

_____. <u>The Divine Triunity</u>. Philadelphia: United Church Press, 1977.

_____. "The Doctrine of Christ in a Process Theology," <u>The Expository Times</u> 82(1970):7-10.

Pittenger, Norman. Goodness Distorted. London: A.R. Mowbray & Co., 1970.

_____. The Holy Spirit. Philadelphia: United Church Press, 1975.

_____. Love and Control in Sexuality. New York: Pilgrim Press, 1979.

_____. Loving Says It All. New York: Pilgrim Press, 1978.

_____. The Lure of Divine Love: Human Experience and Christian Faith in a Process Perspective. New York: Pilgrim Press, 1979.

_____. Making Sexuality Human. New York: Pilgrim Press, 1970.

_____. The Meaning of Being Human. New York: Pilgrim Press, 1978.

_____. Process-Thought and Christian Faith. New York: Macmillan Co., 1968.

Pittenger, W. Norman. Reconceptions in Christian Thinking: 1817-1967. New York: Seabury, 1968.

_____. Rethinking the Christian Message. Greenwich, Ct.: Seabury, 1956.

_____. Theology and Reality: Essays in Restatement. Greenwich, Ct.: Seabury, 1955.

_____. A Time for Consent. London: SCM Press, 1967.

_____. Trying to Be a Christian. Philadelphia: Pilgrim Press, 1972.

_____. The Word Incarnate: A Study of the Doctrine of the Person of Christ. Digswell Place: James Nisbet & Co., 1959.

Pols, Edward. Whitehead's Metaphysics: A Critical Examination of Process and Reality. Carbondale, Il.: Southern Illinois University Press, 1967.

Price, Lucien. Dialogues of Alfred North Whitehead. Boston: Little, Brown, & Co., 1954.

Pope, Marvin H. Job. Anchor Bible, vol. 15. Garden City, N.Y.: Doubleday & Co., 1965.

Rad, Gerhard von. Old Testament Theology. Trans. D.M.G. Stalker. New York: Harper & Row, 1962.

Rad, Gerhard von. Wisdom in Israel. Trans. James Martin. Nashville: Abingdon Press, 1972.

Rahner, Karl, and Thüsing, Wilhelm. Christologie--Systematisch und Exegetisch: Arbeitsgrundlagen für eine Interdisziplinäre Vorlesung. Freiburg: Herder, 1972.

Rahner, Karl. Foundations of Christian Faith: An Introduction to the Idea of Christianity. Trans. William V. Dych. New York: Crossroad, 1982.

_____. Geist in Welt: Zur Metaphysik der endlichen Erkenntnis bei Thomas von Aquin. Ed. Johannes Baptist Metz. 2nd ed. Munich: Kösel-Verlag, 1957. English translation: Spirit in the World. Trans. William Dych. New York: Herder & Herder, 1968.

_____. Hörer des Wortes: Zur Grundlegung einer Religionsphilosophie. Ed. J.B. Metz. 2nd ed. Munich: Kösel-Verlag, 1963. English translation: Hearers of the Word. Trans. Michael Richards. New York: Herder & Herder, 1969.

Rahner, Karl, and Lehmann, Karl. Kerygma and Dogma. Trans. William Glen-Doepel. New York: Herder & Herder, 1969.

Rahner, Karl, and Vorgrimler, Herbert. Theological Dictionary. Trans. Richard Strachan. New York: Herder and Herder, 1965.

Rahner, Karl. Theological Investigations. 20 vols. Various translators. Vols. 1-6. Baltimore, Md.: Helicon, 1961-69. Vols. 7-10. New York: Herder & Herder, 1970-73. Vols. 11-14. New York: Seabury: 1974-76. Vols. 15-20. New York: Crossroad, 1979-83.

_____. "Thomas Aquinas on the Incomprehensibility of God," The Journal of Religion 58 Supplement (1978):S107-25.

Rankin, O.S. Israel's Wisdom Literature: Its Bearing on Theology and the History of Religion. Edinburgh: T.& T. Clark, 1964.

Rattigan, Mary Theresa. Christology and Process Thought: The Decisiveness of Jesus Christ in the Thought of Bernard Meland, W. Norman Pittenger, and Daniel Day Williams. Ann Arbor, Mich.: University Microfilms, 1973.

Reese, James. Hellenistic Influence on the Book of Wisdom and Its Consequences. Rome: Biblical Institute Press, 1970.

Richard, Lucien. What Are They Saying About Christ And World Religions? New York: Paulist Press, 1981.

Ricoeur, Paul. "Biblical Hermeneutics." Semeia 4(1975):29-145.

_____. The Conflict of Interpretations: Essays in Hermeneutics. Trans. Kathleen McLaughlin et al. Ed. Don Ihde. Evanston, Il.: Northwestern University Press, 1974.

_____. Essays on Biblical Interpretation. Trans. Peter McCormick et al. Ed. Lewis S. Mudge. Philadelphia: Fortress, 1980.

_____. Freud and Philosophy: An Essay on Interpretation. Trans. Denis Savage. New Haven, Ct.: Yale University Press, 1970.

_____. "The Hermeneutical Function of Distanciation," Philosophy Today 17(1973):129-41.

_____. Interpretation Theory: Discourse and the Surplus of Meaning. Fort Worth, Texas: Texas Christian University Press, 1976.

_____. "Philosophy and Religious Language," The Journal of Religion 54(1974):71-85.

_____. "'Response' to Karl Rahner's Lecture: On the Incomprehensibility of God," The Journal of Religion Supplement 58 (1978):S126-31.

_____. The Rule of Metaphor: Multi-Disciplinary Studies of the Creation of Meaning in Language. Trans. Robert Czerny et al. Toronto: University of Toronto Press, 1981.

_____. Time and Narrative. 3 vols. Vols. 1-2, trans. Kathleen McLaughlin and David Pellauer. Vol. 3, trans. Kathleen Blamey and David Pellauer. Chicago: University of Chicago Press, 1984, 1985, 1988.

Rike, Jennifer, "Being and Mystery: Analogy and Its Linguistic Implications in the Thought of Karl Rahner." 2 vols. Ph.D. dissertation, University of Chicago, 1986.

Roberts, Louis. The Achievement of Karl Rahner. New York: Herder & Herder, 1967.

Robertson, Jr., John C. "Rahner and Ogden: Man's Knowledge of God." Harvard Theological Review 63 (1970):377-407.

Robinson, James M. and Koester, Helmut. Trajectories through Early Christianity. Philadelphia: Fortress, 1979.

Röper, Anita. _The Anonymous Christian_. Trans. Joseph Donceel. New York: Sheed & Ward, 1966.

Rowley, H.H. _Job_. The Century Bible: New Series. London: Thomas Nelson & Sons, Ltd., 1970.

Ruether, Rosemary Radford. _Sexism and God-Talk: Toward a Feminist Theology_. Boston: Beacon Press, 1983.

_____. _To Change the World: Christology and Cultural Criticism_. New York: Crossroad, 1983.

Russell, Letty M. ed. _Feminist Interpretation of the Bible_. Philadelphia: Westminster, 1985.

Rylaarsdam, J. Coert. _Revelation in Jewish Wisdom Literature_. Chicago: The University of Chicago Press, 1974.

Sanders, Gilbert Lee. _The Christology of W. Norman Pittenger: A Summary and a Critique_. Ann Arbor, Mich.: University Microfilms, 1979.

Sanders, Jack. _The New Testament Christological Hymns: Their Historical Religious Background_. Cambridge: Cambridge University Press, 1971.

Schineller, Peter. "The Place of Scripture in the Christology of Karl Rahner." Ph.D. dissertation, University of Chicago, 1975.

Schilpp, Paul Arthur, ed. _The Philosophy of Alfred North Whitehead_. New York: Tudor Publishing Co., 1951.

Schottroff, Luise, and Stegemann, Wolfgang. _Jesus and the Hope of the Poor_. Trans. Matthew J. O'Connell. Maryknoll, N.Y.: Orbis, 1986.

Schwerdtfeger, Nikolaus. _Gnade und Welt: Zum Grundgefüge von Karl Rahners Theorie der "anonymen Christen"_. Freiburg: Herder, 1982.

Scott, R.B.Y. _Proverbs. Ecclesiastes_. Anchor Bible, vol. 18. Garden City, N.Y.: Doubleday & Co., 1965.

_____. _The Way of Wisdom in the Old Testament_. New York: Macmillan Publishing Co., 1978.

Segundo, Juan Luis. _The Historical Jesus of the Synoptics_. Vol. 2 of _Jesus of Nazareth Yesterday and Today_. Trans. John Drury. Maryknoll, N.Y.: Orbis, 1985.

Segundo, Juan Luis. The Liberation of Theology. Trans. John Drury. Maryknoll, N.Y.: Orbis, 1982.

Sheppard, Gerald T. Wisdom as a Hermeneutical Construct: A Study in the Sapientializing of the Old Testament. Berlin: Walter de Gruyter, 1980.

Skehan, Patrick W. "Structures in Poems on Wisdom: Proverbs 8 and Sirach 24." Catholic Biblical Quarterly 41(1979):365-379.

Sobrino, Jon. The True Church and the Poor. Trans. Matthew J. O'Connell. Maryknoll, N.Y.: Orbis, 1984.

Speck, Josef. Karl Rahners theologische Anthropologie: Eine Einführung. Munich: Kösel Verlag, 1967.

Suggs, Jack. Wisdom, Christology, and Law in Matthew's Gospel. Cambridge, Mass.: Harvard University Press, 1970.

Terrien, Samuel. Job: Poet of Existence. New York: Bobbs-Merrill Co., 1957.

_____. "Toward a Biblical Theology of Womanhood." Religion in Life 42(1973):322-33.

Thie, Marilyn. "Feminist Concerns and Whitehead's Theory of Perception." Process Studies 8(1978):186-91.

Thompson, John Mark. The Form and Function of Proverbs in Ancient Israel. The Hague: Mouton, 1974.

_____. "The Power of Form: A Study of Biblical Proverbs." Semeia 17(1980):35-58.

Trible, Phyllis. "Wisdom Builds a Poem: The Architecture of Proverbs 1:20-33." Journal of Biblical Literature 94(1975):509-18.

Tuttle, Gary A. "The Sermon on the Mount: Its Wisdom Affinities and their Relation to its Structure." The Journal of the Evangelical Theological Society 20(1977):213-30.

Vawter, Bruce. "Prov 8:22: Wisdom and Creation." Journal of Biblical Literature 99(1980):205-16.

Vorgrimler, Herbert. Understanding Karl Rahner: An Introduction to His Life and Thought. Trans. John Bowden. New York: Crossroad, 1986.

Wallack, F. Bradford. The Epochal Nature of Process in Whitehead's Metaphysics. Albany, N.Y.: State University of New York Press, 1980.

Weinsheimer, Joel C. Gadamer's Hermeneutics: A Reading of Truth and Method. New Haven, Ct.: Yale University Press, 1985.

Whitehead, Alfred North. Adventure of Ideas. New York: Macmillan Co., 1933. Reprint. New York: Free Press, 1967.

_____. The Concept of Nature. Cambridge: Cambridge University Press, 1920. Reprint. Cambridge: Cambridge University Press, 1971.

_____. The Function of Reason. Princeton, N.J.: Princeton University Press. Reprint. Boston: Beacon Press, 1962,

_____. Modes of Thought. New York: Macmillan Co., 1938. Reprint. New York: Free Press, 1968.

_____. Process and Reality: An Essay in Cosmology. New York: Macmillan Co., 1929. Corrected edition. Eds. David Ray Griffin and Donald W. Sherbourne. New York: Free Press, 1978.

Whitehead, Alfred North. Religion in the Making. New York: Macmillan Co., 1926. Reprint. New York: New American Library, 1974.

_____. Science and Philosophy. New York: Philosophical Library, 1948.

_____. Science in the Modern World. New York: Macmillan Co., 1925. Reprint. New York: Free Press, 1967.

_____. Symbolism: Its Meaning and Effect. New York: Macmillan Co., 1927. Reprint. New York: Capricorn Books, 1959.

Whybray, R.N. The Intellectual Tradition in the Old Testament. Berlin: Walter de Gruyter, 1974.

_____. Wisdom in Proverbs: The Concept of Wisdom in Proverbs 1-9. Naperville, Il.: Alec R. Allenson, Inc., 1965.

Wilcox, John. "A Question from Physics for Certain Theists," The Journal of Religion 40(1961):293-300.

Wilken, Robert, ed. Aspects of Wisdom in Judaism and Early Christianity. Notre Dame, Ind.: University of Notre Dame Press, 1975.

Williams, James G. Those Who Ponder Proverbs: Aphoristic Thinking and Biblical Literature. Bible and Literature Series, no. 2. Sheffield, England: Almond Press, 1981.

Wilmot, Laurence F. Whitehead and God: Prologomena to Theological Reconstruction. Waterloo, Ont.: Wilfred Laurier University Press, 1979.

Wilson, Barrie A. "The Possibility of Theology after Kant: An Examination of Karl Rahner's Geist in Welt." Canadian Journal of Theology 12(1966):245-58.

Wilson-Kastner, Patricia. Faith, Feminism, and Christ. Philadelphia: Fortress, 1983.

Winston, David. The Wisdom of Solomon. Anchor Bible, vol. 43. Garden City, N.Y.: Doubleday & Co., 1979.

Wong, Joseph H.P. Logos-Symbol in the Christology of Karl Rahner. Rome: Libreria Ateneo Salesiano, 1984.

Wood, Charles M. "Karl Rahner on Theological Discourse." Journal of Ecumenical Studies 12(1975):55-67.

INDEX OF BIBLICAL AND ANCIENT WORKS

INDEX OF PROPER NAMES

The author: Leo D. Lefebure is instructor of systematic theology at Mundelein Seminary in Mundelein, Illinois. He received his doctorate in theology from the Divinity School of the University of Chicago.